WIN

WIN

The Key Principles to
Take Your Business from
Ordinary to Extraordinary

DR. FRANK I. LUNTZ

HYPERION
· · · · ·
NEW YORK

Library of Congress Cataloging-in-Publication Data has been applied for.

ISBN 978-1-4013-2399-8

Hyperion books are available for special promotions and premiums. For details contact the HarperCollins Special Markets Department in the New York office at 212-207-7528, fax 212-207-7222, or e-mail spsales@harpercollins.com.

Book design by Sunil Manchikanti

FIRST EDITION

10 9 8 7 6 5 4 3 2

THIS LABEL APPLIES TO TEXT STOCK

We try to produce the most beautiful books possible, and we are also extremely concerned about the impact of our manufacturing process on the forests of the world and the environment as a whole. Accordingly, we've made sure that all of the paper we use has been certified as coming from forests that are managed, to ensure the protection of the people and wildlife dependent upon them.

To my mom, who gave me the passion, persistence, and desire
for perfection that has allowed me to live a very interesting life.
Now, if I could only get some sleep . . .

CONTENTS

ACKNOWLEDGMENTS

In reviewing all the expert interviews I conducted prior to sending them to my editor for her consideration, I was pleasantly surprised to realize that more than a dozen of the Forbes 400 richest Americans helped contribute. I owe the people on these pages a debt I will never be able to repay for the lessons they have taught me. Their comments, suggestions, and recollections—not just in these formal interviews, but over the years that I have known many of them—explain both my successes as an individual and my shortcomings as a manager. I can't pay them back, but I can pay it forward by sharing their lessons with you.

The idea for this book came straight from Gretchen Young, my editor. I hope I have done it justice. She has made her mission to move me from political commentator to business analyst. A dozen Fortune 500 companies have since signed me up, thanks to her commitment. I hope she doesn't ask for a commission.

Mike Phifer had more to do with the words in this book than anyone else. I could not have completed the initial draft without his help, and I have no doubt that he will soon be recognized as one of America's great new nonfiction authors. Amy Kramer and Lowell Baker also worked their magic on the text—some of my best lines are theirs—as did Liz Bieler and Shepherd Pittman.

More than three dozen incredible business, political, and sports icons sat (or stood) for interviews that are sprinkled throughout the text, among them basketball legend and Hall of Famer Larry Bird, New York Mayor Michael Bloomberg, *Desperate Housewives* creator Marc Cherry, General Wesley Clark, private equity genius Jim Davidson, Amway cofounder Rich DeVos, actor Richard Dreyfuss, J.Crew CEO Mickey Drexler, television legend Sir David Frost, management guru Michael George, Notre Dame's legendary football coach Lou Holtz, radio personality Don Imus, Gibson CEO Henry Juszkiewicz, former chairman of Paramount

Pictures Sherry Lansing, automotive guru Bob Lutz, Discovery Land CEO Mike Meldman, entertainer Bob Newhart, hockey Hall of Famer Mike Richter, former Secretary of Defense Donald Rumsfeld, COO of Facebook Sheryl Sandberg, California Governor Arnold Schwarzenegger, hockey legend Brendan Shanahan, Philadelphia Flyers and 76ers owner Ed Snider, University of Phoenix founder John Sperling, NBA commissioner David Stern, and basketball Hall of Famer Jerry West.

There are several people to whom I owe special recognition, not just for their time and wisdom, which is reflected on these pages, but for their impact on my life:

Roger Ailes, Fox News founder and CEO, who loves America so much and still doesn't realize how much of America loves him back. He's the funniest man in television news (sorry, Brian Williams, you're second).

Stephen Cloobeck, chairman and CEO of Diamond Resorts, for teaching me "The Meaning of Yes" and allowing me to teach him the language of vacation ownership hospitality. A decade from now, the name Cloobeck will rank alongside Marriott and Hilton.

Jim Gray, sportscaster extraordinaire, who has enabled me, on multiple occasions, to combine my love for sports with my passion for communication. The man definitely has opinions. I hope the sports world is listening.

Tom Harrison, chairman and CEO of Diversified Agency Services, the largest component of global marketing behemoth Omnicom, who helped guide my first company's acquisition. To this day he helps guide my thinking. His understanding of instinct and human behavior is unsurpassed.

Mark Montgomery, the youngest rear admiral in the U.S. Navy, for his expert knowledge of national security and his willingness to explain it in terms I can understand. He defines a Great American.

Rupert Murdoch, who has taught me not to think outside the box, but to think as if there is no box. I can't always understand what he says, but I *always* follow what he does.

Jim Murren, the chairman and CEO of MGM Resorts International, for saving more than sixty thousand jobs at a company minutes away from bankruptcy because of his vision, passion, and willingness to fight for his people.

Rob Rosania, co-CEO of Stellar Management, who has changed the lives of thousands of apartment residents for the better by applying principles of customer satisfaction to an industry that heretofore couldn't care less.

Jesse Sharf, the sharpest, hardest-working real estate lawyer in America and a friend for more than thirty years.

Bill Shine, John Finley, and Sean Hannity—all of Fox News. If it weren't for Sean's support of my televised focus groups, I would still be doing them for audiences of a few people rather than a few million, but I owe Bill and John just as much. They don't get the public credit for all they do behind the scenes.

Herb Simon, chairman emeritus of Simon Property Group—which includes the Forum Shops in Las Vegas—who makes everything look so easy when he has worked so hard for so long. He's the nicest billionaire you'll never meet.

Fred Smith, FedEx founder, for being a CEO's CEO. When someone asks how best to study the American Dream, I tell them to study Fred Smith.

Burt Sugarman and Mary Hart, for their ongoing words of wisdom and support in all of my language endeavors. I am informed, educated, and entertained whenever fortunate enough to be in their presence.

Steve Wynn, the greatest linguist of any CEO I have ever met. He is to speech what Picasso is to art.

Mort Zuckerman, chairman of Boston Properties and owner of *U.S. News & World Report* and the *New York Daily News*, who is to written prose what Steve Wynn is to the spoken word.

WIN

1

WHAT IS A WINNER?
The 15 Attributes of Winners

Look at it this way: if winning wasn't so hard, it wouldn't feel so good.
—MIKE RICHTER
STANLEY CUP WINNER AND NHL HALL OF FAMER

To what do I owe my success? Three things: I came to America. I worked very hard. And I married a Kennedy.
—ARNOLD SCHWARZENEGGER

Win is designed to be an unprecedented examination of effective communication in America today as told by America's great communicators.

There are dozens of business books that offer to "give you the edge" or tell you to "seize the moment," but they don't really tell you how. *Win* teaches by highlighting real-world examples of the companies, people, and politicians who achieve greatness, and examines what we can learn from what they say, how they say it, and why. Ultimately, life is a contest in which people play to win. This book addresses the philosophy, strategy, and language of winning from the perspective of America's greatest winners inside and outside the business world.

So before you go any further, ask yourself two simple questions: First, how badly do you want to win? And second, are you willing to do what it takes to move from the ordinary to the extraordinary? If the answers are both yes, then let's begin.

THE DEFINITION OF WINNING

THE 15 UNIVERSAL ATTRIBUTES OF WINNERS

Jim Davidson, the co-CEO of Silver Lake, one of the most savvy and successful private equity firms in America, has a simple philosophy for deciding where his $14 billion fund should invest: start at the end of the process and work backward. That strategy also applies to this book. Allow me to begin at the end. If I were to summarize twenty years of corporate and political communication research and discussions with America's business, political, sports, and entertainment elite into a single, simple checklist, what differentiates genuine winners from everyone else is the following:

- the ability to *grasp the human dimension* of every situation;
- the ability to know what *questions* to ask and when to ask them;
- the ability to *see* what *doesn't yet exist* and *bring it to life*;
- the ability to see the *challenge*, and the *solution*, from every angle;
- the ability to *distinguish* the *essential* from the *important*;
- the ability and the drive to *do more* and *do it better*;
- the ability to *communicate* their vision passionately and persuasively;
- the ability to *move forward* when everyone around them is retrenching or slipping backward;
- the ability to *connect* with others spontaneously;
- a *curiosity* about the *unknown*;
- a *passion* for life's *adventures*;
- a *chemistry* with the people they work with and the people they want to influence;
- the willingness to *fail* and the *fortitude* to get back up and try again;
- a belief in luck and good fortune; and
- a *love of life* itself.

This book draws on more than three dozen private interviews with people who have made it to the very top of their professions, to the top of the Forbes 400 wealthiest Americans list and the Fortune 500 list. They have led their companies to great heights and led their teams to world championships. They are the best known and the most respected in their fields of endeavor. After combing through hundreds of pages of transcripts, a consistent pattern of attitudes and behavior emerges that applies across and throughout their careers. This book harmonizes and synthesizes their "secrets of success"—so you can make them yours.

In my work for dozens of Fortune 500 companies, I am consistently amazed at how many people would rather be working somewhere else—or at least *for* someone else—and yet they don't act on it. Not life's winners. They all love what they do. Most of them call it *fun,* and none of them call it work. Some acknowledge that they *work hard* or that they've had to *sacrifice along the way,* but all of them consider themselves grateful, blessed, and/or lucky to be doing what they're doing, and none of them would rather be doing anything else.

These 15 Attributes of Winners are fundamental to the Nine Principles

---

LUNTZ LESSONS

1. **Winning by communicating:**
   Winners focus on the outcome, not just the process. They *measurably prove* they can lead you to better *results.* For example, they emphasize "wellness," not "health care." Why? Health care is the means; wellness is the end. Health care is a distant, impersonal bureaucratic system; wellness is a personal, aspirational state of being.

2. **Winning by grasping the human dimension:**
   Winners deliver *value* that solves a quality-of-life need, rather than stopping at just price and profitability. They know that their bottom lines are best served *not* by "running the numbers" but rather by *understanding the person.* They recognize that *every* sustainable relationship arises from a personal, human need. So they make products and services that meet those needs—and market them to human beings, not to the amorphous masses.

3. **Winning by focusing on the experience, not the technology:**
   Winners have the vision to see beyond the product and into the desires of their customers. It's not about the iPhone or the BlackBerry; it's about the hassle-free, worry-free apps delivered through the phones that revolutionize how a person lives, works, and *experiences his or her individual world.* And it's done using ordinary language for ordinary people.

of Winning (aka the Nine *P*'s) and all that follows in this book, so let's cement them with specific examples.

Winners are self-aware. They recognize their own strengths and weaknesses, and respond to situations accordingly. Don't underestimate this. From Lehman Brothers to General Motors to Circuit City, countless companies have struggled or gone under because of leaders who stayed in their comfort zones and didn't take the right action at the right time because they were afraid to make the wrong move. "Don't think I've been here for fifty years because we're a great company without having made a lot of mistakes on the way," says Rupert Murdoch from his CEO suite on Sixth Avenue in Manhattan. "How are you going to question yourself? Are you going to look in the mirror? When you see things going wrong, do you try to put them right? Or maybe you can't put them right. You have to say to yourself, 'I was wrong to do this in the first place' and just cut your losses. I know when to cut my losses."

Winners are also tuned in to the needs and desires of others, and this outward focus guides them to deliver revolutionary solutions, not just better mouse traps.* They recognize where their strengths meet someone else's needs and double down on delivering the greatest value while ignoring lesser distractions. In plain English, winners succeed because they foresee and pursue the biggest prize.

Winners recognize that even when they aren't physically selling a product, they are always selling themselves. Every human interaction is an opportunity to connect—and then to sell. So says Tom Harrison, chairman and CEO of Diversified Agency Services (DAS), the largest subsidiary of Omnicom, the world's largest advertising, marketing, and communications company. As one of Madison Avenue's most creative minds, he knows by "instinct" (which just happens to be the title of his seminal book on human behavior) exactly what to say and when to say it. Winners know what makes people tick by effectively tapping into our fears and aspirations. By listening very carefully and then repeating almost word-

---

* Of the 15 attitudes, behaviors, and characteristics of the people we all would define as winners, none so universally transcends every profession as the ability to read others. Whether you're in politics or business, sports or entertainment, knowing what people *really* want and how they will react is the equivalent of being able to predict the future. And if you know the future, you can own it.

for-word exactly what they've heard, winners know how to articulate compelling needs—and products to satisfy those needs—that people didn't even know they wanted. Says Harrison, "As long as I can keep my ears wide open, and my eyes wide open, and literally understand every word that they are saying, then it's about them. The moment I translate it, it becomes about me—and that's why others fail."

Bono is a winner by every measure. He is arguably the most iconic performer of his generation, as well as one of the most well-known people on the planet. A U2 show echoes in your ears for hours after the music stops . . . and the song sales echo in the band's ears for years. But Bono's biggest wins will reverberate for generations. They're wins on a societal scale, and they're what make him a true winner rather than merely a rock legend. Listen to Bono as he sits across from Larry King, or meets with world leaders, or hosts a policy summit, and you instantly realize how his quiet, serious commitment has won billions for the world's hurting. Yes, he has a megaplatform—but so do many other rock stars. He wins where they do not, not because he is powerful, but because he is accessible, compelling, and has a common touch.

Winners don't preach; they persuade. Winners clearly articulate their own principles and kindly, subtly invite you to adopt them. But the choice is yours. Sure, they lead and you follow, but you ultimately come to their point of view on your own.

For winners, it's never about a single game, product, or performance. Winners know how to succeed over the long term because they are persistent. They agree with Mark Twain: "The inability to forget is infinitely more devastating than the inability to remember," driving beyond failure in order to eventually succeed. Or, for those readers who prefer sports to literature, Wayne Gretzky said, "You miss one hundred percent of the shots you don't take."

Another attribute that winners all have in common is how much they hate to lose. This isn't particularly surprising, but what stands out is how they *visualize* it. Like anyone in Room 101 in George Orwell's 1984, they each have their own vivid picture in their heads of what it's like to lose. Never at a loss for words, most winners had difficulty articulating how failing affected them emotionally, and several even refused to answer any questions about it, as though losing wasn't in their mental dictionary, but they could clearly see it. For some, it's a flashback to unpleasant memories of their childhood.* For others, it's a specific moment in time that went horribly wrong. My personal favorite comes from tennis legend Jimmy Connors. *"The worst thing about losing a tennis match was the handshake. I saw the expression on their face after they beat me, and I hated it. The humiliation."*

Winners never give up and they don't accept defeat. They work as long and as hard as it takes to get the job done right. There isn't a winner anywhere who doesn't bring passion to what they do or to how they communicate. Passion is contagious. It's getting others to see what you see, to imagine what you imagine—and then want to do what you do. It's not about high volume for the sake of attention; it's focused intensity. Winners employ "blue heat" because it lasts longer, burns hotter, and is more precise than a wild orange flame.

Winners rarely talk about the bottom line, profitability, or even success. Rather, they talk about a greater purpose—and invite you to join them. They identify and address a weakness or deficiency in the human experience—to fill a void others have yet to notice. They identify the impediments that derail others and move past them.

Jim Davidson, the co-CEO of Silver Lake, a global private investment firm specializing in emerging technology with approximately $14 billion in assets under management, has a slightly more nuanced take: *"The difference between people who are wildly successful and the people who are just plain successful is not in answering the question, it's figuring out which questions are worth asking. The guys that actually figure out what problems are worth working on, what questions are worth asking, are the ones that actually make it big."*

There's one other experience a surprising number of the wealthiest people featured in this book have had in common: poverty. You wouldn't know it by how they live today, but the lack of money, sometimes even basic daily sustenance, clearly scarred their youth and had a significant effect on their unrelenting drive for success. Herb Simon, the billion-

---

* Many of the most successful people of our generation grew up in broken or impoverished homes, moved around often, had serious trouble in school, or had an otherwise challenged childhood.

aire real estate developer responsible for the Mall of America and the Forum Shops, grew up so poor that his greatest fear as a young adult was *"winding up all alone in a hotel room in my undershirt, no room service and no money."* The three-room apartment where he was raised in the Bronx was so small that he slept on a cot in his parents' bedroom until his early teens. Said Simon, *"We never had any money. I heard my mother worrying about money, and I sometimes went to sleep worrying about having no money."* In 2009, Simon ranked #317 on the Forbes list of wealthiest Americans, and he never stays at hotels that don't offer room service.

Legendary Notre Dame football coach Lou Holtz grew up in a single-bedroom basement apartment that had no refrigerator or freezer, but the challenges he faced as a youth played an important role in his life-long mission to be the best. Of the three dozen interviews I did for this book, none left me more motivated than Coach Holtz. Perhaps it was because he was the only interview who served me a home-cooked meal. With an incredible 249 wins against just 132 losses, he was the only college football coach to lead six different programs to bowl games. Sitting in his den, surrounded by artifacts from an incredible career, it's easy to understand why he's not only one of the great icons of college sports but one of the most powerful speakers on the lecture circuit. When I asked him how someone from such a difficult financial background could achieve extraordinary success, he erupted. *"I don't think God put us on this earth to be ordinary,"* he stressed, swinging his arms for emphasis:

> *Life is ten percent what happens to you and ninety percent how you respond to it. Show me someone who has done something worthwhile and I'll show you someone who has overcome adversity. And one more thing. I didn't have it tough growing up. I never thought of myself as poor. I don't complain. Never have. Remember, most people don't care about your problems, and the rest are glad you have them.*

Basketball legend Jerry West had even more humble beginnings. Raised in a 500-person mining community in dirt-poor rural West Virginia, his situation was tragic. He didn't want to talk about his childhood, but he acquiesced when I explained that his triumph over adversity would serve as an inspiration to others. I include it here as a lesson that anyone, regardless of where you start, has a chance to end up on top:

> *In my family, it was a struggle to survive. There were times when there wasn't a quarter in the house. I'm not exaggerating. In those periods when my father wasn't working, we had absolutely nothing. We never had a car. We never had a family vacation. I used to run everywhere. I remember seeing Forrest Gump and thinking how much like him I was. My parents had little or no education, and I had no means to go to school. But I had this love for basketball. I didn't realize I had a skill, because I was so thin and so small. All I had was a strong work ethic and an imagination, and someone who showed an interest in me—and that was enough.*

It was enough to earn him a position on the NBA All-Star team fourteen times in his fourteen seasons, and membership in the Basketball Hall of Fame. By the way, you've seen the official NBA logo with a player in silhouette? That's Jerry West.

Steve Wynn, the billionaire creator of modern Las Vegas, didn't grow up poor, but his father's untimely death left the twenty-one-year-old college senior with more than $ 100,000 in debts and a bingo parlor that was losing money every week. Little has been written about this part of his life, and so I asked Wynn whether he ever considered declaring bankruptcy or just ignoring what his father owed. He paused, looked at me incredulously, and then responded in a soft but determined tone:

> *His last night, my father told me to write down some information that he wanted me to have. He said, "Everything's going to be OK, but just in case, I owe your uncle Frank fifteen thousand dollars. And I owe so-and-so ten. Pay it. And mark this down." And I sat there on the bedside and wrote down what he told me.*
>
> *The next day, the doctors couldn't get his heart started. I had just turned twenty-one and I had a ten-year-old brother. We were broke, and that was the worst possible thing that could have ever happened to me. But when my father told me to do this, to pay these debts, I just felt like I was doing what he told me. I was following his instructions. I never*

thought not to do it. My dad was the kind of a guy that always kept his word.

People that are really fundamentally honest don't think about it that much. It just seems like the only thing to do. Not just the right thing to do; it's the only thing to do. Don't make too much fuss about being honest. You shouldn't be proud of being honest. You should just be honest. You should be ashamed if you're not.

I had my father's partner his seventy-eight thousand dollars back by New Year's. And then I got everybody paid within twelve months.

Now remember, this was a twenty-one-year-old kid whose father owed $100,000 in 1963 dollars. And he paid it all off in one year! That intensity and integrity was why he was able to convince bankers twice his age to give him the money he needed to start his business in Las Vegas and why, today, Forbes lists him as the 616th richest man in the world.

Allow me one more example because this is, by his own admission, particularly poignant. Andy Granatelli is in many ways the father of modern stock car auto racing. A born promoter, his legendary racing spectaculars gave birth to a multi-billion-dollar industry in the 1950s, and his teams won the coveted Indianapolis 500 in the late 1960s and 1970s thanks to engines that he helped design. A prolific automotive inventor and driver, his cars established and then broke hundreds of world records for speed and endurance, and he set many of the records himself. But he is best known as the CEO and spokesman for STP (*"the racer's edge"*) corporation, which, thanks to his persistent promotions, was at one point almost as ubiquitous as Disney and Coca-Cola. He parlayed his love of cars into a fortune estimated at several hundred million dollars, but his financial condition wasn't always so rosy:

I knew what it was like to starve, literally starve. I lived The Grapes of Wrath, *the actual story you see in the movies where people loaded up these little junk cars to drive to California, only to go without a job. I never ever wanted to do that again. I actually believe to myself that I'm fat because I never want to go hungry. I keep my stomach full because I don't want to die with an empty stomach.*

At the time of my interview, Granatelli told me that he weighed more than 300 pounds, though he was well into a diet that would eventually shave more than 100 pounds off his large frame. Most winners would agree that money buys freedom, but Granatelli and others would also acknowledge that it can't always buy freedom from fear.

Win demonstrates *how* and explains *why* winning without communicating is simply impossible. Every winner has prioritized and perfected their own lexicon. This book chronicles and dissects their successes, but more important, it equips you to apply *their* lessons to *your* life, *your* work, and *your* pursuit of the extraordinary.

My 2007 book, *Words That Work,* explored the power of specific words and phrases from a business, political, and personal perspective. *What Americans Really Want . . . Really,* from 2009, is an exposé of who we really are and what we really expect out of life. *Win* examines the common characteristics and linguistic strengths of the world's most successful people—and how any American who wants to win can capture and utilize these communication secrets. This is not the first book to address how effective language has shaped the success of America's finest entrepreneurs and CEOs, the marketing of our most successful products and services, and the cultures of our most successful corporations. What makes this book unique—and why it should matter to people who want to understand what separates the ordinary from the extraordinary—is that it spans the width and breadth of American life, from business to politics, from sports to entertainment. This book compiles key characteristics and language lessons from each industry and leader into a single collection, because we can learn greatness from the most extraordinary among us.

Early on, I set out to determine the specific attributes that contribute the most to success in business, politics, entertainment, sports, and day-to-day American life. My assumption was that once the attributes were identified, it would be relatively simple to connect the most effective language to the most important attributes, giving readers a straightforward how-to guide to take typical situations and improve them with atypical words.

But to my surprise, it quickly became evident in this undertaking that the *style* of communication was just as important to the eventual success as the *substance*. What I failed to address in *Words That Work*, and what you will read on the pages that follow, is more than a primer for message development. In fact, just as much emphasis is devoted to the *way* those messages are communicated as the words themselves.

There are many specific "Luntz Lessons" and recommendations that follow. They are designed to help you apply what you read to your day-to-day life. All of them directly illustrate the nine essential action-oriented principles of winning at every level, from private one-on-one meetings with your boss to public presentations before hundreds of strangers to media appearances that may reach millions.

So grab your highlighter and join me in an unprecedented examination of the Nine Principles of Winning that fuel the art, the science, and the language of life.

2

THE NINE *P*'S OF WINNING

What it takes to get to the top

After climbing a great hill, one only finds that there are many more hills to climb.

—**NELSON MANDELA**

Good business leaders create a vision, articulate the vision, passionately own the vision, and relentlessly drive it to completion.

—**JACK WELCH,**
FORMER CHAIRMAN AND CEO, GENERAL ELECTRIC

There's a big difference between those who want to be something and those who want to do something. About 95 percent of America is made up of people who want to be something, and they cause all the problems that have to be solved by the 5 percent who want to do something. I hope your book is about the 5 percent, not the 95 percent.

—**ROGER AILES,**
FOUNDER AND CEO, FOX NEWS CHANNEL

This book is written for the 5 percent Roger Ailes so wisely identifies who want to do something. Of that 5 percent, it focuses on the lessons and experiences of a still smaller group of people who have done more than aspire; they have actually achieved. They've won. It is my hope that their stories can help you join their ranks.

THE DEFINITION OF WINNING

Winners think differently from the rest of us. *"They're wired differently,"* says Tom Harrison. *"Their DNA is different. The moderately successful person focuses on the roadblocks, on how to get over or around them. The winner focuses on the goal."*

In his 2001 best-selling book *Good to Great: Why Some Companies Make the Leap . . . and Others Don't,* Jim Collins and his team of researchers set out to answer a single question: How does a good company become a great one? They started with a list of 1,435 companies, which was eventually narrowed down to 11 of the very best: Abbott Laboratories, Circuit City, Fannie Mae, Gillette, Kimberly-Clark, Kroger, Nucor Corporation, Philip Morris, Pitney Bowes, Walgreens, and Wells Fargo.* To make the list of great companies, "the company had to show a pattern of good performance, punctuated by a transition point, after which it shifted to great performance. 'Great performance' was defined as a cumulative total stock return of at least three times the general market for the period from the transition point through 15 years."[1]

Collins and company examined books, articles, case studies, and annual reports and they pored over financial analyses for each company they studied, totaling 980 combined years of data. They conducted more than eighty interviews with senior managers and board members, while studying the personal and professional records of more than fifty CEOs. In addition, they analyzed the companies' payment structures and incentives; they reviewed layoffs, corporate ownership, and media coverage; and they examined the role technology played for each of the companies that had made the leap—all the metrics that mattered.

So what did Collins and his team discover? He concluded that there was no "magic moment" that took a company from good to great. Rather, it was the ongoing commitment of the company and its leaders to set

---

* Greatness, like beauty, is fleeting. Presumably the 2008 government bailouts of Fannie Mae and Wells Fargo weren't included in Collins's disqualifiers for enduring greatness. Or Circuit City's 2009 collapse into bankruptcy. Perhaps some within these failed institutions thought that being deemed "great" was "good enough," and rested on those laurels. Then the Great Recession exposed their arrogance.

clearly defined priorities and focus on what really mattered. Based on more than twenty years of work with Fortune 100 CEOs, executive-level corporate managers, Hollywood studio giants, and Washington power brokers, Collins's conclusions seem largely right to me. People who do great things focus on what matters most and just get it done again and again, better and better.

But that isn't winning. Winning is so much more. When I talk about winning, I'm not talking about cumulative total stock returns that outperform the market, or people who rise to the position of senior vice president of a Fortune 500 company. That's *success*. That's *leadership*. Those are laudable achievements, but they are not extraordinary. There are many successful people and companies in America, and many who lead. But by *definition* there is a paucity of extraordinariness—even in America, where we are judged by what we do and not who we are, or who our parents are.

Winning is about getting to the top and making things—great things, unprecedented things—happen. It's about *transforming* and completely *revolutionizing* products, processes, and even people. It's about making an impact that endures long after you have gone. As management guru Tom Peters pointed out in a 2003 interview:

> *Companies that Jim [Collins] calls great have performed well. I wouldn't deny that for a minute, but they haven't led anybody anywhere. I don't give a damn whether Microsoft is around 50 years from now. Microsoft set the agenda in the world's most important industry at a critical period of time, and that to me is leadership, not the fact that you are able to stay alive until your beard is 200 feet long.*[2]

Winning means charting a new course, setting the agenda, and convincing everyone else to follow. Jerry Jones, longtime owner of the spectacularly profitable Dallas Cowboys, will do absolutely anything he can to enhance his team and their reputation. If you told Jerry Jones, in a polite way, "Jerry, we'd like you to go climb up that pole and wave a flag for the Cowboys," he would evaluate it, and if he thought that it was in the best interest of the team, he'd do it. He would do absolutely anything, within the boundaries of good taste, to make every experience memorable. He goes out of his way to make sure the fans feel that

WHAT AMERICANS REALLY WANT TO HEAR FROM THEIR BUSINESS LEADERS

I believe in a simple formula for leadership: listen, learn, help, lead. The best leaders recognize that listening inspires much more than telling, and then they learn. Next, they set an example of responsible leadership by helping. Employees are much more willing to sacrifice and follow when they see that their leaders are right there in the trenches with them. And when they have earned the trust and confidence of their team, they are ready to lead.

they're getting exactly what they want, and that's why he was named sports personality of the year in 2010. Winners like him know it's not about making something new and improved; it's about inventing something superior that stands apart.

The first step is to think differently. If you're a student about to graduate from college and you haven't found a job yet, your number-one focus should probably be on obtaining gainful employment. And have no fear; there is an entire industry set up to help you find that perfect job. But what if focusing on getting the perfect job isn't actually the right priority for you? Maybe it should be "inventing" the perfect job. I hadn't really thought about this point until I spoke with Richard DeVos, the founder of Amway. He tells a story about addressing some college students that will probably make you think twice if you have children coming out of college:

> I was speaking once at Michigan State University where I was given a PhD, and they said I could have a couple of minutes to address the students. All I said to them was, "I bet a lot of you guys are wondering if you're going to get a job when you graduate, huh? Stop worrying about it, and go start a business of your own." And the whole place erupted in applause. It surprised me with its intensity; the whole place just erupted. Wow, starting a business of their own; they hadn't thought about that. Nobody in college teaches you that. They teach you how to be dependent on somebody else, not how to take charge of your life.

For Mary Hart, host of *Entertainment Tonight* for thirty years, attitude is everything. In 2011, she tied Johnny Carson for the longest continuous hosting of an ongoing show. *"I'm blessed with waking up in the morning a happy person and an optimistic person. There's a lot of cheerleader in me. I've always felt I was lucky to have this job, and I take nothing for granted. I go to work imagining that this is my first day doing the show. Each show renews my enthusiasm."*

"Success starts and ends with people. To appeal to a lot of people, you have to have real insight into them," says Henry Juszkiewicz, CEO of Gibson Guitar. Gibson, the makers of the hugely popular Les Paul guitar, had fallen on hard times when Juszkiewicz came in as CEO in 1986 and rescued the company. At a time when digital technology and dramatic advances in consumer electronics have pitted most of the music industry's corporate players against their customers, he is widely respected not just for his business acumen but for his pro-people approach A CEO for more than two decades, he still embraces consumers like a warm blanket on a cold winter day:

You can pursue a paradigm shift that people don't like, and it's just not going to work, because there's no point to it. You have to be holistic and take a broad view with a broad understanding. All the great guys I know who have had that special touch actually developed their products for themselves. Steve Jobs is actually developing products that he wants for himself. He is the customer. And he understands it better because he's one of them.

In the guitar field, I'm developing stuff that I want to play. And as I do, I'm like a kid in a candy store. It's like my favorite thing now. You have to have that intuitive connection with your consumer. If you're trying to go in with surveys and statistical methodology, you'll stumble a lot. It's like looking through little peepholes; you'll only get snippets of factual information. You need to wrap your arms around what's happening to really connect.

Something invariably happens to winners on their path to success that changes their perspective—a bad boss, a poor working environment, a temporary career setback. But they don't make this an excuse for failure. Instead, it becomes a life lesson that they use to get ahead. Says Mickey Drexler, the dangerously candid but highly entertaining CEO of J.Crew:

> I always wanted a boss who drives hard, has high standards, is honest, direct, and is not full of s–t. Someone said to me, "Always remember who you were. You're not a big shot." I remember the big shots when I started at Bloomingdale's; they hardly said hello to you and they wouldn't listen to you. A lot of them are just not confident. A lot of them are self-important. A lot of them are narcissistic. A lot of them are ego-maniacs.

Winners don't make excuses at all. There's an authenticity to the winners featured in this book that is both refreshing and compelling. Radio-personality Don Imus has survived and thrived through four decades of seemingly ongoing controversy by simply being himself. *"I am not full of s–t and people know that. It is not an act. I am what I am. I have never done anything on the air that I wouldn't say or do or isn't the way I act privately. I think that's why I have a real connection to people."*

Because winners live for epic change and radically rethinking the status quo, they must be able to make the case with force and skill. They begin by engaging and inspiring the people who work with them and for them. They persist over the objections of skeptics who are afraid of what change might mean. They prevail over critics who want to shut them down completely. Engage, inspire, persist, prevail—you need them all.

It's not as hard as it sounds. Most winners had certain attributes on the day they were born, but each of the nine essential principles can be incorporated into one's life. Winners are never satisfied with the status quo and always pursue more. Better. Higher. Faster. Easier. That's why they aren't satisfied with the skills they were born with; that's just the starting point on a path to greatness. These principles may not come naturally, they may take years of practice, and you may not get them all right all the time, but the more you master, the more likely you are to win in the workplace and in the marketplace.

So what are the nine principles of winning?

THE NINE *P*'S OF WINNING

1. People-Centeredness
2. Paradigm Breaking
3. Prioritization
4. Perfection
5. Partnership
6. Passion
7. Persuasion
8. Persistence
9. Principled Action

No, the *P*'s are not a simple gimmick. Look again and think about the most successful people you know: what may be just words to you are the principles by which they live.

PEOPLE-CENTEREDNESS

I know more about you than you realize. That's because no matter who you are, what you do, or what you sell, I know what your enterprise is really all about: people.

I have made a career of showing candidates and companies, unequivocally, how their objectives will fail if they refuse to truly listen to, and understand, what people want from them. I've also enjoyed decades of witnessing winners who learn, grasp, and perfect this central principle. *Every* decision about communication, products, and objectives must submit to the central organizational question: *How does this affect real everyday people?*

Let's look at what this means for language. It's often a question of emphasis. For most of the great innovators of recent generations, often the most essential language lessons are a result not of what they said, but of what they didn't say. What you choose to leave out of your communication is just as important as what you choose to include. In business, the most successful people rarely talk about the bottom line, or profitability, or even success. Those are just mile markers along the way. Their message—and their gift—is about seeing a deficiency in our human existence and addressing it by finding a product or service that makes life better.

The best living example: Steve Jobs. He is referenced often in this book because he is among the most influential personalities of the twenty-first century. I have only met him once, and he was decidedly unfriendly, yet he has had a more pleasant, personal impact on the quality of my life than anyone I can think of. One of America's most respected CEOs who knows him well described the people-centered paradox that is Steve Jobs:

> *Steve Jobs is my idol. I've never seen anyone in my life accomplish what he's accomplished, at the scale that he's accomplished it, in terms of changing the world. America needs more people like him. Yet Steve Jobs is not a people person. He doesn't even say hello. He's in his own world. But I admire him more than any other businessperson in history because of his impact on so many people.*

The most successful communicators are charming and charismatic. This makes their task of winning far easier, but it is not essential. Notable exceptions—such as Bill Gates, who is socially awkward, and Jobs, who is often described in private as self-absorbed—overcame their interpersonal shortcomings by developing products that spoke *for* them. Winners like them come from a long line of competitive innovators like Thomas Edison and Henry Ford—people who were notably prickly and irritable, but who were also dedicated and driven to improve the human condition . . . and did.

From the entertainment world, notable examples include Oprah Winfrey and Martha Stewart—both are idolized for their communication capabilities and influence on popular culture, even though their own personal relationships are reportedly complex and troubled. They provide comfort to an increasingly anxious population seeking security in a difficult world. They know how to fill in the missing pieces in the lives of middle-aged and middle-income women in a way that transcends geography, economy, and ethnicity. Oprah's Book Club isn't about selling

books (a product); it's about selling peace of mind (a people-centered solution). Martha Stewart isn't selling recipes (a commodity you can get
anywhere); she's selling quality-of-life solutions you can trust, because
Martha trusts them and women trust Martha.

Quick, answer this: What do you sell? What is your Big Idea? Think
this over before reading on.

If you answered with a thing (like a "widget," or "health care," or your
"political candidacy," for instance), you haven't defined the "So what?"
that's essential to boiling down your idea into something that matters
to—and benefits—someone else. But if you answered with an attribute
("fewer hassles," or "quality time with family," or "better quality of life," or
a "more accountable government"), then you're a step ahead on the path
to winning.

Winners know what makes people tick, and they connect either to
our fears or our aspirations—or both. The job of all winning communicators is to recognize what is missing in the lives of others and then try
to address it. Winners help us imagine the possibilities that change our
realities.

That's one reason I always advocate a more positive, aspirational, hope-
ful approach to advertising and marketing. The people-centered approach
is to address, resolve, and alleviate personal pain—to focus on "solutions"
rather than the management of the problem. It's the same in politics. Voters have come to reject unrelenting negativity. In the 2009 Massachusetts Senate race, Republican Scott Brown's best message was when he
told his opponent, "Stop attacking the past. I am not Bush/Cheney. Let's
focus on the future." Even in Massachusetts—not exactly a prime location
for the George W. Bush legacy library—people wanted to know how this
race affected them *today* and *tomorrow*, not yesterday. While we may all
dwell on our own pasts, nobody wants someone else to dwell there, let
alone their elected representatives. Voters are more concerned about a
candidate's potential than his or her past. They would rather have politicians focused on a better future—for them.

PARADIGM BREAKING

Chapter 4 is about the people and products that dramatically change the way we live. Winners are not improvers; they are game-changers. Three attributes define paradigm breaking:

(1) the *attitude* of never settling for the conventional;

(2) the *practice* of purposeful reinvention; and

(3) the *necessity* of using skilled communication to lead people in a new direction. It's about convincing people that a radical departure from the status quo into a brave new world isn't just a good thing to do—it's the only thing to do. For example:

- There is a big difference between *innovation*, which is the language of the good, and *breakthrough*, which is the language of the great. Americans like innovation because it takes something known and makes it better. But they love breakthroughs—especially in medicine, science, technology, and other related areas—because they throw off the limits that constrain quality of life and replace them with something that shifts our expectations about existence. An innovation simply isn't big enough.

- A *bold approach* is better than an *incremental* one—but importantly stops short of the alarming tone of *revolutionary*. While Americans reject *revolutionary* and *radical* leaders or ideas, they are still seeking faster, more fundamental change than what is currently being offered from either Washington or Wall Street. A *bold approach* says things will change, but in a safe and reliable way. *Bold* people march ahead with purpose, but also with firm footing.

Breaking paradigms is something few can do, but fewer still can explain. Their language often has to overcome vast skepticism, doubt, and sometimes blatant hostility. Remember, as much as we say we want change, it is natural to resist it. As human beings, we innately fear the unknown, even if we simultaneously embrace it. The best communicators know how to position their new product or idea as an improvement that people should expect to have—not a burden they'll have to bear.

PRIORITIZATION

Winners in business and politics have an uncanny ability to prioritize, whether they're part of an organization or team, or are acting individually. They know how to separate what must be done from what should be done—and that has a direct correlation to what they say and when they say it. In fact, identifying and effectively articulating priorities may be the single most important component of successful communication.

The first step is to prioritize your actions so that your enterprise is wholly focused on what you can *win*. Bill Gates hosts no book clubs; Oprah programs no code. We cannot all win at everything. But even more crucially, Bill Gates knew better than to take the *slightly off-course* bait of, say, making microchips. Let Intel produce Pentium processors. Microsoft was going to stick to the *essential*, rather than focus on the merely *important*.

The second step of prioritization is related to language. Words remain at a premium in a world where audiences are increasingly distracted and

LUNTZ LESSONS

YOUR FIRST WORDS ARE MORE IMPORTANT
THAN YOUR LAST

Listen up. You get only one shot to make a good first impression, and what you say first colors everything that follows. It doesn't only color it, but depending on how you frame the context, the initial impression you make will either cast a shadow over your purpose or provide a foundation under it.

Whether you are asking for a raise or trying to raise a million dollars, whether you are working toward a promotion or promoting your candidacy, your first sentence, first thought, first idea, or first impression is by far the most important. So many people spend all their time focused on delivering their final thoughts. Not smart. In most cases, if you blow your opening, no one will be listening when you finish.

their attention spans are dwindling. If you accept the adage that what people hear is more important than what you say, knowing what to omit is as important as what to include. Winners prioritize their messages. For example, successful communicators need evidence to prove a point—but too much evidence is actually worse than too little, because listeners believe you're overcompensating or, even worse, tune you out completely. Brevity is still the soul of wit. In fact, in the era of texting and Twitter, the longer you speak, the less people hear.

PERFECTION

If you're not driven to perfection, you'll never reach excellence. This is the active and therefore better version of the feel-good but insufficient adage, "Shoot for the moon, and even if you miss, you'll end up among the stars." Winners understand this and, whether they admit that perfection is impossible (it is), they nevertheless make perfection their constant mission. Good enough . . . isn't.

As I'll explain in this chapter, there's a great deal of overlap between passion and perfection, because they feed off each other. Without a burning desire to do what you do, it's almost impossible to find the internal strength to strive for perfection. It's one thing to work sixteen-hour days because you have to. It's another to work sixteen-hour days because you *want* to.

Winners who are passionate about their work don't mind a sixteen-hour day if that's what it takes for them to be the best they can possibly be. Oprah didn't become the Queen of Talk by asking mediocre guests mediocre questions. That's how you become Chevy Chase or Ricki Lake. Oprah relentlessly pursues perfection in everything she does, from her TV show to her magazine, and everything in between.

As a business strategy, the pursuit of perfection can help distinguish one brand from another, especially in an overcrowded marketplace. See, for example, Lexus's language advantage over BMW and Mercedes in their ads where their tagline is "the relentless pursuit of perfection." Perfection implies value for the consumer and something worth hearing, seeing, experiencing, or knowing. Just take a trip to Steve Wynn's flagship hotel in Las Vegas to see what I mean. From the minute you enter Wynn Las Vegas, you're surrounded by opulence and elegance. Every detail, every inch of space, from the tiles on the floors to the decorations in the rooms, is meant to convey uncompromising perfection for customers of all tastes. And it does. There's a reason the Wynn name unequivocally stands for quality, value, and luxury.

Even if you aren't selling high-end luxury to high-dollar customers, you'll still be held accountable to the pursuit of perfection. Why? Because if you don't pursue perfection, your competitor can—and will—leave you in the dust.

PARTNERSHIP

No one is perfect. Were you to wake up tomorrow with infinite wisdom, unlimited resources, and a crystal ball, then you might not need other people to achieve the things you want to achieve. Until that happens, you need partners.

When asked about her new TV network in early 2010, Oprah made it clear that one of her biggest challenges was creating the team to help her make it all come together. "The biggest challenge is getting the right people to create the right kind of creative energy and synergy," she said. "It's about getting the right people on the right seats on the bus. And getting the people off of the bus that shouldn't be on the bus."[3] Even for someone like Oprah, who's rumored to have more money than God, there are limitations that only other smart, hardworking people can help her overcome. She aptly expresses an idea that originates with Aristotle—that the whole is greater than the sum of its parts.

Honest, open communication is paramount for a partnership to survive. Without it, trust and respect will simply wither on the vine. Your partnerships must also have balance. If one of you is a big risk taker, the other should probably be more prudent. If one is wildly disorganized, the other had better be methodical. Partnerships thrive on achieving the right balance that maximizes the "good" and minimizes the "bad" that each side brings to the relationship. Preferring collaboration to confrontation and consensus to conflict, women have the clear advantage. Anne Mulcahy, former CEO of Xerox, Irene Rosenfeld, CEO of Kraft

Foods, and Angela Brady, CEO of WellPoint health care, all rose to the top thanks to their partnership skills.

PASSION

There isn't a winner anywhere who doesn't bring passion to what they do or how they communicate. When you look at the expressions of passion of those at the top, there are three clear language attributes at play:

- First, they communicate confidence in themselves and in their products;
- Second, the message always rests on results and solutions; and
- Third, there is a clear call to action at the end.

But passion is about more than just words and language. Effectively communicating passion requires focus on style and delivery. In this case, it's not just what people hear that matters—it's *how* they hear it. Three examples:

- **Don't mistake volume for enthusiasm.** Shouting is one of the worst mistakes communicators make in demonstrating passion. Nobody wants to be yelled at, even when they agree with you. In reality, the most passionate—and persuasive—people speak the softest when it matters the most.
- **Absolutes are deal-breakers.** Never use language that suggests universal or unanimous agreement. Audiences don't like to hear words like *always, everyone,* or *all the time* because it suggests a certainty and uniformity that no one believes exists. In fact, avoid the word *never,* because people will conjure up exceptions in their minds. The minute they find one, you lose.
- **Passion and clarity must go hand in hand.** Doctors are notoriously bad communicators even though they are passionate about their work. They fill up their messaging with technical jargon that confuses rather than clarifies the point they're trying to make. Clear, concise communication will instill more passion than exact but confusing technical terms.

Passion is also about intensity. The two companies that I've seen exhibit the greatest intensity in serving their customers are FedEx and Anheuser-Busch. For FedEx, passion has an actual name: the Purple Promise. It's something every employee learns upon joining the company, and it has a very simple meaning: "to make every customer experience outstanding." It's what they hope differentiates them from UPS. A FedEx driver is expected to find a way to get a package to an individual no matter what it takes. Failure is not an option. The U.S. Postal Service may have a passionate motto—"Neither snow, nor rain, nor heat . . ."—but FedEx actually delivers. You never hear someone complain that "it got lost in the FedEx."

For decades, the motto of Anheuser-Busch wasn't about selling beer. It was about making friends. No one on the outside knew that senior executives at the company were given "sampling allowances" so they could buy beer for strangers at restaurants and bars. But it wasn't just about the beer. It was about the conversation and camaraderie to which that free beer led. They realized that beer is more than the ingredients or the brewing process. It's about the experience of drinking it with friends and family. No words or images can sell a beer better than the experiences you share over it. The executives of AB were among the best corporate communicators because they showed their passion for their product by giving it away. That culture began to disappear when the all-American company became foreign-owned in 2009, but some executives still practice friendship-building even today.

PERSUASION

Winners don't preach; they persuade. They tell you exactly why you should accept their point of view, yet you feel like you came to their conclusions on your own. Chapter 9 is based on the organizing theory behind *Words That Work:* it's not what you say but what people hear that matters. One of the most important components of persuasion is referencing that which people already believe and then using it as a springboard for the leap of faith you want them to take. This chapter explores the five components of any audience:

- **Rejecters.** These are the people who will oppose you no matter what you say or do.
- **Disagreeables.** They oppose or doubt you, but not strenuously, and effective persuasion can render them *neutral.*
- **Neutrals.** They can go either way. Within the typical corporate culture, this is the largest segment of employees, and management misses a great opportunity if it fails to seek their support.
- **Accepters.** They back you—but they're not willing to speak up for you. This is the most important segment of the audience and usually the make-or-break slice of the pie for would-be winners.
- **Embracers.** No convincing or motivation is needed. Whether it's a question of personal loyalty or willingness to be led, they're packed and ready to go. They just need to know what to say and do.

PERSISTENCE

Winning is never really about a single game, or product, or performance. Winners know how to succeed over the long haul. In fact, they know that winning is *defined* by repeat performances and increasing achievements. One-hit wonders experience brief success, but only consistent chart-toppers win the industry. Winners never give up, never accept defeat, and work as long and as hard as it takes to get the job done right. Most successful people have overcome multiple setbacks, often including bankruptcy, illness, and the inability to deliver what was promised, to name a few. From Toyota's failure to respond to its technological deficiencies to Tiger Woods's continued unwillingness to answer questions about his private life, not all icons make the right decisions all the time. The challenge is to communicate persistence even when everything around you is going to hell. Winners commonly say, *"Don't tell me why I can't do it. Tell me how I can get it done."*

PRINCIPLED ACTION

What good is winning at work if you lose at life? In my conversations with some of America's wealthiest, most successful people, their pride in their financial and career accomplishments is dwarfed by their personal disappointment over the condition of their family. In an effort to win it all in the workplace, they lost it all at home.

The concluding chapter attempts to put in perspective the essential nature of a set of the guiding principles that define true winners. It focuses on those who gave up their morality, humanity, and decency in the chase for success—and how they fell from grace because winning wasn't just everything, it was the only thing. From Ken Lay to Jack Abramoff to Bernie Madoff, they will be known not for what they temporarily achieved, but for how they achieved it and, ultimately, how miserably they failed.

What was going through Steve Jobs's mind that inspired him to create some of the most groundbreaking and successful products of our time, namely the iPod, the iPhone, and, most recently, the iPad?

How does Rupert Murdoch continue to astound allies and confound critics with his proficient decision-making on the eve of his eightieth birthday?

What was it about competition that drove Larry Bird to push himself and his team—the Boston Celtics—so hard that they ended up winning three NBA championships, with Bird taking home two NBA Finals MVP awards?

What can business professionals learn from the pre-match discipline, focus, and determination of tennis great Jimmy Connors?

What business skill does Mike Bloomberg respect most?

How does Steve Wynn reinvent himself, and Las Vegas, again and again . . . and again?

How did Amway founder Rich DeVos combine passion, persistence, and deeply rooted principles to build an eight-billion-dollar global marketing empire?

What essential attributes allowed Arnold Schwarzenegger to rise from poverty to conquer the entertainment world, the business world, and the political world?

And how did Ken Lay's and Jeff Skilling's stunning lack of principle take Enron from being one of the most admired and profitable companies in America to a corporate graveyard, costing thousands of jobs, decimating entire life savings, and ruining countless lives?

These are just a few of the questions I explore and answer throughout the pages of *Win*. I'll explain why each of the Nine *P*'s of Winning is so vital and so logical, yet so often overlooked by many business leaders, both in the suites of corporate America and in the back offices of small businesses throughout the country. It's important to understand that not every winner has all of these characteristics. In fact, you may need only one or two of them in a given situation to get the result you want. But you won't find a winner out there today who doesn't exhibit most, if not all, of these fundamental human traits.

3

PEOPLE-CENTEREDNESS
Humanizing your approach

I've seen him do it a million times,
but I can't tell you how he does it, Henry.
The right-handed part.
I can tell you what he does with his left hand.
He's a genius with it.
He might put that hand on your elbow . . .
or your bicep, like he's doing now.
Basic move. He's interested in you.
He's honored to meet you.
But if he gets any higher, if he gets on your shoulder . . .
it's not as intimate.
He'll share a laugh with you, a light secret.
And if he doesn't know you, but wants to share emotion . . .
he'll lock you in a two-hander.
You'll see when he shakes hands with you, Henry.

—THE OPENING SCENE OF *PRIMARY COLORS*, 1998

Say what you will, Bill Clinton is a winner.

In the spring of 1992, while attending a fund-raiser in New York City for his presidential campaign, Clinton was confronted by a very angry man on a very specific mission. That man was Bob Rafsky, a member of the AIDS awareness and advocacy group ACT UP (AIDS Coalition to Unleash Power). Having made his way through the crowd to stand just inches from Clinton, Rafsky said, "We're not dying of AIDS as much as we are dying of 11 years of government neglect." Somewhat taken aback, Clinton simply replied, "I feel your pain."[4] And in a single moment, with a single sentence, Bill Clinton said something that, forever, will cast him in Americans' minds as a preeminent man of the people. Rather than trying to argue with or debate Rafsky about what he was saying, he acknowledged his frustration (his pain), validating Rafsky's feelings and letting him know that the candidate personally cared. In that moment, he temporarily stopped being a politician and instead became a human being.

Clinton went on to win the presidency that year because he, more than any other political figure, understood what was happening in the country at that time, and had an innate ability to communicate it right back. Clinton *was* a man of the people—he felt our pain and knew how to connect with us. In a debate that year, he said that when someone lost a job in his home state of Arkansas, he probably knew the person by name. Of course, that was an exaggeration, but it didn't matter. Bill Clinton was a new type of character in the drama of American politics. He understood people to such a degree, and could relate to them on such a personal level, that he could reach them in a way few politicians ever could. He was smooth. He was confident. And it wasn't by accident. Although his stories, words, tone, and facial expressions appeared to materialize effortlessly, every single gesture, look, and remark were crafted specifically to show that he was listening. He was a master of empathy.

No matter what you may think of Bill Clinton's character or politics, he's the single most people-centered public figure alive today. Regardless of your ideology, when he speaks, you listen. He seems to have weighed the facts, studied the policy, listened to the different arguments, and then subjected all those considerations to a simple question: How does this idea affect everyday people? It's no accident that the Clinton White House was famous for late-night, twelve-round policy fights that were refereed by Clinton himself. He wanted you to know that he wasn't just feeling your pain; he was working hard to heal it. He studied like a wonk, but communicated like a friend. Translating one to the other is the rarest of political talents.

Clinton is the personification of a people-centered leader. He commands his voice and words—and even his face—in a manner that compels listeners, whether auditoriums packed with thousands, or individuals in one-on-one conversations, to stop and look, listen and learn. And whether he's actually in the room with you or simply on your TV screen, you almost always feel like he's talking to *you* and no one else. He creates an authentic connection that can turn even his most ardent critics into momentary cheerleaders. Republican congressmen and senators routinely freeze like deer in the headlights when he speaks to them. Bill Clinton understands people.

Now, note the term *people-centered*. That is *not* the same thing as being a people person. When I talk about being people-centered, I do not necessarily refer to the kind of people we like to hang out with in our leisure time. I don't mean people who know how to "connect" with us and who "get" us. Yes, that's part of the concept, but there's so much more to it. If you're a people person, you walk into a roomful of strangers and in no time you've made three friends. You've probably already networked your way into at least one upcoming soiree, and if you're really good, you've snagged a few business cards, given out a few of your own, and you are already drumming up real revenue before the last overserved partygoer stumbles out the door. You're a connector. You're the kind of person who brings others together. You're invaluable.

But Bill Clinton provides a perfect example of what it means to be people-centered—and every would-be networker can learn from his example. For him, networking wasn't just a matter of passing out business cards, collecting those of others, and making the most of the time at the event before calling it a night. And he didn't rely on charisma alone. Instead he had a *habitual practice* of coming home each night and meticulously recording each conversation in a growing library of index cards. He committed to memory not just where someone worked or what someone did, but *who they were*. So the next time he saw them, asking "How have you been?" wasn't just an empty formality; it was loaded with understanding that allowed him to meet that person's individual need to be known and valued. And no matter who we are, we all have that basic need for connection.

If you met him, he remembered you. What's more, he treated you like an old friend. He did it to me, and I even worked against him. The lesson: do not underestimate the simple power that recall has on an individual. Every person wants to be not just noticed, but memorable. In a world that moves faster and faster, and where people are treated more and more like commodities, the leader who slows it down—who truly treats people like individuals and not interchangeable pieces—wins.

Just being a people person will not make you a winner. Your witty banter and off-the-cuff pop-culture references at cocktail parties might help fatten your list of contacts, but they will not help you discover America's most pressing needs and desires. Those who are people-centered, however, enjoy an advantage that, if bottled and sold, would cost more than a government toilet seat.

No company is more focused on building personal relationships or is better at it than Facebook. With more than 550 million users globally and growing by the day, they have redefined human interaction in the twenty-first century. Along with Google, Facebook is transforming the way people connect and share information in their personal and professional lives, so it makes perfect sense that the process of building partnerships is at the core of what they seek to do. At the core of this effort is Sheryl Sandberg, Facebook's highly accomplished COO. A chief of staff to the U.S. Treasury Secretary while in her twenties, a VP at Google (until Facebook stole her away), and a board member at both Disney and Starbucks, she has clearly earned her ranking on the Fortune Most Powerful Women in Business list. When I asked her for the secret of her success, her response was immediate: *"Blame yourself when things go wrong, and give credit to others when things go right. The process of giving other people credit is what it takes to build a team."* Sandberg, one of America's great team builders, knows exactly what it takes to win.

Sandberg is as focused and people-centered as the company she runs. She has a big poster in her conference room that reads "The Future Belongs to Those Who Are Willing to Get Their Hands Dirty." *"I actually got it from Howard Schultz's conference room,"* she admits. For her, team building is about face-to-face interaction at all levels. *"I visit the clients myself. Everyone should. Things will go wrong when your people lose touch, when they think they've gotten too senior to talk to people. When I do conferences with my sales team, I ask them right up front whether they have talked to a customer within twenty-four hours. If they haven't, they've got a problem."*

Which of the following do you believe is most important for a good CEO to demonstrate or possess?

	TOTAL
Understands people—how to lead them and how to reach them	58%
Strong passion and personal commitment to the company's success	36%
Outstanding communication skills and authenticity	29%
Genuine common sense	29%
Excellent business skills	16%
Knows the products and services inside and out	16%
Great intelligence	10%
Decades of real-world experience	6%

Source: The Word Doctors, 2010

So why do I think that people-centered individuals and companies are so much more likely to become winners than the rest of us? The most important thing to keep in mind is that winning isn't just about achieving a bottom-line profit. No, our people-centered colleagues are so much more likely to make it to the pinnacle of success because they know what makes people tick. They know what to look for, and they know which questions to ask in order to unleash an unknown—and thus unrealized, pent-up demand. That's what led mothers and collectors alike to stand in line for hours at Toys "R" Us in the '80s, literally fighting over the only available crate of Cabbage Patch Kids when it arrived on the sales floor. In the summer of 2007, the same phenomenon was responsible for the lines that formed for months at 7 a.m. each day at Apple stores around the country as shoppers waited patiently (or impatiently) for that day's supply of iPhones. And once again, in 2010, the Apple iPad packed them in, day after day after day.

I asked Henry Juszkiewicz for his take on why Steve Jobs is so effective at developing technological gadgets that people simply love:

Steve Jobs is a great example of an incredibly intuitive mind.
The iPod is an example of his brilliance of mind, because music players

were available long before the iPod. Creative had an MP3 before the iPod. So did several others. They were readily available, but they never really took off. They were talked about, but stayed rather fringe. There were a lot of problems with the way these guys had focused the technology. What Steve did, he took that technology and made it usable. He was able to step into a consumer's mind. That's what his intuitive gift is. He really knows what people want, even before they know they need it, and he can really step into their shoes.

Winning is finding a product or service that meets a need or fulfills a desire—sometimes even one we've yet to recognize. Sometimes it's just a really big marketing victory that people write about in books like this. But it's also about making life better to such an astonishing degree that what you've done truly changes what it means to live the "human experience." Once winners have done their thing, we mere mortals cannot imagine life any other way.

One misconception about being people-centered needs to be cleared up before I explore the communication techniques of these sociological sleuths and business anthropologists. Understanding and being able to connect with people—to know them better than they know themselves— is not the same thing as being charming, charismatic, or even nice. Some of the most successful people-centered individuals in the world— in fact, in human history—have reportedly been difficult, if not dreadful, to be around.

Those who have worked for Anna Wintour, American *Vogue*'s editor in chief, say that the 2003 book and the 2006 movie *The Devil Wears Prada* aren't too far off the mark. Based on Wintour, the character Miranda Priestly is a middle-aged, venomous magazine editor who also happens to be one of the most important people in the nearly $1.3 trillion global apparel industry. A hapless, newly minted journalist becomes her assistant and quickly learns that in her boss's world, limitless success means ignoring the feelings of everyone around you. Granted, such portrayals of excessive executives are often self-serving and indulgent, but the story here is a perfect depiction of the disparity between human decency and business victory. You do not need the former to achieve the latter. Winners may understand what drives people better than anyone else. But that doesn't mean for a minute that they care about your birthday or anniversary when there are deadlines to meet. Anna Wintour has her finger on the pulse of women even as her hands are wrapped around her employees' throats.

It would be a mistake, however, to assume that charm, wit, and grace have nothing to do with one's ability to connect with people and figure out what they really, really want. Those characteristics may not be necessary for you to become people-centered, but they almost always help. They certainly go a long way toward maintaining the loyal, dedicated, and motivated work teams on which your success ultimately depends.

The reason people who can connect have such a stronger ability to

ARE YOU PEOPLE-CENTERED?

Ask yourself the following five questions. If the answer to four of the five is yes, you exhibit the essential attributes of a people-centered person.

1. *Do you look others right in the eyes?* People-centered people are very attentive not just to what you say but how you say it, and they are looking for the emotion behind your language.

2. *Do you repeatedly ask "why"?* Naturally inquisitive, people-centered individuals want to know how others think, and they deconstruct idle conversation the way scientists deconstruct a molecule.

3. *Do you analyze what you can gain from each interaction?* While the first two attributes suggest a person who is focused on others, the reality is often exactly the opposite. They are constantly looking for personal meaning and benefit from interactions with others. It's not that they're selfish. It does mean that they are always focused on achieving their goals by learning from others. By listening to—and caring about—someone else's needs, you can then identify the opportunity to make your service align with that need.

4. *Do you actively look to improve products, results, or situations?* Most people-centered people are also problem-solvers. They are always looking for things they need to fix and then fixing them. They seek opportunity—or create it.

5. *Do you apply your experiences?* Whether it is people, products, services, or experiences, people-centered people have an ability to take what they learn from one situation and apply it to other areas of their life. Everything you've done, experienced, and learned up to this moment is your working capital for winning. Put it to work in every situation, however you can.

win others over lies in one word: *respect*. When someone affords us their undivided time and attention, we feel respected, appreciated, and significant. Most of the winners profiled in this book are more than just believers in the essential nature of respect—they're practitioners. *"You can't ever gain respect until you show respect,"* declares Richard DeVos, the visionary cofounder of Amway and one of the great entrepreneurs of the twentieth century. With his wife and partner of fifty years nodding in agreement, he emphasized, *"Your first act of communication is to show respect to whomever you're talking to. Whatever their philosophy, whatever their flavor, whatever their color, you've got to show that you respect them as a person. When people don't respect you, they don't let you in. They don't tell you their secrets. And they don't give you the information you need to give them what they want."*

It's hard to identify a company today that depends more on effective messaging than Amway. When DeVos talks communication theory, the thirteen thousand Amway employees and multiple millions more independent business owners (IBOs) listen intently. After five decades of success, Amway is consistently in the top fifty privately owned companies as ranked by *Forbes,* and Deloitte identifies them as one of the largest and most successful retailers in the world. Based on those numbers alone, DeVos may be the best salesman of his generation. He certainly created one of the great direct-marketing empires, with global sales of $8.4 billion in 2009.

Steve Wynn is another example of someone who simply "gets" people— and for him it started at an early age. *"My dad told me, and he truly lived by this, 'Steve, these people make our life possible. When you look at them, think of that and be grateful. You should love them.' He heard somebody make a disparaging remark about a heavyset bingo customer, and my father fired the guy. He said to me: 'If you ever look down your nose at a customer, you shouldn't be here.'"*

Wynn knows a lot about hotel design, but he knows even more about people and how to create the perfect resort environment to make visitors feel so at ease that even the most intense people open up and enjoy it. The very tone of his melodic voice is so mesmerizing (my female focus group participants have told me this; I'm just reporting the research—and since women make two-thirds of the vacation decisions, it's their opinions that matter) that you don't mind being put on hold because you get to listen to Wynn himself give you your own private tour of the resort.*

The lesson of Steve Wynn is to understand and embrace the person you have to be to match the business you've chosen. If you're selling GM cars today, you need to have a humble, authentic, "let's get to work" approach. If you're selling Toyota, it's closer to "I'm sorry" and "here's what I plan to do to regain your trust." The American consumer expects no less. But if you're selling the experience of luxuriating at the most opulent casino in Vegas, people expect Mr. Wynn's grasp of showmanship. And if you don't have it, you won't be a winner.

Much like Bill Clinton, former president George W. Bush had the remarkable ability to connect with the "average American," either one-on-one or in small group meetings. Whether this was because of, or in spite of, the creative liberties he took with the English language is a question for another book. Even so, those who talked to him came away saying he was one of the most affable and charming men you could ever hope to meet—nothing like the man who was hopelessly straitjacketed by podiums, teleprompters, and TV. In fact, even the Al Gore presidential campaign team had to admit that Bush had a way with people. After one of the presidential debates, Gore's spokesman Todd Webster conceded, "Look, [Bush] is an endlessly charming man. He's engaging and witty . . . but that doesn't mean that he should be president of the United States."[5] Unlike Gore, whose wooden movements and stagnant speech were boring at best, Bush knew how to connect with people. It was that very charm and human connection that helped him win reelection, a feat neither his father nor Jimmy Carter was able to accomplish.

Whether you like George W. Bush or not, being elected president of the United States twice, by definition, makes you a winner. Personally, I've always thought the main reason John Kerry lost the 2004 election wasn't necessarily that George W. Bush was so much stronger a candidate, but because John Kerry stayed so distant from average people that a majority

---

* People actually admit to *asking* to be put on hold. That has never happened elsewhere in all my work in the hospitality industry.

of Americans simply couldn't identify with him.* To most Americans, he was (and still is) a very liberal, Northeast, blue-blood politician.† In point of fact, writing for Salon.com (not exactly a bastion of conservatism) in 2003, columnist Ben Fritz observed:

> Like [Al] Gore, the Massachusetts Democrat has been characterized, with some justice, as being aloof and cold. On Saturday, when asked about his haughty image during the first debate among the Democratic candidates, he tried to laugh it off (in much the same way Gore unsuccessfully joked about being stiff in 2000) by suggesting he "ought to just disappear and contemplate that by myself."[6]

Great joke, but it's why he wasn't people-centered—and why he wasn't a winner. When Bill Clinton delivered a disastrous hour-long keynote speech at the Democratic National Convention in 1988 that was interrupted with applause only when he said the words *in conclusion,* he immediately understood what he had done wrong and sat himself on the couch next to Johnny Carson the following week to make amends publicly and to laugh it off with several self-deprecating observations. Carson ridiculed him in a three-minute introduction, but Clinton's good humor endeared him to the millions watching and it began to restore his credibility and his people-centered image.

Barack Obama may have been just as *liberal* as John Kerry (if not more so), but he knew how to subvert that image to appear and sound more mainstream in 2008.‡ He could speak to the American people in a language they understood and wanted to hear. Obama, like Bush, could connect. John Kerry could not.

I've witnessed Obama's people-centered approach firsthand when I was invited to meet him in his Senate office in 2006. It was described on his calendar as a "meet-and-greet," but I could tell right away that it was something more. He met me outside his personal office—a rarity

---

* Though admittedly, Bush did an amazing job of making Kerry look weak on terrorism at a time when the memories of 9/11 were still quite fresh and America had just begun a second war, this time in Iraq.

† According to *National Journal's* 2010 ratings, John Kerry is the sixth most liberal senator in the country.

‡ According to *National Journal's* 2007 ratings, Barack Obama was the most liberal senator in the country.

among senators, who generally prefer their guests to see them working behind their desks. He was jacketless and surprisingly casual, again a rarity considering this was only the second time we had met. (Maybe in true people-centered style, he was trying to put me at ease from the outset.) But what immediately grabbed my attention was when he led me not to the sofa where guests always sit when talking to a senator but to *his* chair, as he went for the sofa. Having done hundreds of such meetings, and being stunned by this, I asked him why he had made this seating decision. His response? *"If I knew you a little better, I wouldn't be sitting on this couch. I'd be lying on this couch."* From that moment, he began to quiz me about my beliefs, convictions, and electoral theories, and with every response, he offered a short story or anecdote meant to connect his life with my comments. He didn't just want to learn about me. He wanted to connect with me. That defines a people-centered approach, and it defines a winner.

Now that I've offended most of you by saying nice things about three controversial presidents within three pages, let me offer this notion that undoubtedly rings true: in every presidential election in the television age, the winning candidate has been the person with whom most Americans would rather have a beer and a burger at a barbecue. There's something uniquely American about relaxed, homespun authenticity. We admire it, we relate to it, and it puts us at ease.

So ask yourself, are you capturing that natural affinity with the way you communicate?

Many of the examples are obvious, like Dubya defeating a windsurfing John Kerry and a very cool Clinton beating a very dull Dole. Others are not so clear (George H. W. Bush over Michael Dukakis in the dull and duller election) or reflect a change in prevailing perceptions over time (Jimmy Carter, the Southern peanut farmer, was more credible than Jimmy Carter, the flailing president that followed). Think about it: who would you rather *hang* with—the relaxed, almost jovial Barack Obama, or your cranky uncle John McCain? You may not be an Obama fan today, but millions people went out of their way to hear and see him during the 2008 campaign.

Through our televisions and our home computers, Americans have to *live* with our presidents in our living rooms and bedrooms for four to eight years. It's no surprise that we tend to choose the person we relate to—or at least tolerate—the most.

A CORPORATE CASE STUDY

Why is it so hard for companies to give great customer service? They don't think like the customer, they don't put themselves in the shoes of the customer. They're thinking more about their own organization, processes, and rule book the way it's always been done. Most companies want to make life easier for themselves as opposed to the customer.[7]

—ROBERT SPECTOR,

AUTHOR, *THE NORDSTROM WAY TO CUSTOMER SERVICE EXCELLENCE*

Most companies teach and preach the importance of customer service, yet too often their standards and procedures undermine these efforts even before the first customer walks through the door. If you've ever called any major retail store, airline, or cable company for assistance, you know exactly what I'm talking about. Sure, fewer employees means less overhead and more profitability—in the short run—but the problem with automation and now e-mail is that it is devoid of human contact. As for the workforce, particularly in retail, too often they seem more concerned about punching out than tuning in.

To quote Don Corleone and Aga Khan, "fish rots from the head." The people who fail to effectively motivate their employees are often the same people who fail to communicate effectively to their customers. So if you want to be a winner, know what customers most want from you and what you have to communicate to your people—in order of importance.

Here's your answer. In a 2010 national survey of consumers, notice that *respected* and *valued* actually finish ahead of *well-serviced*. That's as good a sign as any that the process of customer service is less important than the result. Or as Academy Award winner Warren Beatty once said, "People will quickly forget what you said, but they'll always remember how you made them feel."

In the midst of a world filled with ambivalent salespeople, there is one company that has been a winner for three decades because it takes a people-centered approach to everything it does: Nordstrom. The word *no* never entered into their vocabulary. While some of the following are no longer commonplace, the Nordstroms of the 1980s and '90s were known to:

HOW DO YOU WANT THE COMPANIES YOU DO BUSINESS WITH TO MAKE YOU FEEL?

Respected	40%
Valued	29%
Well-Serviced	27%
Secure	24%
Confident	15%
Appreciated	13%
Professional	13%
Comfortable	11%
In Control	11%
Happy	4%
Socially Responsible	4%
Relaxed	3%
Connected	3%
Hopeful	2%

Source: The Word Doctors, January 2010.

- Pay shoppers' parking tickets
- Accept returns without receipt or question
- Rush deliveries to offices
- Lend cash to strapped customers
- Send tailors to customers' homes[8]

Walk into a Nordstrom today and you'll likely encounter salespeople who have worked there more than a decade—some much longer. In an industry that turns over staff every two or three years, Nordstrom has among the most loyal employees, which contributes to an unusually loyal customer base. They really do live by the eight management principles that are taught to every store manager and reinforced again and again:

1. Provide your customer with choices.
2. Create an inviting place for your customer.
3. Hire nice, motivated people.

4. Sell the relationship.
5. Empower employees to take ownership.
6. Dump the rules.
7. Encourage internal competition.
8. Commit 100% to customer service.[9]

Salespeople at Nordstrom are paid a healthy commission and are judged on their performance, not on their ability to pass the time. This approach ensures that customer service is the expectation, not the exception. Another distinguishing factor is the employee hiring criteria. Nordstrom seeks employees who fit a description: candidates who are already personable, not ones the company has to try to mold into nice people. When company chairman Bruce Nordstrom was asked who trains his people, his response was "their parents."[10] And current CEO Blake Nordstrom, Bruce's son, attributes their renewed success to his policy of listening to and supporting his sales force rather than ordering them to perform. "We believe in an inverted pyramid where management is on the bottom and salespeople and customers are on the top."[11] It should come as no surprise that *The Nordstrom Way to Customer Service Excellence,* which divulged the secrets behind their legendary customer service, became a best seller. This book is required reading for each of Nordstrom's employees prior to their first day on the job.

STORYTELLING

People-centered winners expertly employ imagery, metaphors, and stories. They make you step out of your perceptions, if only for a moment, to explore *their* vision on *their* terms. They ask us to "close our eyes," to "imagine," and to "think about what it would be like." In essence, they're linguistic tour guides who take you on a journey to *their* destination—while convincing you that it's a place you want to go.

Without fail, they'll start any presentation or sales pitch with a narrative that both interests and engages their audience—because they know the most efficient inspiration derives not only from teaching, but from *in-*

teracting. It may be obscure—maybe about a business trip or a conversation they had with someone they met in an elevator or at a restaurant. Regardless, the story's impact will be immeasurable because it will set the tone and frame the rest of the discussion. And the story, if told well, will make the lesson memorable by creating a human connection with everyone in the audience and serving as a reference for understanding the larger challenge they're all asked to overcome. Through imagery and a well-told story, a winner can turn a room of skeptics into a room of soldiers, ready to suit up and fight for victory.

Stories are how we understand and interpret the world. They give us place, meaning, and a reference point for figuring out how life is supposed to work.

Hollywood is full of the men and women who've dedicated their lives to telling and presenting great stories. I had the chance to talk to one of those storytellers not long ago. *"I'm an actor. My job is to scrutinize human behavior, and I think I scrutinize it better than most,"* Richard Dreyfuss boasted, with a cat-that-swallowed-the-canary grin, sitting by the pool at the Beverly Hilton Hotel, home to many a sparkling Hollywood event. I include him because he is a people-centered actor, and he has a passion and commitment to perfection for his craft that is unrivaled:

> I always knew I was going to be a movie star. What I didn't realize is that I wanted to be a movie star of the thirties and forties. And that you can't do today. The censorship that existed then forced the films to be better. In the thirties and forties, the story came first, then character and then dialogue. So that you can watch the tackiest MGM Clark Gable, Lana Turner Western and hear more brilliant dialogue than anything being written now.
>
> I grew up knowing every single film that every American studio made. When I was a kid, I would wake up at three o'clock in the morning and I would study Spencer Tracy, and I would study Charles Laughton, and I would study Irene Dunne. I can enter a room exactly the way Tracy did. [At this moment, Dreyfuss leaps out of his chair, waddles back about twenty feet, and walks toward me with a deliberate gait.] Tracy entered the room differently than anyone else in the movie business. He

always hit his mark. [Dreyfuss comes to a halt a few feet from me, pointing at an imaginary mark on the ground, noticing and ignoring the fact that a couple of dozen people are watching him imitate Tracy's walk. To Dreyfuss, the story takes precedence.]

The story always came first. After seeing *Avatar,* I'm not so sure the same can be said today. And that might explain why Hollywood has lost some of its cachet over the years. The people Dreyfuss mentioned, and even Dreyfuss himself, were legends in film because they came to work every day intent on telling the best story possible. Sadly, Americans have now become accustomed to the big studios putting out films that look and sound good, but whose stories are often mediocre, or worse. The experience of going to the movies and getting lost in a great story is starting to fade away.

And if you don't think visuals matter, consider what Bob Lutz—a living legend in the automotive industry and former vice president of BMW, vice president of Ford, president of Chrysler, and vice chairman of General Motors (the man's held more jobs than a utility infielder for the New York Yankees)—had to say when I asked him about how someone's appearance can affect their message. *"I think the initial barrier to the absorption of information can either be drawn down or raised by the person's appearance. The message itself will lose much of its power and meaning if the source looks unattractive or unreliable."* Having designed the look of more vehicles than anyone alive today, he ought to know. How you look matters as much as what you're actually saying, so remember that next time you're having an in-depth conversation with someone you're trying to impress and you are wearing a wrinkled shirt with a tomato sauce stain from lunch on it.

LISTENING AND LEARNING

I've mentioned that people-centered winners understand the fundamental dynamics of human nature. This is a critical factor in their success. People-centered winners respect our beliefs (even if they don't agree with them), recognize the assumptions we make (even if they know we're wrong), and realize how our past experiences influence the actions we take today (even if they can't truly relate to those experiences). But people-centered winners also know how to get inside our minds to figure out what we really want in life. Part of this power stems from their insatiable curiosity. Winners, like Rupert Murdoch, understand that success depends on accurately knowing what the public thinks and what the public wants—and they are always on the prowl for the next tidbit of business intelligence. *"I have to be sensitive to what the public is doing and what they want,"* Murdoch told me in our interview. *"I worry about a lot of things. I am curious about what everybody else thinks and curious about the world. I think that's what keeps me going, constant curiosity."*

Winners want to know what other people are doing, saying, and thinking. They read incessantly. They consume *outside* their comfort zone. I might get in trouble with Rupert, Roger Ailes, and my friends at Fox News for putting this in print, but if you're watching only one cable news station and rejecting every other perspective, you're limiting your potential to win. Winners are in the know, in the loop, and online—and they see the entire picture. But more than simply devouring everything around them, they're always thinking about life in strategic, unique ways.

The next time you're in your local grocery store or Walmart, pay close attention to everything going on around you. Look at the people around you. Carefully eavesdrop on some conversations. Engage a stranger in small talk about a tube of toothpaste or a new type of cold medicine. It may sound silly, but these are the types of experiences and conversations winners have. Where most of us might see a trip to the mall as a hassle, winners relish the chance to observe people—average, everyday, "real" people—going about their daily lives. As a researcher, I've learned as much about people while waiting to board a plane in a crowded airport as I have in focus groups.* In fact, I often learn much more than I'd like to know.

---

* The single best day of the year to learn anything about anyone is December 26. You'll find out how people are doing economically, emotionally, and spiritually. As a behavioral scientist, it is one of my favorite days of the year.

LUNTZ LESSONS

THE VISUAL COMPONENT OF READING PEOPLE

I've been studying language for two decades, but I have to admit that it is often what people *don't* say that matters most. While this book is meant to explain the attributes, characteristics, and words of the most successful people in society, allow me to offer insight into where people often get it wrong:

1. **Looking up and/or away.**

   Making constant eye contact is difficult for all but the most confident people. It's often easier to look down rather than stare straight ahead, so don't think worse of someone if they occasionally drop their glance. (Women are more comfortable with direct eye contact than men, and men are more comfortable maintaining direct eye contact with a woman than with another man.) But people who look above you or around you either have something to hide or are thinking about something else—or are looking for an excuse to get out of the conversation.

2. **Folding your arms.**

   No matter how comfortable it may be, this is a bad visual message to send. CEOs do this quite often, and it communicates a combination of "I don't care" and "How dare you say that"—which is lethal in any situation. In Tiger Woods's second news conference at the 2010 Masters following revelations of his extramarital affairs, he spoke for a full half hour with his arms protectively folded in front of his body. His words may have communicated repentance, but his body was telling a different story.

3. **Checking your watch and/or phone, or texting/e-mailing.**[*]

   It's rude. It's disrespectful. And it is the quickest way to break any bond you might have formed with another person. Most successful people have learned not to do this when others are talking. If you have to answer your phone, explain why (for example, I'm expecting an urgent call from my child). If you explain *before* you look down, you will be forgiven.

---

[*] Warning: Few things bother winners more than the misuse of e-mail. Treat e-mail and texting as seriously as you would a phone call. Interrupting someone important with an unimportant e-mail or text is the surest way to have future correspondence ignored. When it comes to e-communicating, it is often best NOT to have the last word.

4. **Head nodding.**
This is a double-edged sword. It communicates agreement, approval, and that you're paying attention. But if done too often, it becomes distracting and undermines the give-and-take of a successful conversation. Avoid nodding unless you genuinely agree and need to express it before given the opportunity to speak.

THE POWER OF QUESTIONS: ASK AND YE SHALL RECEIVE

There's no better way to learn what drives people and makes them tick than by asking them. I asked Mort Zuckerman, the founder and CEO of Boston Properties and owner of the *New York Daily News* and *U.S. News & World Report*, how he was able to close some of the biggest real estate and media deals in his lifetime. His answer? *"You just have to listen. You have to get a sense of what is in the interest of the other people as they see it. And you have to ask questions."* What's important to remember is that listening is about *them*, not about *you*. It's how you get inside and get people to show you what *you* want to see, not just what *they* want you to see.

Since 1989, I've spoken to more than a million people in focus groups, interviews, and surveys. I've probed them about every topic you can imagine. From underwear and eating habits to financial decisions and movie preferences, I've seen it all and heard it all. I'm certainly not a people person, but I am a people-centered person, and I live for the opportunity to peel away the layers of defense mechanisms people often hide behind. I titled my last book *What Americans Really Want . . . Really*, not because I was born with some deep and hidden knowledge about human nature and the American psyche, but because I have spent years doing two things over and over again: asking and listening.

If there's one thing I've learned in my years researching people and what they want, it's that more often than not, you just have to ask the right people the right questions at the right time. Regardless of gender, geography, age, income, race, religion, education, or any other factor you can think of, most people want to talk. They like to talk. They want to tell you what *they* think and what *they* want. And they want you to listen.

But for many companies, asking and listening are harder than they should be. Many CEOs and corporate executives look down on the idea of "focus grouping" because they think they know what people want better than the people themselves.

I often hear executives and company people claim they know their product better than any customer could. Or politicians say that voters don't really understand the complex policy issues that force them to vote a certain way. Both come to the same wrong conclusion for the same wrong reason: If I know my product better than my consumer, why bother listening to them? That question is not only simplistic, it's arrogant. The correct answer is simple: you *don't* know how your product *intersects* with the real life of a real person unless you ask them.

And asking is not enough. You must listen, understand, and take on *their* perspective. That means eschewing every preconceived notion you possess and putting yourself firmly in your customers' position. It sounds easy, but almost no one can do it. Even in my profession, too many of my colleagues either tell the client what they want to hear, or tell them what they themselves already thought, regardless of what the research says.

The same questions that you should ask customers apply to employees as well. While many assume that a people-centered enterprise is primarily focused on customers, FedEx CEO Fred Smith has spent four decades ensuring that his company is equally or even more attentive to its employees. In fact, when I asked Smith to talk about the language of customer satisfaction, a FexEx specialty, he focused on employee satisfaction instead:

> FedEx is firmly anchored to a set of beliefs about people that have guided us, just like the North Star had guided mariners. That foundation is built on a set of fundamental questions that people ask in every setting that we try to answer. These aren't our questions. These are ques-

tions that all of the great sociologists and psychologists have developed over the years:

When you hire someone, they want to know, "What do you expect from me?"

When they get into the organization, they want to know, "What do I need to do to get ahead?"

They want to know, "What's in this for me?"

They want to know, "How do I get justice if I run into a difficult situation inside the organization?"

And the last thing they want to know is, "Is what I am doing important?"

We constantly try to focus on those questions and answer them for people so that they can perform at a very high level. We do this because it is the right thing to do. But we also do it because in a high-performance service business, it is something that you have to do if you want to perform to customer expectations consistently. It's so baked into our corporate DNA today that it really is almost on automatic pilot.

In this deeply cynical, hostile, anti-CEO environment, the people who work at FedEx still call Fred Smith Mr. Smith out of respect and reverence—because they see him as their advocate. He is their biggest fan, and they are his.

Simplistic questions stifle development, but insightful questions spur even deeper insight. Tony Robbins is one of the smartest and most successful speakers, authors, and business consultants in the world. He serves as the chairman or vice chairman of seven companies, which combined bring in almost half a billion dollars in revenue every year.[12] Tony Robbins is a winner, so listen to his advice. "Quality questions create a quality life," he says. "Successful people ask better questions, and as a result, they get better answers."[13]

LUNTZ LESSONS

THE 9 ESSENTIAL QUESTIONS YOU
NEED TO ASK YOURSELF

1. Am I asking the right questions?
2. Am I truly listening to the answers?
3. Am I acting on what I learn?
4. What more can I do to really understand those I wish to influence?
5. What more can I do to ensure that others understand me?
6. How can I get my people to be more engaged in what I'm doing?
7. How can I make my people feel more invested in our mutual success?
8. Is this truly a journey/mission/task worth undertaking?
9. When (not if) we succeed, will it really be worth it?

THE "TRUTH"

Winners talk to people in order to dig deeper and find the most relevant, transcending, permeating *truth*. Being honest is certainly smarter than lying, but the Truth matters most. True believers know what I'm talking about. I learned this from one of my most talented staffers ever, Lowell Baker, who also helped me with this book. He taught me that the Truth was the single highest value in a person's belief system—and if you could connect to people on that level, you had it made. In a world of claims, assertions, declarations, and affirmations, there is only one Truth. Find it, articulate it, and never, ever take it for granted.

In order to uncover the Truth, you'll have to work hard to find the fundamental dynamics involved in any given scenario. What's the motivation behind what people are or aren't doing? What keeps them awake at night? What are their true hopes, dreams, and fears? If you're not asking the right questions, there's little chance you'll ever be able to fully understand what's driving their decisions. The constant questioning that leads to uncovering the Truth is your key to understanding the human condition—and that is how you will maximize your personal and professional success.

It's too easy to let bad language distract from the search for the Truth. British television's Sir David Frost made this point perfectly when I had the chance to speak to him in London about what it means to conduct a good interview:

> One of the most important lessons is to avoid the language that point-lessly provokes people. If it is a genuine confrontation, and you genuinely disagree with somebody, then you have a genuine confrontation. But it's pointless to have pointless confrontations. No point in heckling people if you don't have the smoking pistol there underneath to deal with it.

Needless confrontation inevitably leads to needless consternation. Often the smartest tactic is not trying to look like you're the smartest person in the room, which means keeping quiet when it makes sense and throwing a softball every now and then to keep things cool and cordial. Winners don't have to win every encounter—just the important ones.

I want to end this section on questioning with another great story David Frost told me. We were talking about Bill Clinton, and I'd asked him about the interview they had together a few years ago. I wanted to understand how he crafts questions that cause his subjects to pause,

ASSIGNMENT: QUESTIONS, PLEASE

Each day this week, have one conversation in which you do almost nothing but ask questions. In fact, your response to every comment must be delivered in the form of a question. Keep them simple: no questions longer than ten seconds allowed. This isn't a rapid-fire inquisition; plan the first question, but make sure you *listen* to the answers. Each question should flow from the *answer* to the last question—until you have uncovered the Truth in your subject. Note: if you are a psychiatrist or psychologist, you are exempt from this assignment.

reflect, and say something they've never said before. I'll let him tell the rest:

> The best questions that you can ask can often be the softly, softly, catchy monkey sort of words or phrases that sort of creep up on people. Bill Clinton was talking after his book came out, and after about fifty interviews, he came to London to do some press. He'd been asked the obvious questions about Monica Lewinsky a lot of times, and I didn't want to ask the questions that Bill had heard so many times before.
>
> So I asked him a question about Monica Lewinsky, a very straightforward question. He answered it, and then I said, "Did you love her?" And that was a really crucial question. After all these fifty or so interviews, he hadn't been asked that, and it's just a simple, casual question. But often, those simple, casual, undisguised, straightforward questions can produce a wonderful answer. "First of all," he said, "I don't think it was that sort of a relationship for either of us." And then there was a long pause. It was a very telling sort of pause because it was a genuine exchange.

Good questions, like good art, don't have to be complex. They're powerful and effective precisely because they are simple, straightforward, and slice through needless confusion and obfuscation like a hot knife through butter. But they're not confrontational. Subversive? Yes. But their intent isn't to cause friction—it's to get a real response. Remember this the next time you want to ask a "gotcha" question. You're often much better off keeping the exchange calm, casual, and friendly.

SOMETHING IS *ALWAYS* MISSING

One of the most powerful benefits of people-centeredness is figuring out what's *missing* in people's lives—the void—and then coming up with a way to fill that void. An essential component of this search for the void is determining whether the solution is a "product" or a "platform." In technology, for example, products are something you use for a specific purpose, such as a Samsung 3D HD big-screen TV, while platforms are things you use for multiple purposes, such as Microsoft Windows. The

Internet has made the difference between products and platforms more confusing, but platforms are fundamentally more valuable and more intriguing for those at the very top because they often involve the engagement of a broader community.

Right now, the leading platform is the App Store. Sure, Apple sells a phone, but it's not really a phone per se—in fact, for many iPhone users, making and receiving calls is an afterthought. The iPhone is a platform to deliver communications technology and content applications technology that pushes the boundaries of imagination and creativity on a daily basis. And while the App Store sells individual "products," Apple's 2007 decision to open up its platform to the world has seamlessly linked creators and users and made the iPhone (and more recently the iPad) much more powerful. For example, fully 98 percent of iPhone owners are using various data services and 88 percent are using the Internet. A mere phone it certainly is not.

We often look at winners who've come up with new gadgets and platforms—the Bill Gateses, Steve Jobses, and Michael Dells of the world—and think to ourselves . . . Why didn't I come up with that? The "why didn't I think of that" complex is compounded with the astounding number of ridiculously commonsense, yet life-transforming, apps that are streaming into the market every day. Whether it's the app that solves a complex issue like paying all your bills with one touch, or simply entertains your kids (and keeps them from screaming) in the backseat, these apps take hard things and make them easy. Consider the rubber duck that squeaks when you tap it. One digitized duck equals countless toddlers entertained for hours. Brilliant. Any parent reading this realizes that a profound need was perfectly met with one simple app.*

In 1982, under the helm of Fred Smith, FedEx decided to shift its strategy to overnight shipping. To communicate its new service and

---

*   On a personal note, I credit Itzhak Fisher, the executive vice president of global product leadership for the Nielsen Company, for first recognizing the limitless business opportunities afforded by app creation for the iPhone. Long before the word "app" became a part of our lexicon, he was encouraging his research colleagues to apply their knowledge of human behavior to meet unmet consumer needs. Those who listened made a lot of money.

value, FedEx launched an ad campaign featuring the slogan "When It Absolutely, Positively Has to Be There Overnight." This resonated with people so quickly that FedEx became the number one company in overnight shipping almost, well, overnight. In one line, FedEx created and then fulfilled a new need. Because it was thought to be basically impossible, no one even thought to wonder if they needed overnight shipping. Today, try to imagine your business without it. FedEx was able to make a "guarantee" to its customers that differentiated the company from its competition—and continues to do so to this day.

Another CEO who knows what it means to be people-centered is Southwest Airlines' Gary Kelly. While other airlines have struggled to stay above water and out of bankruptcy, Southwest has been the only domestic airline to achieve an investment-grade rating and to return consistent profits. Kelly, a savvy businessman and communicator if ever there was one, made it his mission to ensure profits were never put above people. As Christopher Hinton wrote for MarketWatch in December 2008:

> At a time when other airlines were forced to cover rising costs by charging for formerly free services such as checked baggage, beverages and blankets, the hedging program at Southwest helped CEO Gary Kelly avoid such customer-service pitfalls. While passenger patience was being tested elsewhere, Southwest maintained its low-priced, people-centered business model and kept its stock valuation well ahead of its peers, a feat that made Kelly a finalist for the 2008 MarketWatch CEO of the Year award.[14]

Gary Kelly helped Southwest maintain its superiority and winning stature because he focused on people and by asking the right questions. Travelers responded by telling him exactly what they wanted out of an airline experience. Then, he devised a way to deliver their desires— and do it with excellent, cheerful, upbeat service. When you fly Southwest, you can feel how they built an airline around your needs for price, simplicity, and choice. When you fly the other guys, particularly US Airways—which is my own personal Room 101 nightmare from Orwell's 1984—you get the impression you've been shoehorned into a convoluted, hub-driven machine that makes sense to some actuary behind a desk, but not in your own real life. Consumers have spoken, and they love Southwest. US Air—not so much.

It's easy to read stories about winners, their life-changing gadgets, and their bodacious amounts of wealth and fame and think to yourself, They're just better than I am. They're smarter. They understand their field or area of expertise more than I ever will. I'll never become a winner.

Well, not so fast.

I'm not saying you *will* become a winner even if you don't have those qualities. That's up to you. But there's nothing inherently special about these people that gives them some supernatural advantage over the rest of us, other than the fact that they understand and connect with everyone else better than most. They believe in hard work, and they're willing to do whatever it takes to make their vision come to life.

Yet I firmly believe the ability to understand people's hopes, fears, and motivations is the most valuable skill any human being can ever possess.

Winners also understand that it's not just about them. The most successful people in this book are those who are just as focused on improving the lives of others as they are about themselves. This is particularly true in sports. Ed Snider, owner of the Philadelphia Flyers hockey team, is not someone you want to talk to if his team is losing. The fact is, he's not that easy to talk to even when his team is winning. But never, ever interrupt him while his team is on the ice. I have watched him watch his team, and I have never seen someone so focused and determined on behalf of his players and the fans. The game means everything to him—not for himself but for everyone who cares about the outcome. Says Snider:

> If you're not in it to win, get the hell out. Winning is what it's all about. Even though you own the team, you're really just a custodian for the fans. They know if you're trying. They know if you're listening. The bottom line is if you're honest with the fans and you give it one hundred percent, the fans appreciate it, even if you don't win. But what fans can't

stand is when they get the feeling that they're either being lied to, or misinformed, or if there isn't any desire to win. I have never had that problem.

It doesn't matter if you are pursuing success in business, politics, or just life in general. It doesn't matter how many times you burn the midnight oil or how good you are at finance or building hotels. It doesn't matter how unique your vision is or how passionate you are. None of these things matters if you don't understand *people*. Without their support, you'll end up settling for "good enough," stuck in middle management for life. And if you're reading this book, my guess is you want much more for yourself and the people you lead than to become the real-life Michael Scott, Dunder Mifflin's Scranton branch manager in NBC's *The Office*.

I asked hockey Hall of Famer and New York Rangers legend goalie Mike Richter to identify the best team captain in hockey and what made him so special. His answer was Mark Messier because *"he was a people person, and in the end you're dealing with people."* He continued, *"If I know what makes you click, I'm going to connect. Maybe what makes you click isn't the same thing as someone else, so if I beat the crap out of you to get you to respond, maybe that strategy won't work for someone else. You have to be more nuanced, and you have to be more controlled in the way you approach people."* Even winners whose job involves bashing others into Plexiglas walls know the importance of carefully observing those around them. In plain English, winners know how to *individualize, personalize,* and *humanize* what they say and do.

In fact, I'd argue that most of the success we see is due to being people-centered rather than intelligent. From the outside, it looks like winners are brilliant because they unlocked the secrets of a great mystery. Do you think Oprah Winfrey just knew how to create a television empire because she'd been in the business so long? No. Oprah knew how to connect with women. Her audience was made up largely of stay-at-home or unemployed moms, and she connected with them by providing a sense of community that was missing in their lives. Like any good businessperson, she helped fill a void. She became a friend and confidante to her viewers—someone they could depend on to be there for them every weekday afternoon. Better than any other talk show host in history, Oprah understood the missing component in the lives of American women. Her ability to connect with this audience allowed her to topple racial and economic barriers and become one of the most successful and richest women in the world, worth an estimated $2.7 billion in 2009.[15]

Similarly, it's tempting to think that Bill Gates knew computers so well he came up with Windows "just because." Or that Barack Obama became president of the United States at the tender age of forty-seven because he was just so darn smart. Or that Jeff Bezos developed the Amazon Kindle just because he'd been keeping an eye on the moribund publishing industry. From our side of the glass, these scenarios seem to make sense. And for the pundits, writers, and critics whose job it is to help us make sense of the world, they're the easiest stories to tell. But if you look a little deeper and analyze the things these winners have in common, you see the same thing over and over again: they know people, they talk to people, they find out what people want . . . and then they give it to them. Being people-centered lets you look like the genius who saw it coming when no one else did, when in fact you were just asking the right people the right questions at the right time.

While it's one thing to discover an unmet need, it takes another level of skill to anticipate an unmet need. Going even further, it takes someone willing to risk it all to fulfill that need.

That's exactly what GM is doing with its newest vehicle, the Chevrolet Volt. It's one thing to invest heavily in an electric car when gasoline is at $4 a gallon and people are in an uproar over the pain at the pump. It's quite another to bet the farm—the farm you don't even own right now—on such new, expensive, and untested technology when gas prices have fallen back to more tolerable levels and your company has gone through bankruptcy and a very public, very nasty, very unpopular government bailout. But that represents the new General Motors.

For decades GM seemed content to rest on its laurels and rely on mere name recognition and ubiquity while companies like Toyota, Honda, and even Ford pulled even or surpassed them in design, quality, and sales. But the 2011 Chevy Volt—a plug-in hybrid electric vehicle with the ability to run solely on an electric charge for forty miles—represents Chevy's attempt to, for once, get ahead of the market rather than play catch-up.[16] The brass at GM are betting that, given the volatility of gas prices, the limited and problematic supplies of oil, and the growing concerns about climate change, people will continue to demand transportation alternatives that don't rely exclusively on gasoline. Only time will tell if they will be successful, but you have to give them credit for trying to be proactive. And even if it doesn't sell many cars, GM is certainly generating fervent buzz as it lures a new generation of car buyers into its showrooms for the first time.

GM may never turn a profit on the first version of the Volt. At $41,000 (before factory and dealer incentives), it is not selling at a people-centered price. True, the Volt is eligible for a $7,500 U.S. federal tax credit, and GM is offering an attractive $350-a-month lease package, but the real value for GM is in what it will do for the brand. It tells American consumers who are starved for innovation in American cars—and afraid of the next gas spike—*we're listening. We feel your pain. And here's what we're trying to do to heal it.*

ADDRESSING OUR FEARS

To be human is to have both hopes *and* fears. No matter where we are in life, we all hope for the future and fear what it may bring. To ignore what people fear is to miss an essential component of life. If you're ever going to break through, understand, and connect with people in a big way, it cannot just be about achieving the good life. It also has to be about avoiding the pitfalls that we face on our journey. Winning isn't just about understanding all that is good about human nature. It's also about seeing the changing and challenging conditions in which we live and responding accordingly.

People who disagree with my politics routinely accuse me of trying to find some sort of deep, latent fear in the American electorate and then trying to aggravate it. And if I can't find one, the story goes, I'll use words to conjure one up. In fact, I think it's the exact opposite. Fear already exists. It always exists. Thanks to 9/11 and the economic collapse of 2008, people are afraid—for good reason. The world can be a scary, crazy, dangerous place, and a rational response to that is fear. Without fear, we would end up like the gazelle that blissfully imbibes from the watering hole . . . until he becomes someone else's dinner. When communicating with the public, you *absolutely* must identify with people's fears as a *means* of demonstrating that you understand their needs. But the *end* result is the solution—the protection from their fears.

You don't get the communication payoff of "I feel your pain" without there being *pain* in the first place. Ultimately, successful communication is about *acknowledging* fear and finding a way to address or remedy it. Rather than trying to exacerbate fears in the work that I do, I try to come up with language to help my clients address and allay those fears. It's one reason I turned away from politics and went into the business world. I like alleviating pain. Addressing it. Solving it. Helping people find solutions to their problems rather than making them worse.

Truth be told, America's businesses are far better at creating and delivering solutions than America's politicians are. The entrepreneurs with whom I work are taking the great and making it exceptional almost every day. With politicians, if we're lucky, they're making the best of a bad situation.

An example of the language used to address people's fear is the highly positive statement "No one knows___better than you . . ."

"No one knows how to spend your money better than you."

"No one knows what's right for your family better than you."

"No one knows how to educate your kids better than you."

"No one knows how you should live your life better than you."

This simple formulation is so powerful because it puts people in control. You become the vessel for their wishes, not the arbiter of their lives. When it comes to issues of financial systems and government and how our country is run, many, many people fear that they're losing control of their destinies, their futures, and even their own government. A February 2010 poll conducted by CNN found that a majority of Americans thought their government had grown out of control. In fact, 56 percent of people questioned thought the federal government had "become so large and powerful that it poses an immediate threat to the rights and freedoms of ordinary citizens."[17] An "immediate threat" is strong language, and yet a majority identifies with it. And a 56 percent majority invalidates the suggestion that the only people who fear government are right-wing militias. At 56 percent, you've got soccer moms and metropolitan career climbers . . . old and young . . . Republican and Democrat. It's a shocking result.

And this statistic does not stand in isolation. The Vernon K. Krieble Foundation—an organization on the front lines of promoting individual freedom and limiting government control of individuals' lives—recently revealed that a shocking 53 percent of Americans believe they are *less free* than they were just *five years ago*, while only 12 percent believe that they are freer. When Americans are losing what makes them Americans— freedom—they get frightened. And that makes them angry.

Those perceptions *should* give every elected representative in Washington, D.C., an epic case of heartburn (it won't), but it's completely in line with what we know about people's fears and the corresponding language needed to help soothe them. Language consultants like me need not manufacture fear. It already exists. It's American-made, homegrown, and pervasive. To ignore it would be to disrespect the great people of this nation. Americans' fears are real and palpable, and people deserve— and increasingly demand—the right solutions and the right language to help them see a better tomorrow and the best days that lie ahead of us. The person who discovers both, simultaneously, will be a much needed and new iteration of the American winner.

One day, when you're feeling especially bold, ask a few people on the street what they want most out of life. I don't mean money or things (and if they answer that way, make them answer again by asking them a follow-up question, such as "And what will that give you?" until they give you an answer that doesn't involve material things). Ask them what they want on a very long-term, ultimate level. What do they want in terms of their whole lives? I'll bet my convertible you'll hear the words *security, stability,* and *predictability* at least a few times. Winners are able to address people's sense of hope and fear at the same time, creating products, services, and solutions that allow them to feel more stable and secure in their day-to-day lives.

A PEOPLE-CENTERED LEXICON

1. I'm listening
2. I hear you
3. I get it
4. I respect you
5. My commitment
6. You're in control
7. You decide

WORDS THAT WORK

Notice that the words below all focus on the listener, not the speaker. Sure, it's *"I'm this"* and *"I'm that."* But in reality, these words help you demonstrate that it's all about *them.*

"I'm listening" demonstrates that you care enough about your audience to pay attention to what they have to say. If they know you're listening, they'll feel engaged, empowered, and appreciative. It is an active process.

"I hear you" says that you agree with, or at least understand, what your audience is thinking. It is an affirmation of a message received.

"I get it" was once considered slang, but now it is a universally accepted linguistic shortcut that affirms and confirms what you are being told. It is a personalized way to signify not just understanding, but acceptance.

"I respect you" is simply the highest compliment that you can pay a colleague or customer. It's what we want most in our professional lives, yet we hear it rarely. *"I respect you"* makes the listener feel like a winner— and that makes you a winner.

"My commitment" communicates in a serious tone the intention to get it done. When you give your commitment, you put your reputation and your honor on the line. Winners don't use words like *"I promise"* or *"I pledge."* Those terms have no credibility anymore; we've experienced too many broken promises and empty pledges.

"You're in control" is, by definition, empowering. Telling people *"you're in control"* restores the freedom they feel they've lost. Giving control to your listener is the ultimate antidote to the pervasive feeling of helplessness.

"You decide" is the actionable aspect of control. Roger Ailes invented one of the most successful slogans of an era when he coined the phrase *"We report, you decide"* for the Fox News Channel. The network may be mocked by its critics, but millions of Americans have decided that Fox News is the cable news they prefer most—more than all the other news channels combined.

That's what winning is all about.

4

PARADIGM BREAKING
The values of being first

No problem can be solved from the same level of consciousness that created it.
—**ALBERT EINSTEIN**

Einstein had a boyhood dream of what it would be like to ride on a light wave. Is it physically possible? Could you actually ride on a light wave? And then, years later, he comes up with his theory of relativity. He asked one question as a six-year-old—a pretty amazing question. Would it physically be possible to ride on a light wave through space? And the whole world changed because of that one question from a six-year-old.

—**JIM DAVIDSON,**
CO-CEO, SILVER LAKE

Las Vegas is well known for its outsized personalities and its structural superlatives. When the Mirage opened its doors on October 17, 1987, a local journalist described it as "The 8th Wonder of the World." When the Bellagio opened on October 15, 1998, at a cost of $1.6 billion—the most expensive hotel ever built at the time—several media outlets rushed to assert that it was the finest hotel on the face of the globe. But for Steve Wynn, it just meant the bar for his next masterpiece had to be set even higher. For his next hotel, the one that would have his own name on the door, it couldn't just be a little better. It had to break the mold. Since no one tells a story better than Steve Wynn, allow him to describe in his own words how he shattered the existing paradigm and took Las Vegas to a new level:

> It was during the initial process of intellectual challenging and intellectual conversation with myself and my colleagues about my next hotel that we realized that just maybe, for twenty-seven years, we didn't quite have it quite right. It is a startling thing to realize that, having built three great hotels that numbered among the most successful structures in the world of hospitality, maybe we had it wrong, we had made a fundamental miscalculation. The focal point shouldn't be the sidewalk—it should be the hotel itself and the people in it. The people we owe the greatest responsibility to are not the folks promenading up and down the rialto outside, but the people who are staying in our building, eating, drinking, shopping, cavorting inside.
>
> So I was trying to think of how I was going to resolve my new idea of making each space in the hotel an experience unto itself, and I was complaining to Elaine [his wife], "But if I build the front any higher, it'll block people's view from the sidewalk."
>
> And she turned around from her computer and said, "So what?"
>
> I said, "Well, it'll hurt the walk-in business."
>
> And she said to me, "Is that what the walk-in is all about?"
>
> And I said, "The walk-in's about the word of mouth about how wonderful the hotel is on the inside."
>
> And she said, "Then what are you worried about?"
>
> I was sitting at the kitchen table, I still had my jacket on, and I just stopped. [long pause] That was one of the most epiphany-like moments that I have ever had in my forty years of doing this. I had gone along merrily thinking that the Mirage volcano would say, "Could the inside be as good as the outside? Let's go in." Could the Treasure Island pirate show make them go inside? The Bellagio fountains were supposed to get you so riled up that you couldn't stay outside for a second; you'd run into the building. I had accepted this as religion.
>
> But now, all of a sudden, I realized it's the truth of the hotel inside that works. So if I could actually block out the Strip, then my real audience, the hotel, I would have much more freedom to create the theaters

of experience in the restaurants and throughout. It was a freeing, liber-
ating truth that we didn't have to worry about the damn sidewalk
anymore.

I was so excited about the implications of being freed from the side-
walk responsibility with my fourth hotel on the Strip that I couldn't sleep
that night. I was up at four thirty, got out of bed quietly, crept out, and I
get my design partner on the phone and I say, "Listen to this, we'll build
a mountain. It will be a complex structure with lagoons and bayous. We'll
make it one hundred and fifty or one hundred and sixty feet tall, block
out the Strip, and we'll animate it."

He said, "Block out the Strip?" I said, "What's more powerful than a
ship sinking or a volcano erupting or fountains dancing? Curiosity! Mys-
tery! You build a fence and any kid worth a nickel will climb it to see
what's on the other side. We'll build a giant mountain that hides the
place, but we'll leave a hole in the fence that says 'Enter Here.'" And so
we did.

A paradigm was broken by the same man who had created it eighteen years earlier, and, once again, Las Vegas would never be the same.

George Bernard Shaw once said, "You see things; and you say, 'Why?'
But I dream things that never were; and I say, 'Why not?'" Years later,
Senator Robert F. Kennedy ended his presidential campaign speeches
with a similar refrain: "There are those who look at things the way they
are, and ask why . . . I dream of things that never were, and ask why
not?" Winners don't accept the world for what it is. They're driven by
their ideas of how the world should be. Their vision becomes a mission,
and that mission reshapes the human experience. If you're not asking
"*Why not?*," you're not in the winning mentality.

These two men fully understood that 1 percent of the world's dreamers effect exceptional progress that is enjoyed by the other 99 percent of
us who are content to stand back and watch. Notice they even both use
the word itself—*dream*. Unlike other acts, dreams allow us to break free
of our human limitations. In dreams, there are no rules. Gravity melts
away. The sky can be any color we want. Dreams allow us to see a world

that's different from the one we live in now. Prescient or not, they give us the ability to imagine a radically different tomorrow. Envisioning this type of inspired change is what I call paradigm-breaking.

Generally defined, a paradigm is "a set of assumptions, concepts, values, and practices that constitutes a way of viewing reality for the community that shares them, especially in an intellectual discipline."[18] In the simplest terms, paradigms are frames through which we look at the world. They help us organize information and make sense of it all. A paradigm-free world is a Hobbesian world where anything goes and no standards of evaluation exist. You cannot objectively judge things if there is no paradigm in place to create standards for evaluation.

By dreaming . . . by breaking paradigms . . . winners invent new touchstones and benchmarks and then *apply* the rules of the real world to those markers. This added level of creative freedom distinguishes winners from the rest of us and is the wellspring of many of mankind's greatest achievements.

THE NECESSITY OF PARADIGM BREAKING

In my research on behalf of some of the world's most successful entrepreneurs and paradigm breakers, I have interviewed dozens of people who at one time or another appeared on some elite list: the richest, the most powerful, the most influential. These are the captains of industry, Hollywood elite, sports celebrities—icons for all ages. They may have different pasts and different futures, but they all have one thing in common—one regret that no amount of money or power can change. In a word, it's *family*. In five words, it's *the lack of family time:*

> I didn't see my kids grow. They weren't a part of my life and I wasn't there for them, and there's nothing I can do now to fix what I didn't do then. I have plenty of time to make money. I don't have any time to make memories.

Told to me by one of the Forbes 400 richest Americans, that disappointment and discontentment with life has crept into the lives of America's elite is undeniable. Regret, frustration, and disappointment exist even among the most successful, and it transcends economics and politics. Financial success has always been a high priority for an upwardly mobile, well-educated population. But it's not the cash they actually crave. It's not even the financial score card. It's the *stuff*. More money means more freedom, and that manifests itself in the desire to buy more stuff. Millionaire men are much more likely than any other segment of the population to measure their success by the accumulation of material goods: the largest house, the fastest car, the newest technology. Think big boys with even bigger toys.

The problem with the money-at-all-costs mentality is that it inevitably leads to what sociologists call the "failure by success" condition. Financial accomplishment is supposed to bring with it a sense of personal security. But in reality, it often triggers greater stress and anxiety. The more economically successful people become, the more fearful they get that they could lose what they already have—and so they work even harder, earn even more, and feel even worse. For the super-wealthy businessman, life has become a rat race—and the rats are winning.

And that invites the question: What can you do for the person who owns everything but enjoys nothing? Thanks to a recent last-minute vacation decision I made to ring in the year 2010 in Cabo, Mexico, I discovered the solution—and met the developer who broke the vacation paradigm for the world's most exclusive and demanding clientele. Meet Mike Meldman, a fifty-one-year-old entrepreneur who came to his profession not to revitalize the holiday experience for the famous, but to reconnect parents to their children and children to their parents.

Meldman looks and acts much more like a social worker than a traditional suited business billionaire. Developers are almost always known by their last name, but Mike is strictly a first-name guy. He's in great physical shape, but you won't find him or his clothing on the pages of GQ. Mike often shows up to work in T-shirts and well-worn jeans, and one wonders if he even owns a pair of socks. He slumps as he sits, but comes to life whenever his BlackBerry vibrates—which is about once a minute. And every time he attacks the BlackBerry, chances are he's introducing someone new to the Discovery way of life. From the Bahamas to Cabo, from Palm Springs to Hawaii, from private mountains on which to ski to private beaches from which to surf, people of considerable means are discovering the value of family thanks to Meldman's company, aptly called Discovery. They build paradise from the ground up—one house, one club, and one family at a time.

At a time when almost every competitor is in bankruptcy or liquidation, Discovery thrives. Perhaps it's because their projects are designed to take owners to their own private sanctuary far away from the noise and hassles of the everyday world and closer to the true beauty of planet Earth. There are no clocks anywhere, and no one is in a hurry. Everything and everyone is tranquil. Nature is in harmony with humanity. Even the air is pure and intoxicating. The Discovery mission statement may be corny, but it's accurate: "To seek out new lands and to share their treasures, traditions, and their glory with generations and generations to come."

While this may read like a travel brochure, these are second homes, not holidays. But the neighbors aren't just around the corner; more likely they are a mountain over or a river away. But the kids, well, they're right there—sprawled on the living room floor, horsing around at the kitchen table, or resting in the bedroom just down the hall. In a word, they're close—and today, closeness with family is what winners want more than anything.

What makes this paradigm-breaking is the way Discovery aggressively celebrates families. For example, on movie nights at the Kūki'o community in Hawaii, kids and their parents pull golf carts onto the event lawn side-by-side for a Discovery-style drive-in—replete with popcorn machine and concession stand—and there's no cash register in sight. Imagine an exclusive residential club where *every child* is the focus of attention, where the staff's only responsibility is to create unprecedented experiences for the kids and cherished memories for the parents, and where parents and children interact with ease and informality.

There are no other developers anywhere—zero—who offer this kind of private home/club family-building and community-building all rolled up into one. "Discovery didn't happen by accident," says Meldman. "I built it for families. I built it for people who had everything but family memories." For Meldman, crafting Discovery communities is a lot more than designing luxurious second homes. In fact, it was a strictly personal mission and commitment. *"I was a single dad with two young boys, and I wanted to have fun with them and teach them stuff about the outdoors that I frankly didn't know. So I learned fishing, wakeboarding, surfing, and scuba diving right along with them, and now, fifteen years later, we can do just about everything together."*

The program Mike boasts about to anyone who will listen is called Outdoor Pursuits, and it is uniquely tailored to each club, based on area terrain, local sports offerings, and member interest. From getting participants up on wakeboards for the first time to teaching synchronicity in an outrigger canoe, club members are encouraged to engage in physical activity as a family. And more often than not, it is the children who are coaching their proud parents. When a couple at the El Dorado community in Cabo wanted to watch their daughter's first surfing lesson, the professional instructors prepared a full gourmet lunch for the whole family. Staffers then captured the girl's first wave digitally—presenting the family with a memory book that will last a lifetime.

No matter where you turn, there's fun in the air, on the ground, and in the water. The Sugar Shacks sprinkled across the ski slopes at the Yellowstone Club in Montana give away cookies and candy for the kids and coffee and stronger libations for the adults to encourage kids and parents to ski together. The Comfort Stations on the golf courses at Discovery Clubs offer a treasure trove of delectable goodies to famished golfers—all complimentary. The kids' clubs at all the Discovery communities—with their own private restaurant and menu—give teenagers and younger children a safe, friendly place to hang out with friends from across the street and across the globe.

I am a fanatic about this paradigm-breaking company, and I wrote about them in British *GQ* because many of its readers need what Discovery offers—because I know how many financially successful winners have broken families and how Discovery has stitched them back up again. Discovery may pitch "peerless private luxury" in their brochures and the fresh private powder on their ski slopes, but what it actually provides is priceless time with family and friends that simply can't be bought at any price. Says Meldman, *"I'm most proud of the way our projects have enriched so many lives and brought so many families together. The parents may have bought into our communities, but it's seeing their kids have such a good time that makes me happiest."*

FROM COPERNICUS TO KROC

Legend has it that in 1543, as he lay on his deathbed, Polish astronomer Nicolaus Copernicus was handed the first printed copy of his life's work, titled *On the Revolutions of the Celestial Spheres*. In it, he set forth a heliocentric hypothesis for understanding the universe, claiming that the sun was at the center of the universe and all the planets revolved around it. Today, this is completely uncontroversial. But in the sixteenth century, most people thought the sun revolved around the Earth. This idea stemmed mainly from the belief that God had made the Earth (and by inference, mankind) the center of all of his creation. Then along comes a scientist from Poland who says, "Not so fast. The sun is at the center of it all. I can prove it!" And with the publication of a single book, our entire understanding of the universe and our place within it changed.

We thought everything related to the Earth. But *he refused to settle* for convention, and realized that all the rules of relation needed to be rewritten. Now think of everything *else* that must have been just plain wrong because of one faulty, outmoded assumption. The entire study of astronomy to date was rendered junk science. One man, with one earthshaking idea that it *wasn't* all about the Earth, changed it all.

That's paradigm breaking.

Some of history's greatest achievers live on today because they fundamentally changed the way we think about the world or ourselves. When he assembled the first printing press around 1440, Johannes Gutenberg revolutionized the way information was stored and shared. During the seventeenth and eighteenth centuries, philosophers like John Locke, Jean-Jacques Rousseau, and Thomas Hobbes changed the way humans understood their relation to one another—and the state—which ultimately led to the philosophical foundation of the American Revolution and United States Constitution. No longer was there such a thing as "divine right" or the legitimate authority of monarchs to rule people. In the new paradigm, government received its power, authority, and legitimacy only from the consent of everyone being governed (Fidel Castro and Kim Jong Il are two of many unfortunate exceptions). This idea has been one of the most persuasive, powerful, and positive forms of paradigm breaking in all of human history.

In a more modern context, paradigm breaking is about changing the way we think about a product, service, idea, person, or event. Consider the fast food industry and its founder, Ray Kroc. The story of McDonald's is really the story Kroc, the milkshake-mixer salesman who heard of Maurice and Richard McDonald's small hamburger shop in Southern California. Kroc was told that the McDonalds were selling an incredible amount of shakes, often running eight mixers at a time. So he packed his bags and went on a sales call.

What Kroc saw changed his life—and the daily diet of hundreds of millions of people throughout the world would never be the same. Unlike other burger joints, the brothers were serving burgers as if they were assembled by Detroit autoworkers. Kroc had never seen so many people served so quickly. Kroc knew he was on to something right from the start. "This will go anyplace," he thought. "When I saw it working that day in 1954," he reflected later, "I felt like some latter-day Newton who'd just had an Idaho potato caromed off his skull. That night in my motel room I did a lot of heavy thinking about what I'd seen during the day. Visions of McDonald's restaurants dotting crossroads all over the country paraded through my brain."[19]

Kroc saw a paradigm-breaking opportunity and grabbed it by the arches. He suggested to the McDonald brothers that they expand their presence and their business formula to other areas. They hired Kroc as their agent, and the rest, as they say, is history.* Kroc didn't invent the hamburger, but he "took it more seriously" than anyone else, he once said, and his business tactic was to ensure that every hamburger sold from any McDonald's was the same. A McDonald's hamburger would be a McDonald's hamburger anywhere from Toledo to Tokyo.

The main takeaway is that it all started *simply*: people like hamburgers, so how can we make hamburgers better and faster, and deliver them to more people? The primary ingredient in the fast food revolution: standardization. It had to taste the same wherever you went.

---

* Kroc realized early in the history of McDonald's that the company was sitting on a gold mine. In 1956, he set up the Franchise Realty Corporation, which bought the land on which the restaurants would sit, and then leased it back to franchise owners. The revenues that the company received from the franchisees made it easier for Kroc to raise capital in the financial markets for faster and faster expansion.

And the necessary ingredient for standardization is perfection. As Kroc himself once said, "Perfection is very difficult to achieve, and perfection was what I wanted in McDonald's. Everything else was secondary for me." *

Paradigm breakers convert *their own dreams* and visions into widespread public *demands*.

Because the new fast food paradigm has so drastically changed our expectations about food and meals in general, our behavior has also changed to match our new worldview. In 2009, the average American spent just twenty-seven minutes a day on food preparation and another four minutes cleaning up. That's less than half of the time Americans spent cooking and cleaning up when Julia Child first debuted on our TV screens in *The French Chef* in 1963.[20] Despite how the Food Network's Rachael Ray amazes audiences with her *30 Minute Meals* every day, we're still doing a lot more eating out than ever before.†

How do you turn long-held standards and expectations on their heads? Best Buy founder Dick Schulze, ranked number 102 on the Forbes list of wealthiest Americans in 2007, did it successfully by radically changing the shopping dynamic. After trying to differentiate his electronics stores from the others and getting lackluster results, he knew that more drastic changes were in order.

He succeeded by rejecting the standard *incremental* retail expansion philosophy of the time—"more locations is better"—in favor of a *radical* "more stuff is better" approach.‡

Still, the birth of Best Buy happened by accident. The modern-day electronics superstore was born out of adversity: a tornado had leveled one of Schulze's small retail stores. To sell off remaining merchandise, he held an aptly named "Tornado Sale" with an unusually large selection of goods collected from his other stores, but sold at a single location

---

* Grinding It Out: The Making of McDonald's, Ray Croc, p. 80.
† If you've ever made it through one of her shows without wanting to throw a brick at your TV, tell me how. Hosting a focus group of moms in Las Vegas, I made the mistake of asserting that it was "relatively easy" to prepare a home-cooked meal in less than thirty minutes. The moms almost threw me through the one-way mirror.
‡ Don't use words like "incremental" and "radical." They are meant to describe the process of paradigm breaking, but they should not become part of your lexicon.

with low prices and heavy consumer advertising. That sale was a huge success, proving the adage that out of adversity comes opportunity. But more important, Schulze realized that concentrating more products in a single location was a prototype for a new way of doing business. He opened an unprecedented 18,000-square-foot store in 1983 and adopted the name Best Buy—America's first electronics superstore. The name reflected its marketing strategy: whatever the product, it would be a good deal.

The paradigm-breaking superstore concept proved instantly popular with consumers. In its first year, the one Best Buy superstore sold more than Schulze's entire chain had sold the previous year, and it took just fifteen years for Best Buy to become America's top-selling consumer electronics company. Why?

First, for time-sensitive customers, Schulze made the stores bigger so consumers knew that their first stop would also be their last.

Second, for those who knew exactly what they wanted, there was a greater opportunity for self-service and less dependence (that is, wait time) on salespeople.

Third, for people who didn't like the high-pressure environment of the commissioned salespeople stores (the norm in consumer electronics at the time), he hired a knowledgeable, noncommissioned sales staff.

Fourth, instead of a "grow at any cost" store opening strategy (which is primarily what put Circuit City out of business in 2009), he insisted on smart real estate planning and strategically placed locations.

And fifth, he did all this while charging less than his competitors.

But the story doesn't end there. In 2002 Best Buy acquired Geek Squad, a trendsetter in electronics customer service. While their competition was trying to disconnect from their consumers in a misguided effort to reduce employee costs, Best Buy's Geek Squad extended and revolutionized the customer relationship from the store to the home with installation, problem solving, and ongoing service, bringing an additional revenue stream (and greater customer loyalty) to the company. Circuit City, RIP.

Schulze's successor, Brad Anderson, shared the same commitment to out-of-the-box thinking. He also shared Schulze's open-door policy with lower-level employees, encouraging his in-store staff to customize each store to meet the needs of the surrounding community and act on their ideas. Here's just one example:

> We've got a wonderful team of eccentric people working in our Manhattan store on 44th Street and Fifth Avenue. Now, there's a large Brazilian community near the store, and the manager said, "Hey, we don't do anything to cater to them." So he hired folks who spoke the language in the store. They wound up discovering that there are cruise ships of Brazilians that come to New York City, so they contacted the travel company and found that the store was a desirable stop for them. So all of a sudden we have buses of tour groups pulling up on Sundays. If we waited for someone in Minnesota to come up with that idea, we'd still be waiting.[21]

I cannot leave the retail component of paradigm breaking without making reference to Target, a company that has outlived and outsold a dozen competitors to carve out its own space in the retail landscape.

Let's start with a truism to set the competitive context properly: Walmart has long been the chain to beat when it comes to rock-bottom prices and sky-high success. Most other discount retailers have attempted to compete with Walmart by fighting to match its low prices, therefore accepting Walmart's paradigm and competing on Walmart's terms. Their stores are immense, cavernous warehouses with fluorescent lighting and drab linoleum flooring. When a shopper walks into a discount chain and immediately witnesses a bare-bones aesthetic, they are reassured that they are paying the lowest possible price. I don't mean that negatively; all it takes is a quick look at Walmart's profits or stock rating to see that shoppers love the chain.

But rather than accepting Walmart's paradigm, Target broke it. They pioneered a new approach, combining value with affordable style. The difference is immediate and unmistakable—wide, clean aisles and shelves; colorful, appealing displays, and vibrant images. The genius of Target is that it gives shoppers the almost-as-low prices of a bargain store without the sense that they are slumming it.

There's a product difference at Target that's just as important as the decor. While its competitors struggle to slash prices and highlight the cheapness of every item, Target enlists name-brand fashion designers to create new lines. In a highly touted partnership, Isaac Mizrahi created a fashion line for Target in 2002, and his designs were tremendously popular almost from the start. In five years' time, sales volume for Mizrahi's designs tripled, as the line extended to bedding housewares, and pet products. Mizrahi's work for Target solidified the chain's style credibility and revived Mizrahi's struggling career. It's not an accident that as you walk into Target, you're also greeted by another champion of luxury for the masses—Starbucks. Giving you the option to order a venti iced latte to enjoy while you shop is just another example of Target's savvy bid to combine affordable and classy. It's not surprising that people affectionately refer to the chain with a French pronunciation—"Tar-jay"; they sense that it's different and more stylish than its price-obsessed competitors. And it works. Target roared past every single Walmart wannabe to become the second largest discount retailer in the United States, ranked thirtieth on the Fortune 500 list in 2010.

The corporate culture at Target actively rewards paradigm breaking. Chairman and CEO Gregg W. Steinhafel has pushed the retail envelope every day since assuming the role of president in 1999. Michael Francis, executive vice president and chief marketing officer, holds a "Big Idea" contest every year, challenging the entire company to come up with an innovative solution to address a specific problem. The result is not just a corporation that is committed to breaking paradigms, but employees on every level who are engaged in the quest to reject the norm and come up with something fresh and new.

Paradigm breakers are the Magellans of our time, and like the great explorers of the sixteenth and seventeenth centuries, their names and the impact they have on our lives and our world live on. These modern-day paradigm breakers are mapping new horizons of quality of life, helping people discover new ways to make life easier.

THE PARADIGM BREAKERS

Most people assume that the people at the top of their profession simply do things better than everyone else. Not necessarily. In some cases, they simply do things differently from everyone else. Allow me to use a sports example from future hockey Hall of Famer Brendan Shanahan—one of the toughest players of the modern era:

When I started in the NHL I could score from six feet around the net—basically tip-ins and garbage goals. But when I played with Brett Hull, I studied him and copied him—how to get open. When you talk about getting open in any sport, you assume that getting open means that you're more athletic, running faster, being quicker to the spot. Brett learned that it was often about going slower, and always about going at a different speed. If everyone's going slow, Brett would go fast, like if he had a breakaway, and he'd never get caught. But if everyone was back-checking, he would slow down, straighten up, and everyone would pass him by. And once they were all past him, then he'd come into the play. He did everything differently. He figured it out. That's how he always found open ice.

An enormous part of paradigm breaking is mental. You have to do whatever it takes to effect change, and often that means clearing your mind of past failures and preconceptions and focusing anew on groundbreaking ideas. Andrea Jung, the CEO of Avon and one of the Forbes 100 Most Powerful Women in the world, strives to continually refresh her outlook and her role: "Fire yourself on a Friday night and come back in on Monday morning as if a search firm put you there as a turnaround leader. Can you be objective and make the bold change? If you can't, then you haven't reinvented yourself."[22]

Strategically, Jung does two things here: First, she regularly changes her attitude and approach to reflect a bolder purpose—revitalizing her company and the role she plays in it again and again. Second, she reinvents the expectations she puts on herself, moving from a status quo CEO to a leader driven by a greater purpose. Indeed, paradigms are broken when expectations change and behavior is modified. Most ultrasuccessful people and businesses revolutionize our way of life following this process of continuous questioning, challenging, and transforming. Cher did it. Madonna did it. Richard Nixon and Hillary Clinton each did it. Any collection of people that diverse must be on to something.

Notice also that it all starts with one person—you. No one is going to push you to break paradigms like you can push yourself. It's not easy, comfortable, or even natural for a person to "fire herself" on a Friday and spend the weekend planning to come back newer, different, and transformed. The more natural approach is the easier approach: "It's Friday. I survived. Now I can finally *stop* thinking about work. And then next week, I'll try to survive too." But is survival enough? To *thrive* . . . to *win* . . . you have to push yourself and eschew comfort for its own sake. Winners are their own to toughest bosses and harshest critics.

Paradigm breaking can be as much about style as it is about substance. Here, allow me to use another sports example because it applies perfectly to business. In the early 1970s, the quality of the professional tennis circuit was arguably the best it had ever been, but it still wasn't attracting big money, big sponsors, or a big television audience. Jimmy Connors changed all that. Love him or hate him, you just had to watch him. People came to the matches just to see the outbursts, and they were rarely disappointed. So I asked Connors to explain his on-court behavior, and whether it was all really necessary. To my surprise, the answer was . . . yes:

> I'd rather spit it out than keep it in. If I would've kept it in I would've had a heart attack twenty years ago, because when I blew, I blew. But I blew for fifteen seconds and it was over. I was able to spew it out, get it over with, and then come back and play just as good if not better.

So what does this have to do with paradigm breaking? Connors understood better than the sponsors, the television executives, even his tennis friends and foes that to raise the level of interest in the game, he had to take a radical approach:

> The outbursts were real. The length of them, well, I did pull a little bit more out of it. But if you're to pay big money to go watch guys running around in white tennis shorts with a tennis racquet hitting tennis balls back and forth, you want more.
>
> Why did tennis explode and become sponsor-driven, and television-driven, and player-driven, and young-kid-driven? It certainly wasn't by mistake. Don't take this the wrong way, but I take pride in taking tennis from the country club to the gutter, and the reason being is because that's where everybody was. We were getting the purist tennis fan from the country club. That was OK if you wanted to play in front of two thousand

people and for $1,200 in prize money. But if we were going to become any good, we had to get the real sports fan. They wanted to come see guys kill themselves, bleed and get dirty, and tell somebody to f--k off.

History certainly proved him right. The same people who booed him years ago during his tantrums now run up to shake his hand and ask for his autograph. To their surprise, he always says yes—with a smile. The bad boy of tennis is really a quiet, gentle soul.

Henry Ford's 1909 Model-T made vehicles easy to produce and affordable for the working class for the first time. There's an important lesson in his aspirational language:

I will build a car for the great multitude. It will be large enough for the family, but small enough for the individual to run and care for. It will be constructed of the best materials, by the best men to be hired, after the simplest designs that modern engineering can devise. But it will be so low in price that no man making a good salary will be unable to own one—and enjoy with his family the blessing of hours of pleasure in God's great open spaces.[23]

He broke the horse-and-buggy paradigm. Once cars could be mass-produced for a reasonable price, more and more Americans could enjoy the benefits that came with them. And once they got used to those benefits, they came to expect them. And once they came to expect them, they came to use them and incorporate them into their daily lives. First cities, and then nations, transformed their plans and scales to revolve around the car. To invoke Copernicus, the car became the sun, replacing the horse-and-buggy Earth at the center of the human experience.

Ultimately, paradigm breaking is the difference between innovation and breakthrough, between incremental and transformational. It's not just about making something "new and improved," it's about reimagining the entire purpose of the original. But beware—transformation begets transformation. Even after you've broken a paradigm, you must continue to challenge yourself, because if you don't do it, others will.

As the president of 20th Century Fox and then CEO of Paramount

Pictures, Sherry Lansing was the most powerful woman in Hollywood for more than a decade. But it's her work for the organization Stand Up for Cancer that is making the most waves and having the greatest impact. Their 2010 one-hour commercial-free live telecast raised an unprecedented $80 million, primarily because it was broadcast on every network and every news channel—the first time these sworn enemies of entertainment cooperated, well, ever. So how did she break a Hollywood paradigm to get it done?

We began by wanting to do it differently. And because we're from Hollywood, we tend to dream a little more than most people. So we thought maybe we could do a telethon on one network. But we didn't know which one, so candidly, we told each network that the other one was doing it. And when they ALL said yes, we knew something special was going to happen. And now it's embedded in the culture.

We wanted to pitch Bud Selig, the commissioner of Major League Baseball, to ask him for ten million dollars over three years. We asked and asked, and finally he gave us fifteen minutes—fifteen minutes! How do you ask someone for ten million in fifteen minutes! I've asked people for a thousand or two thousand dollars, but never ten million. But I made the pitch, full of confidence, and he starts to hem and haw. "I really don't know" and "Well, we really can't do that now." Right then, his wife hits him in the arm with her shoulder and says, "Bud, just do it already." So he does, and when he said yes, we all started to cry. Seven women crying. We knew how bad it looked, but we just didn't think he'd say yes. And from that day, we vowed we would never cry again at a pitch.

Lansing was kidding, of course, but she raises a point that deserves additional focus. Men and women not only receive messages differently, they deliver them differently. Sheryl Sandberg, COO of Facebook, is one of the most accomplished business leaders in America today, but she still sees and acknowledges the unique issues facing female communicators and paradigm breakers:

Women have communication challenges that men don't have. There is a negative correlation between success and likeability depending on whether you are a man or a woman. Men appear more likeable as they get more successful, while women appear less likeable. A woman can say something really smart and simple, yet she will still be seen as too assertive. Even when they are softer in their approach, they will still seem harder. Take two people of equal competence and success: Howard and Heidi. Howard, you'll want to spend the day with. Heidi, you'll feel she is out for herself. And every woman I know who I tell this to, they all say, "Oh my God, that's exactly how I feel."

Entertainment is one area where women and men are on equal (slippery) footing. Mary Hart may be one of the most recognizable faces and voices on television, but it wasn't always wine and roses. For her, the earliest, toughest days were an advantage:

I had the great fortune of starting at the very lowest level, where I did everything from set the lights and sweep the floors to run the commercials and book the guests. Then when I started at ET, I went around from affiliate to affiliate, from station to station. I did promotion like crazy, and it worked because it created a personal connection between the show and the local stations that really mattered.

In some of America's oldest and most stodgy boardrooms, female participation is in itself paradigm-breaking. But regardless of gender, effort, commitment, and persistence pay off.

Let's consider an example from a less-than-sexy business sector—the shipping industry. While attending Yale University between 1962 and 1966, a young man from Mississippi wrote a paper for his economics class articulating his plan to provide overnight delivery service in what he saw as the computer information age. As a charter pilot at the Tweed New Haven airport, this young man flew frequently to airports in the area near high-tech companies such as IBM and Xerox. He would hear those companies' pilots talk about how they spent more time flying airplane parts and computer parts around than they were flying passengers. To the pilots, it was a distraction from their mission. To Frederick Smith, it was the birth of an idea. Ultimately, to the world, it was the birth of FedEx, the company that turned package delivery on its head by ensuring customers that their precious materials would "absolutely, positively get there overnight."

In an era when people went to office buildings to do their work and life moved at a much slower pace, getting funding for this paradigm-breaking idea was not an easy task. As Mr. Smith explained:

> It was a hard sell in certain ways. The FedEx proposition came along when the venture capital business was really looking for more prosaic types of investments, where you didn't have to create a product and a market all at the same time. By the time we finished the financing, we had three independent marketing studies that indicated that [our] original premise was correct.
>
> We didn't have to create some completely new technology. We used existing technology—planes, trucks. And then once we put the network in place . . . the secret was to get the network up fast enough to have a product to sell. But from the minute we started operations, with almost no exceptions, the traffic continued to rise.[24]

Today, with annual revenues in excess of $35 billion and more than 280,000 employees across the globe, traffic still continues to rise. What started as a parts-shipping business quickly turned into the overnight shipping of documents. But when the advent of fax machines and the Internet created a new paradigm, FedEx reinvented itself yet again. There was soon an unprecedented need to ship goods quickly (because FedEx had forever changed our expectations about speed of delivery) and in quantities greater than ever before. FedEx seized this opportunity to take the lead in the global shipping of e-commerce purchases.

Winners, by their very nature, don't invent once and call it a career. They're engines of reinvention, continually pushing forward. Innovation is at the core of what FedEx does. If we have learned one thing about paradigm shifts, it's that they keep coming. FedEx serves as an example of a company that has managed not only to break paradigms, but to ride the wave of change.

If you ask Tom Harrison of Omnicom what it takes to be a winner, he'll tell you the secret is *intuition* and *innovation*. Widely recognized as one of the most innovative strategic thinkers and advisers in his field, the description he gives about other paradigm-breaking winners fits him perfectly:

> *If there were a characteristic thread that might run through the one hundred different models of DNA among winners, it would be the ability to intuit, the ability to think around corners, and to know where you will need to be in three years to be successful. Anyone can be successful today, because we all know what's going on today. The people who are going to continuously make it and be successful are the people who understand where they need to be in three years.*
>
> *Innovation is different now. Every company went through a period where it was the bottom line, the bottom line, the bottom line. And once you are done thinking about that . . . think about the bottom line some more. What I'm telling people now is to not turn your back on the bottom line, but turn your eyes toward the top line. Because I think everyone has already created all the efficiencies and downsized and right-sized, and done all that stuff. So we can't shrink to grow. We have to grow to grow. That's what innovation is about now.*

So it's more and more about being able to see what's coming—anticipating what the trends are going to be and setting them, rather than just reacting after the fact.

The world's medical-device manufacturers and pharmaceutical companies also have a record of genuine breakthroughs, though you wouldn't know it by how they're treated publicly. Along with health insurance companies, they have become Washington's most recent whipping boy. But without them, most of the congressmen and senators doing the whipping would have passed on to that great cigar bar in the sky years ago.* Unfortunately, too often winning paradigm breakers must achieve *in spite* of government policies that entrench us in the old way

---

* On a personal note, my father was kept alive an extra twenty years because of two high-blood-pressure pills that, in the 1980s, cost him three dollars a day. Was it expensive? Sure. But it was worth every penny. And as for the people intent on destroying one of America's truly great paradigm-breaking industries by overtaxing and overregulating—let's hope they can be stopped. I can only imagine the life-saving medications that won't be invented or come to market because of shortsighted government policies.

of doing things, not with the support of a government that encourages genuine progress.

Writing for the *Washington Post* in 2009 about the great leaps and bounds modern medicine has made, George Will pointed out how new technologies have fundamentally changed the way hospitals operate as businesses: "When the first baby boomers, whose aging is driving health-care spending, were born in 1946, many American hospitals' principal expense was clean linen. This was long before MRIs, CAT scans and the rest of the diagnostic and therapeutic arsenal that modern medicine deploys."[25] Clean linen?! That doesn't even break the top twenty most costly hospital expenses today. New technologies like MRIs, CAT scans, and ultrasounds may be expensive, but does anyone want to go back to the days before we had them? Of course not. We like to complain about the high cost of modern health care, but for what exactly are we paying? We're paying for scans that find cancer before it has a chance to kill us. We're paying for medications that keep our hearts beating, our lungs breathing, and countless types of infections at bay. Without these breakthroughs, where would we be? Dead or ailing.

Modern medicine has broken the paradigm of life itself. Until the advent of antibiotics, a simple cut of the finger while out enjoying the seventeenth-century English countryside could have taken your life in a matter of days. Infection would lead to sepsis, which would lead to organ failure, and *bam*—you were dead. Today, however, you put some Neosporin on the cut, cover it with a bandage, and get on with things. Or what about women who die due to complications during childbirth? In 1915, roughly 608 women died giving birth for every 100,000 live births in the United States. In 2009, that number was just 17. We still have a way to go, but we have come very far. For the vast majority of American women, the very thought of not surviving childbirth hardly crosses their minds, because new medicines and twenty-first-century technology make such a horrible occurrence almost unheard of.

We are living under a new paradigm, one where both children and mothers nearly always live through birth, polio doesn't even exist anymore, and HIV/AIDS has become a chronic, treatable condition and is no longer a death sentence. And more Americans are fighting and surviving all types of cancer than ever before. The average life expectancy in the United States in 1915 was 54.5 years. If you're born in the United States today, you can reasonably expect to celebrate 78 birthdays.

We have rewritten the rules of life. Who's to say that our life expectancy can't be one hundred years or more, one hundred years from today? We can already transplant major organs or enjoy completely artificial ones. It's not that hard to imagine a world where doctors and scientists will be able to grow new organs, genetically identical to the ones we have now, so we can perpetuate ourselves ad infinitum . . . at least in theory. The point: all of this has become part of your reality. You expect it to be true. But one hundred years ago, visions like these would have been labeled as anything from hokum to heresy. There is a scientist, a medical researcher, a winner right now waging his or her own war against convention—and your children's lives will be forever changed as a result. Do you have the courage to step outside the mainstream, critically analyze it, and then redirect it to something higher and better? If you do, here's how to start talking about it.

ILLUSTRATING PARADIGM BREAKING

New paradigms give us fresh ways of thinking about, understanding, and experiencing our world. They also can make life a lot more fun. Winning is about being aware of our world and the people in it, understanding our paradigms, and then finding ways to shatter them.

The television ad that best illustrates paradigm breaking comes from the Sprint 4G phone. The words are powerful, but the images are unforgettable. Imagine a row of falling dominos, only the dominos are made of up of recognizable technology from the past. A stone wheel rolls into an old-fashioned bicycle . . . which knocks over the engine of a steam train . . . which rolls into and pushes over a gramophone record player . . . that knocks over an old-fashioned microscope . . . that falls into a typewriter . . . that knocks over a vintage telephone . . . that pushes over a Model T Ford . . . that rolls into and scatters a wall of old black-and-white televisions . . . that fall into and push over the Wright

Brothers' plane . . . which falls into a small rocket . . . which knocks over the space shuttle . . . that falls hard to the ground, knocking over a series of computer chip boards . . . which morph into computers . . . and then cell phones, one model after another . . . until you get to the still-standing HTC EVO 4G phone. And while this is happening, the announcer says:

> First is the beginning.
> First kicks open the door, and possibilities follow.
> First resets everything.
> First moves us forward, fast.
> We all want first.
> First isn't later. It's now.
> What will you do first with EVO, the first 4G phone?
> Only from Sprint, the Now Network.

Paradigm breaking requires defying the old guard and asking people to change the way they think. Doing this means taking a risk; it therefore requires the ability to persuade. This is something businesspeople face all the time, especially when trying to launch something new and revolutionary. Henry Juszkiewicz, CEO of Gibson Guitar, told me a story that perfectly underscores what I mean when I say you're going to face some harsh critics. *"People usually hate the idea of our new products. They hate it,"* he explained with a look of bemused frustration.

> *I remember when we introduced a new product called the BFG. The intention was to introduce a minimalist product, and we intentionally made it a little bit ugly. It was like a Volkswagen Bug emotional play; inexpensive, but it had character. And people looked at that product and said "it's not a Gibson. It's not shiny. You might as well just put strings on a tree." And we got a lot of negative comments like that.*
> *But that product went to number three, and we sold a gazillion of them. Nearly ninety percent of the rants were before the product hit the marketplace. But after the product hit the marketplace, people who tried it talked about it and loved it. And very slowly, you saw social media*

go from ninety percent negative to twenty percent positive, thirty percent
positive, and within weeks it went to eighty percent positive. Almost all
of our products that were paradigm-shifting, people initially recoiled and
didn't like them conceptually.

If you run your own business, you're probably aware that your employees won't passionately devote countless hours of their personal time to your whims about how to corner the market on new superwidgets. Unless your idea is wrapped in notions that resonate with their needs, it is dead in the water. So don't expect consumers to act any differently. You're not even paying them!

To make things worse, how on earth are you supposed to convince consumers that they need a new superwidget? They don't even know what it is! And remember that all the people who are employed making regular widgets are going to do everything they can to keep you and your superwidgets off the market. Effective communication is necessary to inject paradigm-breaking ideas into the public bloodstream.

Moreover, breaking paradigms often involves creating discontent. I know I'm going to get beat up for that line, so let me explain.

No one *needs* an iPod. No one *needs* an iPhone. No one *needs* an iPad. No one *needs* the ability to download any book ever written to their e-reader in sixty seconds. Heck, back when horses and trains were our main forms of transportation, no one *needed* to drive a car. (In fact, passersby on the streets often yelled out "Get a horse!" to the intrepid early drivers of Model Ts). No one *needs* to know that the Earth revolves around the sun and not vice versa. Humans managed to thrive without any of these things or this knowledge. But once they're here, more and more people view them as needs, not just luxuries or "nice-to-haves," the defunct Concorde notwithstanding. The reason these items slowly evolve into "needs" lies both in how they changed our lives and in how their founders and supporters communicated their necessity to us.

They entice us with the language of freedom, convenience, ease of use, discovery, and exploration. They paint a picture of a better, more exciting, more enjoyable tomorrow. And before we know it, we start thinking something is missing. "Why *can't* I have every song ever recorded in my pocket?" "Why *shouldn't* I be able to download any book I can think of anytime, anywhere?" "Why *don't* we have the right to drive through a restaurant on the way home and pick up dinner if it makes our lives easier?" You see, Shaw and Kennedy were right. Dreamers—winners—challenge the status quo.

Every big idea—every paradigm shift—has to be sold to the larger public if it's to be accepted. You have to convince people to throw out the old and embrace the new. And the best way to do that is to help people imagine their lives with it so they'll realize why their lives aren't as good or fulfilling without it. Your job, as a winner, is to create value in the new paradigm where none may currently exist—and you start by building trust. Without it, neither the people necessary to fulfill your vision, nor your target demographic, will have any reason to waste their precious time on your little obsession. Similarly, you must communicate carefully so as not to offend or raise suspicions. It's difficult to convince people to do things in a radically different way, but it's *easy* to scare them into complacency.

Winners don't always want to communicate exactly what they're trying to achieve. Sometimes language needs to soothe and calm rather than excite and upset. This is the linguistic equivalent of one of my favorite *Far Side* cartoons by the great Gary Larson. In it, he depicts a zebra leading a herd of other zebras past a lion that has caught and killed another zebra, possibly one of their friends. The caption is classic: "Move along everyone, nothing to see here." Subtle, quiet subversion aims to do exactly that. You want your communication to be docile so it doesn't set off any alarms or worry people. The more you make them think about big, scary change—or at least a change that isn't grounded in "hope"—the more they're going to fight it. They should hear what you have to say, and think to themselves, "Oh, nothing to see here" (read: nothing to worry about).

Allow me to use a political reference.

The 1994 elections, when I helped congressional Republicans win the House of Representatives for the first time in more than forty years, were "change" elections. It was, in fact, quite similar to what we saw again in 2006, 2008, and 2010: people were tired of the status quo and wanted something fresh, new, and different. They didn't vote for a revolution. They voted for change. The two are not the same. The Republican leader at the time, my friend Newt Gingrich, really messed up on Election Night by defining the election as a "revolution." That word frightened people—particularly those who voted Republican for the first time—because they only wanted to send a message to the Democrats, not upend the entire social structure of the country. They were unhappy with the ossified Democrats who had grown arrogant and corrupt, but they certainly didn't give a mandate to the Republicans or want a "revolution." His language of change—the language of the new political paradigm—was too heated and over-the-top, especially given how drastic and complete the change really was. That night, a majority of Americans experienced the election of a Republican Speaker of the House for the first time in their adult lives. Because of the importance of the event, it needed to be communicated with subtlety, humility, and sensitivity— not anger.

There were consequences. As Charles Krauthammer deftly wrote in the *Washington Post* in November of 2004:

> In 1994, when the Gingrich revolution *swept Republicans into power,* *ending 40 years of Democratic hegemony in the House, the mainstream* *press needed to account for this inversion of the Perfect Order of Things.* *A myth was born. Explained the* USA Today *headline: "ANGRY WHITE* *MEN: Their votes turn the tide for GOP." Overnight, the revolution of* *the Angry White Male became conventional wisdom. In the 10 years* *before the 1994 election there were 56 mentions of angry white men in* *the media, according to LexisNexis. In the next seven months there were* *more than 1,400.*

Americans wanted a comforting, commonsense hand at the wheel. But with one linguistic misstep, Gingrich, arguably the most brilliant political mind of his generation, gave ample ammunition for a hostile press to label his movement something it was not.

Here's what it boils down to: while human progress is achieved best through revolutionary change, it is rarely accepted through revolutionary rhetoric. Winners are not incremental progressives; they are revolutionaries. *However,* the public wants methodical progress, not revolution. Remember the strong desire for "stability" and "security" discussed earlier? Here's where the rubber meets the road. Paradigm breakers need the individual drive to transform and the common touch to connect with the expectations of the masses.

I was delighted when Henry Juszkiewicz touched on this point from a business perspective, because it's so critical to understanding the relationship between the right message and paradigm-breaking products or service:

> *People don't understand the emotional context of the human mind. Paradigm breaking, at its core, will only be successful if you make people feel better about themselves.*
>
> *Marketers often miss that boat entirely. You've got to get inside a person's head to give them what they want. We found they wanted automatic tuning, but we called it robotic tuning—because automatic made our consumers feel stupid. The emotional context of a word like automatic, when it comes to guitars, is bad, but buying something that's robotic is very hip.*
>
> *So the first thing we did to advertise were five YouTube videos that had nothing to do with the product. One of the videos was especially funny because it featured a robot guitar that hypnotized a guard and escaped from the factory. It was the real guitar but it had nothing to do with the function of tuning. It was just this robot guitar—this personality. We even had another YouTube video where the robot guitar destroys a Fender guitar. Those have nothing to do with the function and everything to do with imagination, and people really like it because it makes it fun.*

Too often businesses focus almost exclusively on the "thing" and forget to focus on the people who are going to eventually buy and use the "thing." The creative component is just as important as the technical particulars, which is why imagination is critical to developing products that don't just meet our needs, but completely redefine them.

PARADIGM-BREAKING WORDS TO LOSE

"Imagine being able to integrate any third-party or legacy application to create a centralized online marketing dashboard."

"We grow your business by taking the proverbial black box out of the conversion flow."

"Our multi-channel path to conversion technology has generated an increase in our advertiser's ROP over the past comparable years' sales."

THE SINGLE WORST MARKETING SENTENCE EVER

"We are continuing to build our tool kit for performance marketers and by extending advertiser capabilities into search, e-mail, and social media, we are connecting them with more points of distribution for their ads." (Thirty-four words when a dozen would do.)

PARADIGM-BREAKING WORDS TO USE

"Spend efficiently. Optimize effectively. Grow exponentially."

THE LANGUAGE OF PARADIGM BREAKING

Paradigm breaking isn't just about the product. It is often just as much about the language and marketing used to sell the product. For example, jeans are jeans, right? Wrong. For clothing entrepreneur Gene Montesano, coming up with the right name for his jeans was either a stroke of inspiration or a "lucky" guess, but either way, it worked beyond his greatest expectations:

I had a successful company called Bongo Jeans. I was married at the time, had a beautiful wife and two children, and I had no education, and I was just thinking about how lucky I was. So I was sitting in this Chinese restaurant and I looked across the street and I saw this sign that said Won Luck Dong. I then looked down at the soy sauce in my hand that said Lucky Soy Sauce—it said Lucky Brand Soy Sauce, and I thought Lucky Brand Jeans, this could be great.

Armed with a solid name, Montesano was looking for a way to make his jeans stand out against the dozens of other brands. Once again, he fell upon a language strategy that would propel his jeans from ordinary to extraordinary:

Putting "Lucky You" on the fly was a pretty good stroke. I've always liked women, and I just thought it was a very tongue-in-cheek appropriate place to put that phrase. My only issue was whether it is "lucky me" or is it "lucky you"? And I decided I'm going to do "lucky you," which was even more fun. And that was really a pretty big turning point. All of a sudden I started hearing that people were wearing the jeans because of that design. It was something people would talk about.

Montesano built a nationwide brand in a few short years not just by creating a product people wanted to buy but by labeling it in a way that made it stand out from every competitor. Before him, the only example of clothing where the style number was readily known to consumers was Levi's 501 jeans. So Montesano, short on marketing dollars, came up with a novel idea: Why stop at just a number? Why not add a message to every pair of jeans? And the ideas just started to flow. Says Montesano:

When we started Lucky Brand, we thought, "How could you hear about us? How could people learn about us?" So on the back of every jean I had the label with the style number and a description on the back flap that said "Wear us, be lucky," so you would never take that cover off. People thought it was supposed to be there, and if I cut it off, maybe I won't get lucky anymore. So everybody started ordering the jeans using the style number. It was all designed into the project.

Finally, realizing that the retail outlet was just as much the consumer as the shopper, he did something no other clothing manufacturer had ever done. He made his products desirable to those who sold jeans, not just to those who bought them:

I wanted the stores to want the jeans, so I designed this white box with clovers and it said "Good luck and long life to the opener of this box," and sometimes we'd throw a hat in there. So here you are, you're working in some shipping department for Nordstrom, and you've got to open all the boxes, but this one says "Good luck and long life to the opener of this box." We put fortunes in some of our jean boxes, so you found them and said, "Wow." (Pause) We had to stop using those boxes because Lucky Brand became so hot that people would rob the UPS trucks for all the white boxes with the clovers.

So let's get specific. Winners don't just imagine the future. They explain it. The words that follow should become core components of your lexicon because they will help others visualize a more compelling future.

KEY PHRASES OF PARADIGM BREAKING

1. You deserve/You have the right to . . .
2. Life-changing impact (instead of "transformation")
3. Breakthrough
4. A forensic approach
5. Re-engineered
6. American ingenuity
7. Consumer-driven technology
8. Patent protected
9. The new normal
10. Wow

"You have the right to . . ." raises expectations and gives audiences license to demand more than the status quo. It also affirms an inherent desire in most human beings to seek constant improvement. *"You deserve"* achieves the same objective, but it isn't quite so affirmational. The *"right"* to something is stronger than *"deserving"* something, but both touch on a sense of desired empowerment (more about this later).

"Life-changing impact" communicates the permanent personal benefit of a paradigm break in an individualized, personalized, humanized

context. For me, TiVo was just such a technology a decade ago. For kids today, cell phone texting has radically altered relationships and day-to-day life. If you can prove that what you offer is *"life-changing,"* you will have demonstrated extraordinary value (but only if you actually can achieve this—use this language without backing up your claim, and you'll lose credibility). The problem with the more often used *"transformational"* is that nobody really knows what it means, what it does, or why it matters. It has always ranked near or at the bottom of the attributes people want.

"Breakthrough" is the most radical, significant form of innovation, and it suggests a game-changing event. When people hear the word *breakthrough*, they assume it indicates something they have never seen or experienced before, and that the change is compelling and meaningful on many levels.

"A forensic approach" owes its credibility to the CSI franchise and the popularity of crime-solving detectives on television. People consider *"a forensic approach"* to be a step above comprehensive—more precise, clinical, and detailed. It is the best way to demonstrate the seriousness of your effort.

"Re-engineered" is a favorite term of the automotive sector, but it is also applied effectively to other areas of cutting-edge technology. Frankly, it's a more sophisticated way of saying *"new and improved."*

"American ingenuity" is about personalizing and patriotizing the American *process* of paradigm breaking. Most of the key phrases in this chapter are about the end result for the end user, because most people are far more interested in results than process. This is the exception. *"American ingenuity"* communicates the extraordinary steps it took/takes to get there—and adds a patriotic theme that will be appreciated by the vast majority of Americans.

"Consumer-driven technology" immediately answers the question *"What does it mean for me?"* Innovation, technology, and engineering all suggest an improvement in a product, service, or experience, but when it's consumer-driven, people assume that they'll be able to feel and appreciate that improvement. For example, prior to their bankruptcies, most of the American automotive companies were great at providing technical specs, but inept at demonstrating the value of their engineering improvements. They finally realized that unless the public understood

what it meant to the driving experience, they would not appreciate or even recognize the technological effort.

"Patent protected" is much more powerful than *"proprietary"* because it indicates a long-term legal guarantee for the ongoing viability of the technology. *Proprietary* suggests exclusive, but only for now. People will pay more for a patent protected technology or product.

"The new normal" is not something you currently hear in casual conversation, but it is something people immediately understand. In the 1990s, it was about *"reinvention,"* signifying constant, ongoing, positive improvement. In 2009, the word *"reset"* entered into the lexicon to describe how our attitudes, expectations, and behavior would need to change (i.e., go backward in time) in light of ongoing economic hardships. *"The new normal"* is more positive than *"reset"* because it also suggests stability. It can also be aspirational. A technology, product, or service *"breakthrough"* leads to a better *"new normal"* human condition.

"Wow." Frankly, the word says it all. When someone says *"wow"*—such as when they see their first iPad—nothing else matters.

"Customized" probably belongs on the big list because it is such an essential part of the human experience. One of the common traits of paradigm-breaking winners is their ability to affect people on an individual, one-to-one basis—regardless of whether they've met you or even know you exist. So much of what we buy today—and this trend is accelerating—is individualized and personalized to us. We may still be unable to choose the exact cable TV line up we want, but we can now customize our cars and our sneakers (thank you, Nike) to make them just as personal as our iPods. Winners provide customization in everything they do, and their language reflects that.

More On "You Have the Right to" and "You Deserve"

Earlier in this chapter I talked briefly about the need to create an artificial scenario of discontent to help people understand where your product or idea fits into their lives since, by definition, your paradigm-breaking superwidget is foreign to them. You have to create that demand. You have to create the demand for the Amazon Kindle before people are willing to shell out $250 for an electronic version of what they can get for free at the library. You have to create a demand for 3-D television before people will spend thousands of dollars and put on those silly glasses. And the best way to create demand is through the use of language that creates a sense of entitlement—explaining to people that they can have more (time, money, choices, whatever aspect of your superwidget you can link to their core desires) than they have now if they listen to what you have to say.

In contrast, people trying to sell things not yet heard of—or even yet conceived—have a much steeper hill to climb. They have to create a sense of entitlement—getting a consumer to say to herself, "Hey, why *don't* I have that yet?" Until people believed that they were actually worse off without the iPad or the Kindle, there wasn't much reason for them to buy either. They probably had a portable CD player that worked just fine, and books have been doing their thing pretty well for the past five hundred years.

From a language standpoint, there are two phrases that best capture this sense of entitlement: "you have a right to" and "you deserve." A good political example of this was the State of the Union response in 2006 delivered by then Virginia governor Tim Kaine, the current chairman of the Democratic National Committee. It was the first and only time in my eleven years of testing speeches that the *response* to the State of the Union did better than the State of the Union itself. Read these words and you'll understand why:

> No matter what political philosophy you hold or what state you call home, you have a right to expect that your government can deliver results. When there's a crime or a fire, you expect that police and firefighters have the tools to respond. When there's a natural disaster, you expect a well-managed response. When you send your children to school, you expect them to be prepared for success. And you have a right to expect government to be fiscally responsible, pay the bills, and live within its means.

With effective language like that, it's not surprising that he was a finalist for vice president under Barack Obama and the hand-chosen leader of the Democratic Party.

LUNTZ LESSONS

THE RULES FOR *BREAKING* THE RULES

1. **Embrace risk.**
   Accept the truth that you might fail—knowing that you can still fight on. Do not *expect* to fail, because then you will. But anyone who engages in paradigm breaking is stepping out on a limb. Today's rules exist for a reason, usually because they've become rooted in human habit, which is a powerful force to overcome. Your new idea might not actually be better. And even if it's better, it might not be accepted. Or it might change the world. If you're uncomfortable with those stakes, paradigm breaking isn't for you.

2. **Paradigm breaking is about focused exploration.**
   Without focus, your *activity* will not translate into *action*. Relentlessly pursue new rules for making simple things simpler and truer. Identify the need. Distill the quest to its purest form. Synthesize a new and better solution. Paradigm breakers are as much chemists as they are artists.

3. **Paradigm breaking is *still subordinate* to putting people first.**
   There's a reason the people-centeredness chapter came first. Winners don't shatter paradigms for kicks. They do it to improve the human condition (which ultimately sells a product or wins an election). Before asking, *"Why not?"* (the quintessential paradigm-breaking question) you must first look at the human condition as it exists today and identify its insufficiency.

4. **Communication matters.**
   The best revolutionary leaders communicate as if they are incremental progressives. Individual innovation by winners moves at the speed of light, but social adoption moves at a snail's pace. The best paradigm breakers use communication to balance the two.

5. **Have the *courage* to defend your new and better approach.**
   Have the guts to stand by your discovery. Expect people to resist, question, and ridicule. Whether you're upsetting articles of faith or simple human habit, you're touching on a nerve. Expect pain to precede the payoff.

LUNTZ LANGUAGE LESSON:

Each of the following statements has been made by one of America's leading CEOs about navigating the future in these difficult times. Knowing nothing else about the CEO, which do you respect and admire most based on their statement?

The Best Language

We will never stop innovating. Delivering better products will always keep us ahead. No matter what line of business a company is in, there is always a better way to do what you're doing or a better way to reach a new market or unmet need. In an economy as competitive as this, it really is "innovate or die." I'm committed to never resting on our laurels. I will always ask: what will customers need tomorrow, and how can we deliver it today?

The Worst Language

We're not looking at the stock price in terms of how we're making our decisions. We want to make long-term decisions that will add long-term value to our shareholders. Obviously we're gratified that we've had a very good year in terms of turning the company around, getting back to the core business.

5

PRIORITIZATION

Creating confidence one step at a time

I don't know the key to success,
but the key to failure is trying to please everybody.

—BILL COSBY

Overall, in the scheme of things, winning an Emmy is not important.
Let's get our priorities straight.
I think we all know what's really important in life—winning an Oscar.

—ELLEN DEGENERES

The key is not to prioritize what's on your schedule, but to schedule your
priorities.

—STEPHEN R. COVEY

If you're like me, you spend a lot of time traveling, living in hotels, and eating whatever you can find whenever you have a chance.* This often leads to embracing buffets as a last-resort source of nourishment. A common staple in hotels, the lineup usually boasts countless varieties

---

* I should seriously pitch the Mars candy company on creating the M&M Diet, since they've been keeping me alive since 1995. Every focus group facility proudly serves M&M's, and many offer them from the M&M guy—pull down his arm and you get a handful of M&M's. It almost lures you into thinking you're actually getting exercise.

of mystery meats, "vegetables," and pans of dessert-like gooey sweets that immediately make their home on your thighs. The buffet is as American as you can get—it is choice, freedom, diversity, and abundance all in one place.

Because you *can* have it all at a buffet, you usually do. But somehow in the process, you don't end up with much to show for it—except a massive stomachache. Substitute "a buffet" with "American life" and "stomach ache" with "stress and headaches," and you understand why buffets lead the chapter about prioritization. More does not equal better. In fact, it's often worse.

The reason even the best buffet can't hold a candle to a meal at Thomas Keller's French Laundry, Michel Richard's Citronelle, or Jean-Georges Vongerichten's J&G Steakhouse is that it is trying to do too many things. As a result, it ends up doing many things poorly rather than doing a few things extremely well. With limited resources and a limited budget, you can't have thirty dishes that are all exceptional. But pare that down and you've got a shot. Any buffet that charged you what it *actually* costs to deliver a universally quality product would jeopardize your mortgage payment. And to make matters worse, we usually go to buffets when we *want* a lot of food for little money. Enter mystery meats and secret sauces.

Pay attention the next time you go to a gourmet restaurant. The menu is focused, coherent, and flawless in execution. At most it will be two pages—though often only one. Any successful restaurateur who has actually surveyed his patrons knows that the perfect length of a menu is two pages—one page for appetizers, soups, and salads, and one page for entrées. Anything less is considered too restrictive or uncreative. Anything more and it is assumed that there will be good dishes and bad dishes.

So what exactly does all this talk about food have to do with winning?

Winners in politics and business have an uncanny ability to prioritize: to separate what *must* be done from what *should* be done. Winners are able to focus intensely on their priorities, and then pour all of their resources into those priorities. That enables them to underpromise and overdeliver. In an era of broken trust in institutions—where everyone promises the world and delivers peanuts (and that's not a political poke at Jimmy Carter)—doing the opposite immediately distinguishes you.

Not surprisingly, the ability to define what matters most, to order tasks and allocate resources based on commonly understood priorities, hinges on clear communication. You can accomplish the right things in the right order at the right time only when your entire organization understands what is important and why.

SEVEN SECONDS

Another essential trait that separates winners from everyone else is time management. You can't show me a winner in any profession who isn't remarkably efficient and effective in how they allocate their time. To the untrained eye, what they accomplish in a typical day is unfathomable. In reality, they are *always* thinking, working, and doing—and they do it faster and better than anyone else. There are entire books written about how to get the most out of every day, so I won't devote much time to it here. But I do have a time-management lesson from Rich DeVos, Amway's founder, that is worthy of a brief reference:

> It is fun to be in management. You sit in your big office and people come to see you. But that takes time, a lot of time, and I finally decided that I wouldn't see people in my office any longer. If somebody came to see me, I would say, "Fine, I will be right down." And I would go meet them by the front desk to find out what they wanted—money, a job, whatever. I would stand and talk to them right there, it would take five minutes, and then I'd return to my office. But if they sit in your office, they are going to take five minutes just telling you what a beautiful office you have. By the time they get around to talking about what they want, it's a half hour or forty-five minutes later. That's not an efficient way to manage your time.

Articulating your priorities quickly is one of the most important components of communication. First words build first impressions—impressions you have only a few precious seconds to make. Your audience walks into the room with their own set of priorities; time spent with you is time they're not spending on existing commitments. Thus, for you to get inside their heads and earn their attention, you have to move fast. If your first impression is powerful enough, people will never forget it. If not, they will—and you as well. Without the help of Google, you can probably correctly identify the authors, actor, and singer associated with the following opening lines:

- "It was the best of times, it was the worst of times . . ."
- "Call me Ishmael."
- "Rosebud."
- "I'm dreaming of a white Christmas."

That's because they are indelible first impressions—powerful, concise, visual statements that grab your attention and refuse to let go.

People judge you—the person—in seven seconds, and they judge your ideas in thirty seconds. If their eyes stay with you, they're giving you a chance. But the minute their eyes start to wander, it's over—the mind tiptoes away first, and the eyes go chasing after. It's not an accident that the most effective means of political communication is the thirty-second commercial. That is the exact attention span of most Americans when it comes to making a sale. But you won't get even thirty seconds if you don't start off strong.

Brevity is the hallmark of good communication—and it is in very short supply. No one knows more about the importance of immediacy and clarity than former movie executive Sherry Lansing.

The perfect pitch had passion, clarity, and simplicity—all in five minutes. It used to annoy me when I'd say yes to a pitch and fifteen minutes later they'd still be pitching. I'd think, "You know what, I don't like these people as much as I did a few minutes ago; maybe I don't want to do their film!"

If the first priority is about you, the second is about them, to determine exactly what matters most to the most people. FedEx CEO Fred Smith neatly summarizes his priorities in a single two-word catch-phrase that can be explained in just one sentence: "If you talk to anyone who works for FedEx and ask them, 'What's the Purple Promise?' they will tell you 'I will make every FedEx experience outstanding.' There is not a lot of extra verbiage in there. It just says what every one of us has to do, every single day." His number one priority: predictability—which happens to be America's top priority as well.

Smith is one of the most public of CEOs, appearing frequently in the media to promote the value of effective corporate leadership. But internally, his mission is promoting effective communication:

> So much of what goes on in the corporate setting is gobbledygook. People don't understand what you are saying. That is why the Purple Promise is such a perfect phrase. It encapsulates everything because purple is the common color of FedEx. It just tells everybody what you want to do. You have to have very clear communication skills. In fact, if you can't communicate, won't communicate, and put in the time and effort into communicating, then you really can't be a leader for FedEx. You really can't be a first level manager. Communications capability is essential. It is a responsibility.

Smith recognized from the earliest days of Federal Express that prioritizing effective communication was essential not just for consumers but for employees as well.

Since this is both a business and a political book, it makes the most sense to address what Americans want most economically in their day-to-day lives. The answer in our current economic situation is, by far, stability.

With all that has happened on Wall Street and Main Street, people want a return to simple normalcy, allowing them to regain some control over their daily lives. As important as "opportunity" has been to the American character, that's secondary right now. "Stability," "predictability," and "no surprises" constitute a more deeply held emotional need that is often articulated in my focus groups but rarely by corporate or political leaders. It is said that life offers no guarantees, but that's what millions of Americans are begging for right now. Those individuals and businesses that can demonstrate that what they offer smooths out the

AMERICANS ARE SHOUTING OUT FOR "PREDICTABILITY!"

Which of the following do you want most in your day-to-day life?*
(Choose 2, Combined Answers)

Stability	49%
Opportunity	34%
Revitalization	27%
Return to economic freedom	27%
Security	22%
Prosperity	13%
Steadiness	9%
Renewal	8%
Success	7%
None of these	5%

*   Source: The Word Doctors, 2010.

highs and lows and provides a greater degree of certainty will find very receptive employees, customers, and shareholders. In fact, I have no doubt that a new generation of winners will be born from the "no surprises" school of marketing and communication. Just wait.

A CORPORATE CASE STUDY

How does Johnson & Johnson—a legacy company with 125 years of history and habits—manage to consistently outrank innovative and unfettered giants such as Amazon, Southwest Airlines, and Microsoft as one of the world's most admired, respected, and reputable companies? The answer: clearly defined priorities. They know what matters and in what order. And they stick to their priorities day in and day out, no matter what. Consistency is the cornerstone of great brands: it builds trust, sales, and, ultimately, profits. Perhaps that's why J&J consistently beats the performance of the S&P, and why they've delivered seventy-six consecutive years of sales increases and forty-seven consecutive years of dividend increases for their shareholders—even in times of economic distress.

It starts with their credo. Notice that unlike most companies, it's not a vision, a mission statement, or even a mission. A *credo* is a system of principles or beliefs—and that's what guides the actions and decisions of the 114,000 people in 250 operating companies and 60 countries around the world. It tells everyone inside and outside the company what *always* comes first, and it can be summarized as follows:

We believe our first responsibility is to the doctors, nurses and patients, to mothers and fathers and all others who use our products and services. In meeting their needs everything we do must be of high quality.

Adhering to this credo, J&J goes further to publicly communicate the priorities of its entire organization on their Web site for all to see. There can be no doubt what matters most. These "Growth Priorities" that chairman and CEO Bill Weldon highlighted for J&J's common focus in 2010 each fits nicely into at least one *Win* category:

- **Innovative Products**—Our growth has always been based on scientific innovations that serve unmet patient and customer needs in a meaningful way. This has led us to be a market leader, #1 or #2, in many of our businesses. We will stay focused on bringing forth innovative, accessible and effective products—and entirely new business models—that address the most prevalent health care needs of the day. *(People-Centeredness)*
- **Robust Pipelines**—We must continuously target, invest and manage the development of a robust pipeline of new medicines, devices and products. We plan to use a mix of internal and external sources to sustain pipelines that provide a competitive advantage. We fully expect the new products coming out of our pipeline today to accelerate the proportion of our sales driven by newer products. *(Paradigm Breaking)*
- **Global Presence**—As a global health care leader, we must continue to expand our presence and execute our strategies in the appropriate way for diverse markets and customers. Our approach will be strategic, effective and cost-efficient to address the local needs. *(Prioritization)*

- **Talented People**—Our extraordinary and diverse workforce is still our cornerstone and we must develop our people, challenge them, motivate them and reward them to achieve success. *(Persuasion)*

How does prioritization help J&J to be a consistent winner? Consider the Tylenol crisis in September 1982, when seven people were killed by cyanide-laced Tylenol capsules. J&J didn't sit back or ignore the mounting evidence of real problems, like Toyota did with its accelerator issue in 2009, or wait and see if it would blow over. They didn't fight over whose fault it was, like BP did with the Gulf oil spill in 2010, or minimize the public concern. They didn't assert their innocence or attempt to employ their market superiority, like Goldman Sachs did, as a way to avoid blame. Instead, they took immediate action—because they knew that their "first responsibility is to the doctors, nurses and patients, to mothers and fathers and all others who use our products and services."

If personal responsibility wasn't enough motivation, J&J's 18 percent stock decline and the increasing demand for competitors' products such as Datril and Anacin-3 added urgency to the actions they took. They immediately recalled *all* Tylenol products from store shelves and canceled all Tylenol advertising. In fact, even after the FDA determined that the product tampering occurred at the store level and not during the manufacturing process, J&J continued to take responsibility for the consumers affected by this tragedy.

Then the company executed a three-pronged crisis response campaign. First, rather than keeping the press at arm's length, they worked closely with them to keep the public up-to-date and dispel rumors before they began. Second, J&J ran a one-time ad that explained how to exchange Tylenol capsules for tablets or refunds. And finally, to make amends for a tragedy that hurt them, not just their customers, Johnson & Johnson offered a $2.50 coupon off any Tylenol product in newspapers across the United States to reimburse consumers for Tylenol capsules they may have discarded as a result of the product tampering. The coupon not only showed a sense of corporate responsibility that is all too rare today, but it gave both existing and new consumers incentive to purchase Tylenol products in noncapsule forms.

Weeks after the crisis, the FDA issued guidelines for tamper-resistant packaging for the entire food and drug industry. To regain consumer confidence, J&J employed three layers of protection, two more than recommended. Only months after the incident, J&J was well on the road to regaining its market share for pain relievers and shortly regained more than 90 percent of its Tylenol customers. Their strategic, honest, and open management of this crisis earned the then CEO, James Burke, a place in the National Business Hall of Fame, which he was awarded in 1990. Burke was so successful at averting the demise of Tylenol because he knew how to analyze the problem, find a solution, and execute, execute, execute.

In fact, according to Michael George, corporate efficiency guru and author of *Lean Six Sigma,* the highly successful business strategy to cut waste, cut costs, grow revenue, and empower employees, Burke is the model of a successful executive. He explains: *"A successful executive is a person who analyzes a problem, describes a strategic concept for a solution, has minions that translate strategies into specific tactics, defines metrics for performance to achieve that strategic objective, and then makes damn sure that it gets done. He may have to fire his best friend to get it done, but he would apply the necessary resources to achieve that objective."*

Wow, brutal. Then again, you can't really address a crisis like the Tylenol scare without the willingness to do whatever it takes to make the situation right again—no matter what. And because Burke was able to do just that, Tylenol is still one of the most trusted brands in America today.

Unfortunately for Johnson & Johnson, history repeated itself in 2010 when J&J faced an anxious public and an angry congressional hearing as a result of the recall of forty-three over-the-counter children's medicines, including liquid versions of Tylenol, Motrin, Zyrtec, and Benadryl. The FDA found several "manufacturing deficiencies" that appear to have been occurring for some time. While no adverse medical events had been reported as a result of the quality-control issues, J&J once again announced a voluntary recall of all products in all affected countries, including the United States. And once again, J&J came clean. In a May 27 hearing before the Congressional Committee on Oversight and

Government Reform, Colleen Goggins, worldwide chairman, Johnson & Johnson Consumer Group, was clear and contrite:

> *The quality and process issues that we found at McNeil, those which led to the recall and others, are unacceptable. On behalf of McNeil and Johnson & Johnson, I apologize to the mothers, fathers, and caregivers for the concern and inconvenience caused by the recall. Johnson & Johnson embraces the work of this Committee, and we hope that today's hearing will be an important step in furthering public understanding of the recall.*
>
> *. . . Johnson & Johnson and McNeil take these issues seriously, and we are committed to taking the steps necessary to bring McNeil's operations back to a level of quality that Johnson & Johnson demands of its companies, and the public rightly expects from us.*

She did what Goldman Sachs CEO Lloyd Blankfein refused to do when facing the elected representatives of the people. She began with an apology—and she made it personal by referencing "the mothers, fathers, and caregivers." How they handle the situation going forward—including the discovery of *burkholderia cepacia* bacteria on some manufacturing equipment—remains to be seen. But given this company's record of belief-driven behaviors, clear priorities, and effective crisis resolution, chances are they will teach Toyota, Goldman Sachs, and BP a lesson in winning communication.

The American people demand that you deliver perfection, and they expect that you prioritize them before yourself. When you mess up, own up. When you cause harm, make it right, and then go a step further. In the transaction, you may actually end up ahead of where you started. But if you pass the buck, expect them to withhold their own.

PRIORITIZING POLICY AND POLITICS

The challenge of message prioritization occurs in politics and public policy as well. Take the issue of education reform as an example. In nationwide surveys, Americans give the public school system a B- or C+—hardly a ringing endorsement. Yet despite the mediocre evalua-

THE TRUTH ABOUT
PUBLIC SCHOOL EDUCATION

- American fifteen-year-olds rank thirty-fifth out of fifty-seven developed countries in math and literacy.
- 30 percent of public school students don't graduate from high school.
- Every day, 7,000 kids drop out of high school.
- Of the 50 million children currently in public school, 15 million of them will drop out.
- 25 percent of all public school math teachers did not major in mathematics or a math-related subject at a college or university.
- Less than two-thirds of high school graduates are accepted to college every year.
- One half of all African American high school students will not graduate.
- By eighth grade, U.S. students are a full two grade levels behind their international counterparts in math.
- The high school graduation rate for Latino/Hispanic students is just 58 percent.
- 15 percent of high schools produce 50 percent of the dropouts in the country.
- 87 percent of adults in the United States have a high school diploma. By comparison, 97 percent of adults in Korea have a high school diploma.
- Today, only 17 percent of low-income fourth-graders are proficient in reading, while 50 percent are below basic level.
- More than 5 million students are attending more than 10,000 schools that are failing under the federal No Child Left Behind Act.
- Every twenty-six seconds, a student drops out of high school in the United States.
- Nearly 50 percent of children in our nation's largest cities do not graduate from high school.
- 70 percent of eighth-graders are not proficient in reading, and most of them will never catch up.
- Each year, more than 1 million high school seniors fail to graduate.

tion, no one has prioritized precisely what should be measured, tested, evaluated, quantified, or assessed to determine school success. In fact, data ubiquity is part of the problem—there is a statistic available to prove every point. Allow me this example: consider the facts in the gray box and pick the two or three that matter most to you (but don't circle them). Odds are, it won't be what matters most to someone else. Try it.

Can you guess which embarrassing statistic came in first or second? Probably not (the answer is five paragraphs away). But does it really matter? Absolutely. So how do we fix the problem?

The first step is to break through the noise. The only way to get past the ideological rancor fueled by this deluge of data is to prime the conversation with areas of consensus.

First, find the facts or figures that everyone agrees on—the words, phrases, and messages that break through the clutter, grab our attention, and are easy to agree with—and dump everything else.

Second, begin with a statement like, "If you remember only two things from my presentation, remember this . . ." or "The education debate boils down to two tragic facts . . ."

And third, enumerate plainly. (Note: Whenever you mention a number in the beginning of your statement, it's important to follow through by enumerating your points as you make them. This accomplishes two objectives. First, it builds your credibility, and second, it holds your audience's attention as they wait to hear your final points.) If you can't prioritize your facts into several salient points, how can you expect others to agree with you and then follow your lead?

So what matters most to Americans? Based on extensive research for the Bill & Melinda Gates Foundation and the Broad Foundation, there are, in fact, two numbers that matter more to more people and are guaranteed to capture hearts as well as minds:

- Fully 70 percent of eighth-graders are *not* proficient in reading, and most of them will never catch up. To parents, if their child is failing in their early teen years, it means failure for life.
- Each year, more than 1 million high school seniors fail to graduate. Everyone understands the consequences of education failure, and this number quantifies that failure in black and white.

These are powerful statistics. I bet every parent who reads this book will remember them. When you start the discussion with two life-changing facts, people pay attention. When you connect the fact to a personalized consequence, the message resonates. And then when you shift to solutions, people *listen closely* and add your message to their personal perspective. That's exactly what communication winners do every day.

THAT'S MY STORY, AND I'M STICKING TO IT

The other common prioritization faux pas is to change messaging again . . . and again . . . and again. That's exactly what happened with America's health-care debate in 2009 and 2010. From the beginning, there was no clear narrative from the Obama administration about why health-care reform was so critical to the national interest. It started, just after the financial crisis, as a necessary response to the economic downturn. Health-care reform was supposed to help our economy recover by getting the skyrocketing costs of medical care under control. Then the story changed: it was now about our moral obligation to the people without health insurance. Then it became about deficit reduction. Then, well, no one really knows.* We were told we just had to get it done—now. As a result, most polls pegged public support at somewhere between 37 percent and 42 percent, and it passed without a single Republican vote in the House or Senate, along with some Democratic opposition. Never in our history has such a sweeping piece of legislation been passed without a single opposition party vote.

There is an important lesson here regardless of your political persuasion. It was clear from the outset that President Obama's priority—health-care reform—didn't match up with the public's priority, which every poll showed was jobs, jobs, and more jobs. Sure, thanks to the sheer size of the Democrats' congressional majorities and willingness to bend the procedural rules, they succeeded in their legislative agenda. But it was the Republicans whose narrative was much clearer ("say no")

---

* The Bush administration's case for the war in Iraq suffered from the same helter-skelter, ambiguous narrative. First it was Iraq's denying access to the international community and weapons inspectors. Then it was the threat of WMDs and Saddam Hussein to the American people. Then it was the link to al Qaeda. Finally, it was to liberate the Iraqi people from their own dictator. Too many reasons, not enough focus—especially at the expense of American lives.

LUNTZ LESSONS

ESTABLISHING MESSAGE PRIORITIES

I'm going to borrow a line from *And the Band Played On*, a book by Randy Shilts about the discovery of and response to the AIDS epidemic:

"What do we think? What do we know? What can we prove?"

The doctors who were fighting to raise awareness knew the public tolerance for the truth about AIDS was limited and perilous. That meant they'd better put their *best* faces and facts forward. There was no room for error. If they couldn't unequivocally prove it, they'd better not say it.

You can and should consider a wide universe of communication priorities. Analyze them. This is the "what do we think?" and "what do we know?" part. Yes, many things are important. Consider them fully. But then focus all your energy on the essential—the things people want most that you can *prove*.

Prioritization is about identifying that critical nexus between your paradigm-breaking knowledge, your ability to prove it to the public, and the public's desire to know.

---

and more compelling ("stop the government takeover of health care"). Republicans regained control of the House of Representatives in November 2010 thanks to ongoing clarity and opposition. For those of you who supported the legislation, it must be frustrating to witness such a historic victory achieved without the support of the majority of your countrymen—but now you understand the importance of message prioritization. Without it, people just don't hear you. And for those of you who opposed the legislation, it is surely a hollow victory to have won in the court of public opinion but not on the floor of Congress.

PRIORITIZING ACTIONS

What exactly do you want to achieve?

To arrive at your destination, you need to know exactly where you want to go. What does "there" look like? The surest way to doom any fledgling effort is to try to be everything to everyone. Instead, people and products can benefit most from sticking to what they do really, really well. Whether it's the highest quality, most durable paper towel (I'm looking at you, Brawny) or a perennially clutch field-goal kicker (and you, Adam Vinatieri), the most successful people and products prioritize what they want to do, hone in on a specific goal or skill, and completely dominate it.

Look no further than the Amazon Kindle, a device I'm still fascinated with. In interviews with Amazon's founder, Jeff Bezos, you hear the same theme over and over again: the Kindle, in its final form, had to "disappear" the way a book does when you're reading it. In an interview with Charlie Rose the day the Kindle was first released on November 19, 2007, Bezos explained what he meant:

JEFF BEZOS: You know, the physical book is so highly evolved and so elegantly suited to its purpose that it's hard to improve on. It isn't like some other artifact, some other object. It's something very, very emotional and personal for people. But the book has a feature which I think is hard to notice, but it's the book's most important feature. And that is that it disappears.

CHARLIE ROSE: What does that mean?

JEFF BEZOS: So when you are reading, you don't notice the paper and the ink and the glue and the stitching.

CHARLIE ROSE: You just feel the story.

JEFF BEZOS: All of that dissolves and what remains is the author's world. And you go into this flow state. And that ability for a book to disappear is something that became our top design objective for Kindle. Because we knew if we couldn't replicate that aspect of a book, that nobody would use this device. And if you think about it, there are a lot of things that have to go into that, to get something to disappear like that and to vanish so that you can get into that very pleasurable mental flow state that readers know and love.[26]

Bezos and his team at Amazon understood what the final product had to look like and what they had to achieve for the product to be a success. Of course they could have made the Kindle play music, take pictures, wake you up in the morning, and remind you to take your meds. Technology wasn't the issue—it was delivering a unique experience to the customer in a way that no other product can. All of the ringtones, pixels, and memory space in the world couldn't make up for that type of uniqueness. Too many features detract from the clear goal that products like the Kindle possess. Bezos had a shared understanding of what they were making—an eBook version of the iPod—and anything that got in the way of that singular goal had to go. The Kindle had to "disappear" in your hands and become an organic part of your life, which meant the bells and whistles that would make it more than a book had to disappear as well. But if Steve Jobs and Apple have their way, the iPad will eventually put the Kindle out of business, thanks to all those bells and whistles that make the iPad so compelling.

Or think about Google. Way back when, Google was just a search engine. That was it. It wasn't even "the one" search engine. It wasn't even a verb yet. But today, Google is everywhere—literally. Next time you look up at the sky, no matter where you are in the world, there's a chance your picture is being taken and uploaded to Google Earth. If that's not creepy, I don't know what is. More important, Google, while still performing at an amazing rate, could begin to suffer from their loss of focus. Jim Davidson brought this point up in our discussion about what makes a company great, and what makes a great company fail. *"Did you know that Google was like the twentieth search engine to be invented in the nineties? The twentieth one!"* he told me, his voice rising with emphasis.

> So why is Google different? Why is it that Google became so successful as a search engine? Why didn't others? It was there for everybody, anybody could have done it. Sure, Google had a different business model. But it wasn't even the business model that was better. Overture, which was bought by Yahoo!, had the same business model, and other people had similar search engines. But Google had them both right. They had a better search engine, they religiously went to AdWords—and they had the discipline of not searching around and rambling around. They were focused.
>
> But now look at Google. Google is now very unfocused. Google is doing voice, they're doing applications, they are taking on Microsoft Office,

and they've got Android. They are taking on the cell phone world. They are building high-speed fiber to the home to try and accelerate broadband connections across the United States. Google is taking on China over their political censorship. But what made them better than anyone else was great technology and their religious focus on a business model.

Google had such a meteoric rise because it did one thing better than anyone else on the planet—search. That's all it gave you, and it was great. And then Google expanded it, and customers benefited. And then it went public, and hundreds of people became millionaires overnight. But the path ahead isn't so clear. Any company will face ups and downs, but Google's trend has been increasingly volatile, and it's not so certain anymore that it'll conquer its rivals as many once envisioned. Just days before this book went to print, more people spent more time on Facebook than Google—and the trend is in Facebook's favor. If Google is going to remain number one for the long-term, it should never forget what made it so successful in the first place. Winners always remember their first job, their first paycheck, and their first setback.

Before you start a business, launch a new product, start up a new blog, or run for elected office, you have to sit down with your team and define success. By define, I don't just mean spouting an assertion like, "We want to be number one in our industry." It's more than that. What customer need will you meet? What products will you sell? To whom will you sell them? What will they look like? Feel like? How will they perform? What experience will you deliver? How will you make people want to buy from you? How will you be different—better—than your competition? This process can be agonizing and frustrating, but it's necessary.

That's a long list of questions that may lead you to believe this process must be complicated. No doubt about it: there are no *easy* answers to winning. But there are (indeed, must be) *simple* answers. You must find these and underpin your business with them. For each and every question above (and by all means, don't limit yourself to these questions), *force* yourself to write a one-sentence answer. No more. The answer— your priorities—should be about attributes, feelings, and experiences, not the detailed line items of your eventual business plan. These *principles* become the foundation of your product.

Let's practice, using what might have gone through the minds of the geniuses at Amazon.

Q. *What customer need will we meet?*

A. We will make the experience of reading easier and more natural than ever, or we won't make this product at all.

Q. *What products will we sell?*

A. Just one: an electronic reader that calls no attention to its electronic platform.

Q. *To whom will you sell it?*

A. People who love reading and want to enjoy it more—whether they like electronics or not.

Q. *What will the product look like?*

A. So simple you don't even know it's there.

Q. *What will it feel like?*

A. So comfortable it feels natural on the couch, in bed, or anywhere else books have already made their homes.

Q. *How will they perform?*

A. Since books don't malfunction, Kindles can't either.

Q. *What experience will you deliver?*

A. Total simplicity to use and complete intimacy with the story.

Q. *How will you make people want to buy from you?*

A. By providing an experience with the reader that sells itself within three minutes of trying it out.

Q. *What will make you better than the competition?*

A. Pioneering the greatest leap forward in "disappearing" the reading device since the book was invented.

No, those answers aren't long on specifics. And that's the point. Instead, they are deep on meaning. They're organizing principles that will inspire and unify the legion of engineers and marketers who, together, have to produce and sell something that is both revolutionary in purpose and effortlessly easy to use. That's a big task; best to start simply.

When I started my first business, the Luntz Research Companies, I had to decide which services I would offer. I had to focus. I could do traditional polling, focus groups, ethnographies, image consulting, ad testing, media training—you name it—a full smorgasbord of market research and communication services. The problem with that approach is, like the all-you-can-eat buffet, you end up doing everything decently instead of doing one or two things exceptionally. As a result, I chose to focus my time, energy, and resources on one skill, one that few others were delivering: message optimization. My firm focused on messaging and language—finding the exact words, phrases, and articulations of ideas that really stood out and got people excited about a cause, product, or service. By focusing on a single element of public opinion, and then perfecting an innovative research technique—the focus group dial session—I was able to build a reputation as "the word guy." My firm brought objectivity to what was, up to then, a fairly subjective art. We made language development a science. And as time went on, I became known as an authority on messaging because I had built expertise in that one area rather than spreading myself too thin across too many disciplines. It allowed me to differentiate my skills in a field that was brimming with competent but undifferentiated talent.

I didn't become an expert on messaging and communication by chance. I also got to where I am today because language, messaging, communication, and words have been my obsession since childhood. By playing to my strengths and skills—working with language to make it more efficient and more effective—I was able to create a more powerful, desirable product because no one else offered it. No one had truly focused on the language of issues and politics at the emotional, visceral, granular level like I did. That left the field wide open for me to work with clients and define what message consulting should look like. I left the more mundane horse-race polling to others. No knock on them—they're numbers geeks; I'm a word geek. Knowing what your strengths are—and what they're not—can help you determine what your product should look like and whose help you need to get it there.

Focus is vital to winning, but it's not as easy as it sounds. When I sat down with Mike Richter and Brendan Shanahan, two of ice hockey's greatest players, it was reassuring to hear them echo the exact same thoughts. *"Focus is the single hardest endeavor you can have as a human. Anyone can get into the zone. The truly great know how to stay in the zone,"* Richter said as we sat in the owner's box watching the Philadelphia Flyers come from an unprecedented 3 to 0 deficit to win the Eastern Conference championship in 2010. Then, as if on cue, Shanahan jumped in:

> *What's frustrating for me when I make a poor decision or a mistake is when I don't trust my instincts. I think most athletes at the professional level have good instincts. It's when you do something and it doesn't work out, and you say, "I f-ing knew it, but I let other factors talk me into it." That's where players say that they're in the zone. When you're in the zone, you're not listening to any other voices but the one that you really trust and know. Your own.*

Focus forces you to be better because it helps you eliminate the noise, the doubts, the voices, and the distractions that keep you from achieving what you could otherwise achieve. Without it, you can easily find yourself meandering around trying to take on too many challenges and attempting to be everything to everyone, which is a recipe for disaster.

One of the biggest mistakes I've watched CEOs and candidates make over the years is neglecting to recognize their weaknesses as they prioritize their strengths. Until you're willing to have an honest conversation with yourself, you can't prioritize correctly. This applies on both a personal and institutional level. Unless you're a one-man show who enjoys the luxury of self-made status (and even a self-made man or woman usually relies on the support and teamwork of others), you probably have to deal with a larger organizational structure and all the advantages and disadvantages that come with it.

When I think of a company that knows exactly what it's good at, Walmart immediately springs to mind. Founded in 1962 by Sam Walton in Rogers, Arkansas, Walmart is now the largest company in the United States, with fiscal year 2010 sales of $405 billion.[27] In 2007, the megaretailer changed its well-known slogan from "always low prices" to "save money, live better." This was meant to signal a shift internally and become a mission for the company: help Americans save money so they can have better lives. It was simple. It was powerful. It was effective. They realized, correctly, that just being the lowest price retailer wasn't enough anymore. But it worked only because Walmart knew what it was good at and capitalized on its strength. No other retailer in the United States had been able to match Walmart's prices. You have to give Walmart credit for knowing what it can do well and avoiding what it cannot. And give them credit for letting others (I'm looking at you, Target snobs) mock them for what they aren't. To date, they've never taken the bait to move "up." Instead, they're driving deeper to the hearts of their customers.

When you go into a Walmart store, it's a spartan experience. Yes, they've gotten a bit warmer and stylized in recent years, but it's still a relatively bare-bones operation. Walmart's raison d'être isn't the shopping experience; it's friendly frugality. The store's very layout and design are intended to keep you focused on what you're there for—spending money. They don't pretend to be something they're not. And they certainly do not try to appeal to higher-end consumers by offering amenities, like the Starbucks I mentioned earlier at Target. When you go to a Walmart, it's to save money, not sip on a caramel macchiato. By prioritizing the "save money" experience and making it their guiding light, they've taken more than their fair share of criticism over the years. Each new Walmart store is branded by critics as the beginning of the end by whichever poor sap of a community is unlucky enough to host it. Yet as the measurable savings become clear, passions inevitably cool and the surrounding community settles down.

In fact, Walmart's moves to save money—including paying employees less than many critics and employees would like—has painted a bull's-eye on its back. That's why it was somewhat surprising when Robert Reich, former labor secretary under President Clinton, offered a quasi-defense for the megaretailer:

Condemning Walmart for not giving its employees better pay and health benefits may be emotionally gratifying but has little to do with the forces that have impelled Walmart to keep wages and benefits low and bestow good deals on Walmart's customers and investors. Walmart, like every other capitalist player, is, as I have emphasized, following the current rules of the game.[28]

Actually, they're not just following the rules; they're making the rules work for *them*. They understand that for their customers, value drives all, and have subordinated every other consideration to value. In their case, customers first, and the rest be damned.

In this case, that means doing whatever it takes to offer consumers the lowest prices because that's what they demand, especially in the aftermath of the Great Recession and unprecedented unemployment. Part of that equation has meant offering lower wages and less generous benefits to employees, especially part-time individuals, because the suits in Arkansas know it's either that or raising their prices. When you've based your entire business model and reputation on always being the least expensive, you have to find ways to play to your strengths. You stick to your guns even when it's not popular among your critics, because it's more important to be popular with your customers.

PRIORITIZING COMMUNICATION

Who is your audience? It sounds like a simple question, but almost half of the Fortune 500 companies and executives I've worked with got it wrong.

To find the right answer, start with the "what" and "how" of your goal. What do you want to create? And how do you plan to create it? Once you've answered these questions fully, then you can begin developing a communication strategy for moving forward.

Think carefully about the people you're addressing. What is important to them? What's driving them right now? Where do they come from— geographically, ideologically, and economically? What are their hopes, dreams, and fears? What baggage do they bring to the conversation? How are their experiences different from yours, and how do those experiences color the way they see the world and the way they see you? These are the kinds of questions you have to ask yourself before you develop a communication strategy.

Don't make the mistake of thinking your only audience is your customer base. If you are a company leader, you have an internal audience of employees that is often more important than your external customers. You have to get the internal stuff right before you can hope to connect with the marketplace.

Employees don't care about shareholders, and they don't care about corporate profits, except when the lack of them could lead to job cuts. They *do* care about their jobs, and the good employees care about customers. Too often, my firm is brought in to tell executives to stop explaining their next quarterly dividend targets to employees who have just suffered pay cuts. After twenty years of talking to employees in every industry, I can tell you with certainty: no employee gets up in the morning and jumps out of bed thrilled to go to work because they are propelled by a desire to increase shareholder profits. (Well, they might if they work in the finance department, but in that case, shareholders are their customers.) Numbers that are not tied to a mission and that do not convey progress against priorities aren't motivating. They're just numbers. Being the best matters. Quality matters. Customer satisfaction matters. And, most of all, people matter.

Corporate communicators and campaign consultants often tell their bosses what to say without taking even a minute to think about how those messages will come across to the people listening. If you don't take the time to perform an accurate appraisal of your audience, you can almost count on saying something that rubs them the wrong way. And trust me, all it takes is one verbal misstep to sink an entire product line, big idea, or candidacy. Just ask Howard Dean.

Winners get this essential order right: First you need an idea that sets you apart and fulfills a human need. *Then* you need a communication game plan that resonates on a personal level. By *first* focusing on your strength and delivering an *individualized, personalized, humanized* message, you earn the credibility and loyalty of your audience—first internal and then external. It's the difference between being a flash-in-the-pan gimmick and having a lasting, transformative presence.

ENUMERATE, ENUMERATE, ENUMERATE

You may not have thought about it, but there's a reason there's so much enumeration in our Constitution, especially in the Bill of Rights. There were significant concerns among many of the delegates to the constitutional convention that without a "bill of rights" to help limit the size and scope of the federal government, the new nation would quickly fall under the same tyrannical thumb it had just fought so hard to escape from. To help bring the factions together, James Madison proposed the first set of amendments that make up the Bill of Rights. They took effect on December 15, 1791, after three-fourths of the states ratified them.

The Bill of Rights is enumerated to eliminate doubt, uncertainty, and confusion. It also puts the amendments in order of importance. And each numbered amendment is tied to a principle. While no amendment of the ten is technically more important than another, the First Amendment—the freedoms of religion, press, speech, assembly, and the right to petition—has been the most fundamental in ensuring Americans' liberty since the nation was founded. Then, as you work your way down, each amendment becomes slightly further removed from the one before it, until you reach the Tenth Amendment, which says any power not given to the federal government expressly in the document is reserved to the states or to the people. In other words, if the federal government wants to do something, it *has* to be in the enumerated powers contained in the Constitution. Otherwise, the national government just plain can't do it. It was our original attempt at holding the government accountable.*

The point of enumeration, whether in the Bill of Rights or in a five-year business plan, is clarity. It doesn't matter how strong or compelling

---

* Did you know that our Constitution limits government authority to *only* those things specifically listed in the Constitution? If so, congratulations—you are a part of a stark minority. According to a 2010 Krieble Foundation study, only 38 percent of Americans correctly identified that *"The federal government can only do those things that are specifically authorized in the Constitution itself. Anything else is not allowed."* The plurality (43 percent) wrongly say that *"The federal government can do whatever necessary to improve the well-being of the people, as long as Congress passes the bill and the president signs it legally."* Another 20 percent incorrectly say, *"The Constitution does not specify the power of the federal government. It is up to the president, the Congress, and the people to decide."* One wonders how long America can keep winning with results like this.

an idea is if it's communicated in an incomprehensible way. Even worse are vagaries—communicating your ideas in platitudes will always, always hurt you. The act of enumerating lets your audience know exactly what you have in mind. It allows them to section off each individual idea, contemplate it on its own, and then put it away as they consider the next idea. It also creates a sense of accountability by making it easier for them to track your accomplishments—and, frankly, your failures. Just as enumeration holds an audience's attention while you speak, when you enumerate your plans or say, "I'm going to achieve one, two, and three by the end of my first term in office or after five years as CEO," you invite your audience to hold you accountable—and you keep their attention—over *time*. It signals your seriousness about the issue and your commitment to what you say.

Treat your business plan or corporate mission *exactly* like the Constitution:

- Put your accountability rules down on paper and then keep them inviolate. Refer to them often, and don't bend or break them just because things get tough.
- Limit your activity to *only* those things authorized in the plan so that you don't find yourself, years later, lost and adrift doing something you don't do well and contrary to your stated mission. The most successful people are inevitably the most disciplined.
- Establish a high threshold for *changing* those enumerated priorities. Listen to your audience. Put the idea through a system of checks and balances to make sure it's what they really want. Flexibility is important, but consistency is essential.

From the political perspective, say what you will about Barack Obama and his Chicago campaign team; they knew how to stay on message. In all of my years in business and politics, I don't think I've ever seen a person or organization as disciplined as Obama's 2008 presidential campaign team. The constant drumbeat of "hope" and "change" was so deeply beat into the American psyche that it crept into nonpolitical conversations and remained part of the American lexicon long after the election was won. No matter what happened during the campaign, nothing could push the Obama team off their message. Granted, they were faced with a mainstream media apparatus that was more cheerleader than fact-checker but regardless, they had discipline.

Similarly, companies that stay on message have more staying power in the public memory than those who constantly change it up. Ask people what the slogan for Fox News is and they'll tell you "Fair and Balanced," even if they don't think it is either. Similarly, Visa has always been "It's everywhere you want to be." By emphasizing convenience in the form of ubiquity, you, as the consumer, feel comforted and secure. Their slogan promotes the peace of mind of knowing that wherever you go, Visa will go there with you—and they'll always have your back. And, of course, Nike continues to implore us to "Just Do It." Preaching proactive behavior has helped Nike become not only a household name, but *the* household name among all sportswear brands. It will always and forever be associated with the cutting edge of athletics, fitness, and competition, thanks to its consistency and never straying too far from its marketing roots.

There's a reason why every two years, you will get sick and tired of the same ad from the same politician cluttering your TV viewing experience between Labor Day and Election Day. The reason is, it works. They are branding your brain. Just like hot metal on bovine flesh, the repetition isn't pleasant, but it leaves an indelible mark. Or at least, the mark will last to Election Day, which is all they really want.

Stop complaining about those ads and start applying the lesson to your own enterprise. The simple truth is, but for a handful of immensely successful brands, *just about everyone* needs to do more to consistently hammer home their core brand promise.

LUNTZ LANGUAGE: PHRASES THAT HELP PRIORITIZE

This is one area where you should spend more time doing it than talking about it. Some of the language below communicates your ability to prioritize. Other phrases emphasize how to prioritize. And still others demonstrate that you have the right priorities. But they all have one thing in common: they are words that work.

PHRASES THAT PRIORITIZE

1. First principles
2. First things first
3. Prevention/protection
4. Getting our house in order
5. If you remember one thing
6. A straightforward approach
7. Optimize (efficient and effective)
8. Scalable
9. The bottom line

"First principles" is an uncommon but powerful way of explaining what really matters from a philosophical perspective. About 90 percent of this book is about getting you to focus on your audience. This is the exception. First principles explain the *who* and the *why* from your perspective—and it generates appreciation, builds credibility, and establishes common ground with your audience for your efforts. Always close your public presentations with a focus on the benefits to your audience, but open with a credibility-building story about yourself.

"First things first" is simply articulating the order in which something must be done and your acknowledgment that you recognize what matters most.

"Prevention/protection" neatly links the deeply felt anxiety about day-to-day life with the core benefits of a product or service. No longer are we seeking all the advantages that life offers. Frankly, the lighthearted exaltation to *"keep your feet on the ground and keep reaching for the stars"* of American Top 40 DJ Casey Kasem no longer appeals to a nation that is more likely to respond to the ominous warnings of *"be afraid; be very afraid."* Let me be clear: I am not advocating prioritizing the negative. But it is a fact that Americans today are looking just as much for things that will prevent harm and protect them from it as they are looking to seize opportunities for something better.

"Getting our house in order" could indicate simplifying, streamlining, right-sizing, or reorganizing, but it clearly indicates in a positive way the

desire to fix something that has gone wrong. Consequently, it should be used in situations where your audience is aware of an existing problem, and your credibility depends on acknowledging it. Americans today sense that the major institutions they used to depend on are untrustworthy—and this phrase speaks to their underlying desire to have things set right. Audiences will assume that if you fix the big things, the little things will fix themselves.

"If you remember one thing" is about getting the listener or reader to pay particular attention to that which matters most to you. I'm not a proponent of "burying the lead"—saving the most important point for the middle or end of a speech or document. I have found this phrase particularly effective when preparing comprehensive reports or presentations to a CEO. For me to convince them that what I'm offering is worthy of their precious time, I have to grab them at the start with the one lesson or recommendation that matters most, and then conclude my opening with **"the bottom line is this . . . ,"** which addresses the likely result or impact. If it resonates, they'll stick around to hear more.

"A straightforward approach" prioritizes the style of communication as well as the language. When asked how they want to receive information about things that matter to them, Americans only give *"reliability"* higher priority. President Obama prefers the *"let me be clear"* formulation, though he says it so often that it has lost its appeal. In fact, when Americans hear that phrase, they now assume he will be anything but clear. Lesson to readers: even the best words and phrases can be worn out if used improperly or too much.

"Optimize" was once *"maximize,"* but in today's digital world, a new way is needed to express how people can get the most out of something. "Maximize" means more, but "optimize" means better. *"Optimize"* is particularly powerful in a business-to-business relationship. For consumers, however, the more personal *"more efficient and effective"* is preferable.

"Scalable" is what every successful entrepreneur thinks about every business opportunity every day. When something is *"scalable,"* it means that hundreds can become thousands, tens of thousands, and perhaps millions. *"Business without limits"* is another way to look at scalability. Traditional bricks and mortar businesses are often the least scalable because

they are limited by the size of their showrooms; they simply cannot grow beyond their physical limits. Conversely, Internet-based businesses like Amazon and eBay have no limits other than their ability to reach, communicate, and deliver product to potential customers. What happens when you use Google and Facebook has nothing to do with their office space, location, or even time of day, and everything to do with their limitless content and connection capacity. That's scalability.

One final point: The essence of prioritization is that you can't do everything or say everything or be everything to everyone, so please don't try. It's not just a language lesson—it's a life lesson that winners have learned again and again.

6

PERFECTION

Why great is not good enough

We are what we repeatedly do. Excellence, then, is not an act, but a habit.

—**ARISTOTLE**

Have no fear of perfection—you'll never reach it.

—**SALVADOR DALÍ**

Perfection is not attainable,
but if we chase perfection, we can catch excellence.

—**VINCE LOMBARDI**

If you've ever had the fortune, or misfortune, of watching famed British chef Gordon Ramsay do what he loves, you've seen the paragon of perfectionism run amok.* Known for his immeasurably short temper, crudely colorful language, and globally unrivaled cooking acumen, Ramsay is a force of nature. He currently owns twenty-two restaurants, from New York to Dubai to Tokyo. With more Michelin stars to his name than most chefs could even dream of, it's hard to say Gordon Ramsay has been anything short of wildly successful. He's become a household name, and not just among well-read and well-fed foodies.

---

* For those of you who have had any experience with English food, he singlehandedly disproves that the term *British chef* is an oxymoron.

In addition to building a worldwide restaurant empire, Ramsay has become a mainstay on both British and American television over the past decade. In the United States, the Fox network has brought three of these shows—*Hell's Kitchen, Cookalong Live,* and *Kitchen Nightmares*—to an American audience eager to sop up Ramsay's bombastic style while watching him wrap a shell of profanity around any poor soul who sets him off. Now one of the most familiar faces on TV, he's also written nearly twenty books, ranging from seafood soliloquies to dessert diatribes. In spite of his faults, flare-ups, and fighting words, Gordon Ramsay is one of the most powerful names in the culinary world today for a reason: when the plate arrives, it delivers culinary perfection.

You don't attain Ramsay's status, recognition, and level of success by merely putting on a good show. Yes, the theatrics surely help with the TV ratings. But he got the chance to broadcast to the world because he'd made a name for himself as one of the world's most demanding chefs. His showmanship tops it all off, but without meticulous attention to delivering perfect plates—every time, year in and year out—you would never have known Gordon Ramsay from Gordon down the street.

For Gordon Ramsay, every day is a new day—a new challenge to be the best, to outcook, outserve, and outshine everyone else in the industry. His insatiable thirst for absolute standards has led him to make not only some of the best food in the world, but also to develop one of the most talented and attentive staffs in the world. His relentless pursuit of perfection is what makes him great. It's what makes him a winner.

So what can a foulmouthed TV chef teach us about winning? Quite a bit, actually. It turns out Gordon Ramsay isn't alone in his crusade for uncompromising excellence. The more time I've spent with CEOs, business magnates, powerful politicians, sports legends, and Hollywood's elite, the more I've realized yet another trait they all have in common: there's no such thing as good enough. Ever. Steve Wynn is the best hotel designer on the planet. He created the Mirage, Bellagio, Wynn, and Encore—each new structure even more spectacular than the last. You'd think he'd be satisfied, even proud of his accomplishments. Think again:

My thing, that aspect of my life that describes my passion and gives me the most pleasure, is in dreaming up this stuff. I guess that's because I've always thought of myself as a student of all this. So when the places are done, whether it's Mirage or Bellagio, Treasure Island or Golden Nugget, unfortunately, I would see the mistakes we had made, or the opportunities that we hadn't really taken advantage of properly. And I'd say, "Boy, oh, boy, I wish I could do that over again. I wish I had one more chance." Because I'm always thinking that if I could do one more hotel, maybe, just maybe the next time I could get it right.

Many assume, incorrectly, that perfectionism is simply never being satisfied with what you're doing. But there's more to the story. Rarely will you find a perfectionist—an eccentric artist, a diligent writer, a world-renowned musician, a savvy businesswoman, an energized campaign volunteer—who goes around saying, "Yeah, that's good enough." For these people, the words *good* and *enough* never appear in the same sentence.

Anyone can criticize something, or say that others' work isn't good enough, or go around nitpicking the work that everyone else does. And from time to time, these criticisms can be completely warranted and worth a second look. But what makes perfectionists different—and allows them to be winners—is that they take criticism and action a step further. They make excellence the standard by which they judge their work, the people around them, and even themselves. They move us closer to the world as it *could* be, not just as it is.

For my first book, *Words That Work,* General Colin Powell granted me two interviews—and both times he stressed the essential nature of communication perfection. In fact, Powell's words on the matter apply to almost every area of human endeavor. "If you are going to achieve excellence in big things, you develop the habit in little matters. Excellence is not an exception, it is a prevailing attitude." True, excellence is not perfection, but it's what motivates you to come as near to perfection as human endeavor allows. It's not so much *being* perfect that makes one a winner; it's the *driving need* to be perfect that sets winners ahead of the rest.

We all know the stories about the megastars and celebrity CEOs who keep ungodly hours, demand that their staff do the same, and refuse to let people go home until everything is done just right. In politics, the hardest-working person I ever saw firsthand is Newt Gingrich. When Gingrich was elected the first Republican Speaker of the House after forty years of Democratic control, he forced not just his staff, but the entire House Republican congressional staff—thousands of people— to work nights, weekends, whatever it took to satisfy the commitments made in the Contract with America. Many were working eighty-hour weeks or more for three months straight to get the job done. And sure enough, against all odds, he got it done.

From a scientific perspective, the need to be perfect could actually be a medical condition—though there is sure to be disagreement about whether the medical community should diagnose compulsive over-achievers as having medical conditions. What we do know is that per-fectionists "not only harbor unrealistically high standards, but also judge themselves or others as not living up to their elevated expecta-tions," says psychology professor Gordon Flett from York University in Toronto, Canada. "Perfectionism is the need to be, or to appear to be, perfect. Perfectionists are persistent, detailed and organized high achievers," he explains. "Perfectionists vary in their behaviors: some strive to conceal their imperfections; others attempt to project an image of perfection. But all perfectionists have in common extremely high standards for themselves or for others."[29]

Speaking as a perfectionist myself, I can say this is undeniably true, and nowhere is this more evident than in my live focus-group modera-tion for the Fox News Network. I have been known to lash out at a focus group participant who failed to speak when spoken to. In fact, my Fox camera crew has hours of tape of me berating my participants for not talking, or for talking too much, for being too agreeable or for arguing too much, for being unaware of what I assume everyone knows, or for speaking like an expert about an issue that is irrelevant to the audi-ence. In my effort to create informative, compelling, must-see TV, I have a tendency to blow up at my participants—though up until now, only off-camera. When the red light goes on and my producer says "Go," I am the epitome of frumpy professionalism. But moments before and moments after, even my staff suggests I appear certifiably insane. I can't help it. I want everything to go just right.

But my worst demonstrations of perfectionism, the incidents that convince my editor I am not emotionally or professionally fit to write books, always come at the very end of the process—those final hours when I am frantically perfecting individual words, adding obscure references, and otherwise trying to polish a text that is already overedited and overdue. For *What Americans Really Want . . . Really,* I made so many last-minute edits that I was still cutting and stapling words, sentences, and entire paragraphs onto the final manuscript as the truck was leaving the FedEx office in Santa Monica, California. I offered the driver $100 to wait ten minutes (I figured $10 a minute was a good incentive), but he turned me down. I then had to race to LAX airport and beg with a $20 bill in my hands to get them to unlock the door and accept my package—and yet I still hadn't made all the changes I wanted. And so I bought a $2,100 one-way first-class ticket on the Los Angeles to New York City red-eye so that I could make my final text adjustments and still get the manuscript to the publisher on time. What appeared to my editor as procrastination and a blatant disregard for deadlines was, in my mind, a commitment to doing things right. I understand that I will probably never convince her. Perfectionism has its price.

WHY "GOOD ENOUGH" . . . NEVER IS

Procter & Gamble ranks sixth in *Fortune* magazine's ranking of the world's most admired companies and has appeared in the top ten for most of the past ten years. It ranks first in its category, ninth in "quality," and regularly appears on all the corporation reputation lists. Why do people regard a company that sells soap, shampoo, toothpaste, and twenty-three brands of various consumer items so highly on a global scale? Perhaps it's because P&G exemplifies most of the *P*'s of success on which this book is based. For them, "the power of purpose" is their perfection, which, by their definition, *"promotes a simple idea to improve the lives of the world's consumers every day."*

For them, the pursuit of perfection is a daily passion that knows no local holidays or international borders.

Regardless of what "business" you're in, whether it's corporate takeovers or taking back the White House, any competitive environment fosters perfectionism. It's no surprise that perfectionism has found a home in America. Since the nation's founding, both our economic and political systems have been based, to a large extent, on the idea that "the best man wins." It was this sense of unbridled competition that helped drive and shape the American ethos through the nineteenth and twentieth centuries. The free-market economy, coupled with strong assurances of individual liberty, helped create the wealthiest and most prosperous collection of people in human history by promoting relentless competition among a new American workforce and the products and services it creates.

The next time you get in your car, take a look around. What do you see? Depending on the model and how new it is, you probably have a CD player. You may even have a dock to connect your MP3 player. If you drive American, the quality of the materials both inside and outside are noticeably better than any American car you owned in the 1980s, 1990s, or even the early 2000s. Built-in DVD players and navigation systems are becoming the expectation, rather than the exception. Ford now offers vehicles with a technology Microsoft developed called SYNC, which allows you to operate several of your car's functions—radio, GPS, phone—simply by speaking into the air. This is available not just to the rich and famous, but in cars focused on the middle class like, well, the Ford Focus.

Long the innovator in automotive technology, GM has OnStar, an interactive wireless technology that is responsible for saving thousands of lives since its introduction in model year 2004. Under the hood, miles-per-gallon has improved dramatically since the gas-guzzling days of mid-twentieth-century models. From 1980 to 2009, the average fuel efficiency of domestic passenger vehicles in the United States increased from 22.6 to 32.6 miles per gallon, five miles per gallon higher than the government's CAFE (Corporate Average Fuel Economy) standard.[30] In 1997, Toyota began selling its Prius—a hybrid-engine vehicle that automatically switches between gasoline and electricity it generates and stores in a battery—to consumers in Japan. The car is so "smart" that it knows when to use the right form of energy, giving it gas mileage of around fifty miles per gallon, nearly double the current CAFE standard. Since the Prius debuted, Toyota has sold 1.6 million of the gas-sippers globally.[31]

But a competitive auto industry demanded more from Toyota and its rival car makers. In early 2010 Nissan introduced the Leaf—the first fully electric vehicle that doesn't use a drop of gasoline. It doesn't even have tailpipes. You charge the vehicle overnight at home and at soon-to-be-built charging stations when you take longer trips. According to Nissan, the Leaf will travel about one hundred miles on a single charge. That's a pretty big step since the days of the Model T.

What has caused the personal automobile to change so quickly in such a short amount of time? The answer: competition. These are all innovations geared toward creating the perfect car. Eliminating gasoline, for so many reasons, is an essential step toward perfection. And so everyone is on the case, because companies like Toyota, Honda, and Ford have to compete for consumer dollars to keep their doors open. They spend billions every year finding ways to make their products more innovative, efficient, and appealing to drivers around the world. True competition forces them to be perfectionists. The suits at Honda know if they release a subpar product, more people will go out and buy Toyotas or Hyundais. This continuous competitive pressure forces companies to go the extra mile or pay the price—and sometimes that price is bankruptcy.

More than any other force, the reality, fear, and threat of competition has led the great entrepreneurs, innovators, athletes, and leaders of the world to strive for perfection in everything they do. Winners, by their nature, are highly aware of their surroundings. They're always focused on what their peers are doing, and how they're doing it, in an attempt to stay one step ahead. Take Larry Bird—the "Hick from French Lick"—as an example. His nickname might tell you more than you think. Bird was exceptionally talented, to be sure—though he did not have all the physical gifts of his contemporaries. But he managed to outwork every one of them (except Michael Jordan, the world's most competitive person—ever). Universally considered one of the best forwards in the history of the National Basketball Association, Bird is legendary for his fierce competitiveness on the court. But he is also legendary for his work ethic. There's no doubt his upbringing in a small, blue-collar town in Indiana contributed to his drive to succeed and his recognition of the need to work harder than the next guy. However, Bird also faced incredible competition that pushed him—even before his NBA career started.

Much has been documented about Bird's rivalry with Earvin "Magic" Johnson, with whom Bird competed in the 1979 NCAA National Championship game. Bird, with his small-town roots and his Indiana State Sycamore teammates, competed with Johnson's Michigan State Spartans, who hailed from one of the most powerful conferences in college basketball, the Big Ten. Johnson drove Bird to try harder, push further, and achieve more. Great competitors like Bird have to pit themselves against someone or something. Bird, upon arriving in the NBA, arguably used the specter of Magic Johnson to get his Boston Celtics to the next level. After all, you don't shoot five hundred free throws every day for your health, and you don't push yourself to drain thirty-foot jumpers for hours on end unless there's a competitive spark driving you to win.

Larry Bird agreed to let me interview him for this book, which was a big honor. I have always believed the greatest sports legends have a lot to teach those in business and politics about the art and science of winning. Historically reticent to talk much about his career, Bird really opened up about what drove him to work so inhumanly hard, which he attributed almost exclusively to his success. *"I didn't care about the MVP, but I wanted to be the best in the world—the best in the world,"* he said in such a matter-of-fact way:

How many people do you know who have been considered the best in the world at what they do? That's what I wanted. It mattered the whole world to me. That is why I played. I played because I loved it. The things I put myself through were because I wanted to achieve the highest goal possible and to be considered by my peers as the best in the world at what I did. I would get up in the morning at six o'clock knowing that I had to go out and run five miles as hard as I could. I didn't want to do that, but I had to do it to achieve the goals that I wanted to achieve. I wanted Magic Johnson to say, "Hey, you are the best, you are the MVP this year, you are the MVP of our league in my mind." If you are the best in our league, you are the best in the world.

I have achieved one of the greatest achievements—at least in my mind, it may not be in anyone else's—but in my field I have achieved the one goal that I was after. And once you get that, you want to do it every year. A lot of people were just happy with doing it one time. I never was. Because I always felt that if you did it once you have got to do it again and, if you do it again, you have to do it yet again.

Perfection pushes you to work a sixteen-hour day so you can read more, study more, learn more, produce more, create more, and sell more. It makes success something you *want* to achieve, not just something you feel you *must* achieve. But without passion—the burning desire for perfection—without heart, you just can't go all the way. Perfection demands so much of us as individuals that we need something stronger inside us to keep us going. Returning to my conversation with Larry Bird, he said something that made this point come to life:

A lot of success is heart, but how much heart do they have? Do they really have the drive to do it?

The other thing is whether they have a lot of pride. You take a player with a lot of pride and a big heart but with less skill, and I will take him any day, because I know he will get better. I want a guy that will push himself to the limits—a guy that wants to get better every day, not just every year. I want a guy that will give the extra effort to get the loose ball, not someone who thinks, "I have got my rebounds tonight and that's enough, I don't need to get any more." I heard a player one time say, "If I average twenty-five and fifteen, fans will expect it every night." And he could do it. But he said, "I will get my twenty and eight and that's enough." I have seen him do it. I have seen guys do it. It's wrong. It's just wrong.

Hockey's Mike Richter would agree. In fact, Richter believes passion can be just as important as talent:

I've never met anyone who is a winner that doesn't have passion. It's a skill in itself to be able to manufacture passion when you need it most. Winners have passion on demand. I know coaches that look down the bench and take the fourth-line player when it really counts and everything's on the line because they have passion. They're so disciplined mentally that they persevere.

You need passion to exceed excellence and approach perfection because perfection always demands so much more than the minimum. That's why passion, perseverance, and perfection are inextricably bound together.

The reason I was able to work eighteen-hour days, flying back and forth across the globe as if a Boeing 767 were a shuttle bus, and spent months helping craft the Contract with America in 1994 with almost no financial reward was that I was deeply passionate about it. I wanted it to be perfect, and there was nothing that was going to keep me from making that happen. I didn't care how many focus groups I had to conduct, how many surveys I had to analyze, how many fights I had to have with people who didn't believe in it or understand it, how much sleep I

LUNTZ LESSONS

A TALE OF TWO COMPANIES

Meet GM, circa 2008. After decades of pursuing a "good enough is good enough" standard, the company had decayed. They made too many kinds of cars . . . and made none of them well. They wrongly thought the way to compete with Ford and foreign companies was, well, not to compete at all, offering lower-quality cars for the "masses." Well, the masses had other, better choices—and they made them. So when the hurricane of the Great Recession hit, a weak-rooted GM was an easy victim.

Meet the GM of today. The company has replanted and trimmed all the dead branches. Its new mission is excellence—of aspiring for perfection. It's doing less, but doing everything better. And as a result, they've already paid off their government loans.

Here's the point: Perfection must always be your standard. Even if you're appealing to a "downmarket" audience (say, people buying a $20,000 car instead of a $40,000 one), you still have to make it the *best* car for $20,000 you can. If you don't, someone else will. Walmart is selling to people on a budget, so they have to squeeze their *own* budget better than any competitor. They often do, so they win—except when Costco undercuts them.

No matter what your product is, or who you sell it to, if you don't make perfection your standard, you're going to get beat by someone who does.

lost or how many pounds I put on; I wanted to succeed. I wanted the contract to succeed. In fact, it had to succeed. That meant it had to be so appealing and so well crafted that no attack from the Democrats could tear it down.

Perhaps more important, true passion never lets you stop at good enough. When you care about something so much that you're willing to give up most of your personal life to pursue it, why would you give it only half or even 80 percent of your effort? In all my years as a political and business consultant, I've yet to meet a true winner who didn't commit themselves "110 percent" to everything they did. Whether it is FedEx's Fred Smith and his Purple Promise "to make every customer experience outstanding," or former AT&T and GM chairman Ed Whitacre's commitment "to design, build and sell *the world's best* vehicles," the most successful corporate leaders refuse to settle for anything less than perfection.

To become great, you have to strive for perfection in every aspect of your business and every element of your calling. If you're not passionate about what you do, perfection will always be just out of reach.

THE PURSUIT OF PERFECTION

When you're watching TV and a Lexus ad comes on, you probably pay attention. There are few companies today that do such a compelling job of making you feel like they say what they mean and mean what they say. Lexus's famous tagline, "the relentless pursuit of perfection," certainly isn't new. And you'd think that over time it would have lost its punch. But when I've asked consumers about the Lexus motto, I hear roughly the same thing no matter where I am in the country: it works. When I dig deeper to see what about those five little words makes people respect and admire Lexus, I usually hear things like "You can tell they take quality seriously" and "Lexus is about affordable luxury." Lexus has actually done the impossible—they've developed a tagline that both embodies their brand and tells the brand story in a way that's credible to most consumers, even the ones who can't actually afford to buy a Lexus.

The truth is, you can get a Lexus or a BMW or a Mercedes-Benz for about the same price. But while the BMW "ultimate driving machine" marketing folks are busy talking about "joy" and "pleasure," and the Mercedes ads talk about . . . well . . . nothing consistently, Lexus reminds you of their "pursuit of perfection" every single chance they get. Why? It works because of one word: *pursuit*. Lexus has never said, "We are perfect." In essence, perfection *is* the pursuit of itself.

As of April 2010, Lexus, which is part of Toyota, had been "the top seller of luxury vehicles in the U.S. on an annual basis for 10 years in a row."[32] You read that right. More than BMW, Mercedes, Cadillac, Lincoln, Audi, or Land Rover. That's huge—and that's fast. Look at it this way: When Lexus was founded, our president was George H. W. Bush. When BMW was founded, our president was Woodrow Wilson. The man in office when the world saw the first Mercedes? Grover Cleveland. So if you do the math, from its U.S. premiere in 1989 until the time it became the number-one-selling luxury car in America was eleven years. Some more context: In the time it took President George H. W. Bush to break his pledge of "no new taxes" and President Bill Clinton to get himself impeached, Toyota's luxury division outsold two German brands assumed to be forever untouchable in the high-end market.

Detroit, are you paying attention?

The power of a phrase like "the relentless pursuit of perfection" is its ability to set the standard for everyone else. And perfection is a standard that no one can truly reach. So by owning that mantra, and producing products that give it credibility, Lexus has forced the automotive industry's old guard to play by its rules instead of the other way around. But again, let me reiterate: you can't say you're perfect; you have to prove it. If you want to find the quickest way to lose a sale, just try telling consumers you, or your product, is perfect. I don't care how strongly you believe it; they won't. Your product's alleged superiority can't rely on your words alone. It has to be demonstrated. Hearing an ad in 2011 that says a product is "perfect" is just as jarring as hearing an ad today that originated in the 1950s saying, "Four out of five doctors smoke Camel cigarettes." "Nobody's perfect" is a maxim for a reason. You can talk about the journey, the effort, and even the rewards of perfection, but you must never, ever, ever claim you've actually achieved it. To do so would be settling for a result, thereby ending the "pursuit."

A conversation with Mickey Drexler, CEO of J.Crew, is never easy, but it's always worth the challenge. I love him because he is a walking, talking billboard for passion—just try to get him to sit in one place and talk about one topic for more than a few minutes. It's simply impossible. In this case, we ended up discussing Levi's, which has gone from American icon to a case study on how not to run a company. *"Levi's is the worst managed company in the world,"* he began. But rather than trashing Levi's, he used their situation to illustrate a more important point—the vital importance of focusing on the future:

> *Levi's went from $8 billion to $4 billion—they should be a $200 billion company. It's like a nightmare. Levi's just doesn't see the future. If you want to do anything in the world today, you must go to where the world is going. They don't. It's as simple as that. Every day that we come to work, it is my job here to keep raising the bar. What is happening today is not what's going to happen tomorrow. I love J.Crew because every day it's changing. As you can probably tell, I get bored very quickly. I love leaders who get mad, who show their anger, who care so much, because then it drives the troops to care that much.*

Levi's lost their way because they surrendered their pursuit of perfection. They stopped caring as much about what they made as they did in the heady days of Levi Strauss supremacy. They stopped paying attention to the future, and as a result it completely passed them by.

Apple's iPod is the "perfect" MP3 player because it addresses exactly what people want—ease of use and simplicity—not because the thing itself is perfect. My own iPod freezes on occasion, requiring me to Google "how to reboot an iPod" because I keep forgetting the rather simple process. Apple doesn't claim iPods or iPhones or iPads are perfect, but they do sell the value they provide—their being user-friendly—as aggressively as they sell any physical product they make. From a communication perspective, the best strategy is to acknowledge nothing is perfect, because that buys you instant credibility, even if it's painfully obvious.* Perfection is never truly attainable, but it should

---

* You'd be surprised how often "painfully obvious" actually isn't.

be our relentless aspiration. To inspire your audience, you must let them know that you will never stop trying to get as close as you possibly can.

And if you get it wrong, admit it. Steve Jobs learned this the hard way. Perfection and expectation are twin blades of the same razor. When you've built a mega-career on creating some of the most astonishing, cutting-edge electronic devices in the world, criticism piles on quickly when reality fails to meet expectations. That's exactly what happened when Steve Jobs launched the iPhone 4 in the summer of 2010. Some people—even if just a small fraction of total users—began reporting dropped calls when they held their brand new iPhones a certain way. Unfortunately for the hard-working folks at Apple, most of the news stories about the iPhone 4 focused on the device's reception problems rather than its incredible innovations.

The blogosphere was abuzz. YouTube was inundated with handmade videos from irate customers. The new iPhone, Jobs's latest attempt to give the world a game-changer, didn't work. Well, not exactly, but that's the story bloggers wanted to write, so they did. One writer, blogging for breakingglobalnews.com, had this to say: "Widely covered across the net, the reception of the iPhone 4 seems to drop out when holding the phone with the left hand. No problem, says Steve Jobs— 'Stop holding it like that.' Thanks, dude."[33] According to Britain's *Daily Mail* newspaper, Jobs's response was perhaps a bit more nuanced: "Jobs issued his bizarre advice as he responded to an email from a user on the Ars Technica technology news site who had complained about the sudden loss of signal. In an astonishingly blunt response, Mr. Jobs replied: 'Just avoid holding it in that way. All phones have sensitive areas.' "[34]

After three weeks of media attention, negative stories, and the birth of "Antennagate," Jobs finally held a press conference on July 16 to address the issue. But Apple admirers and apostates alike were sorely disappointed if they were expecting an apology from the company's iconic and occasionally irascible CEO. Jobs began the press conference by playing the "iPhone Antenna Song," a YouTube hit, with a grungy Apple apologist singing, "The media loves a failure in a string of successes." It only went downhill from there. Jobs took the stage to serve up a mountain of facts, figures, and statistics to assert that the reception problems weren't at all unique to the new iPhone 4. Jobs boasted that Apple had sold more than 3 million iPhones in its first three weeks, yet only 0.55 percent of purchasers had contacted the company to complain about reception issues. He then touted that very few people are returning the phone, and that the return rate on the iPhone 4 to AT&T was only 1.7 percent, compared to 6 percent for the iPhone 3GS. Using a BlackBerry Bold, a Samsung Omnia II, and an HTC Droid Eris, he showed that other phones experience the same issues people were raising with the new iPhone. "Most smartphones behave exactly the same way," he said. "This is life in the smartphone world—phones aren't perfect . . . It is a challenge for the phone industry, and we are all doing the best that we can."[35]

I've written so much in this book about Steve Jobs because I think he is the greatest entrepreneur of my generation. One hundred years from now, the name Steve Jobs will be as significant and as appreciated as Alexander Graham Bell. But demigod or not, the way Apple's communication team and Jobs himself handled the iPhone 4's antenna problems is, as President Obama would say, "a teachable moment."

One of the first things I tell corporate communicators when something goes wrong is to admit that something has gone wrong. Point blank. This is especially true when the facts are incontrovertible and well known. In Apple's case, once there were YouTube videos going viral showing exactly where and how the phone lost reception when held a certain way, there was really no other appropriate course of action. Think Bill Clinton claiming innocence after the blue dress. You have to own the problem if you're going to fix the problem. You cannot remedy something that you deny exists in the first place.

So rather than taking twenty frustrating, passive-aggressive steps to get from A to B (i.e., all smartphones have these problems, our reception indicator formula was faulty, we put an indicator where you were supposed to hold it, the media are out to get us, etc.), he could have taken one: "We messed up." In three single-syllable words, Jobs could have stopped the issue dead in its tracks. The problem with all of the excuses and obfuscation is that Apple is Apple. The "it's the physics" argument doesn't hold water when you're one of the most profitable and successful technology companies of the twenty-first century. Had Jobs been more humble, he could have avoided technology writers penning diatribes.

Yes, Jobs was probably right. There wasn't really a "*problem.*" But it looked as if there was a problem, and the media were reporting there was a problem, so there *was* a problem. His tone was defensive and irritable, when it should have been understanding and empathetic. By simply acknowledging the problem as soon as it started happening (not three weeks later), laying out a very clear plan for how the company was going to fix it, and what customers could do in the meantime, Jobs could have avoided a large and embarrassing PR headache for a company so keen on its own awesomeness, and the iPhone 4 flap would have been much less dramatic than it was.

People aren't surprised when Microsoft comes out with some new program that (initially) disappoints. You expect Windows to crash, have bugs, and get viruses. It's just the way the world is: the sun will rise tomorrow, and your PC will freeze up at the most inopportune moment possible—such as when writing this book. Sure, they eventually get it right—emphasis on the word *eventually*. But when it comes to Apple, our expectations are much higher, precisely because Apple has spent so much time and money making sure their products are unrivaled in design, innovation, functionality, and quality. When was the last time you encountered the blue screen of death on your MacBook? Exactly.

When you reach a level of success where the purchasing public expects perfection, act accordingly. At the dizzying heights of the Steve Jobs/Apple stratosphere, you have to accept responsibility for damn near everything that goes wrong, even if you know you're right. That often means learning new, hard-to-pronounce phrases in exotic foreign languages, such as "*I was wrong,*" "*I accept full responsibility for what has happened here,*" and "*I'm sorry.*" It also means never sounding defensive, upset, or annoyed at consumers for having the audacity to complain about something that doesn't quite satisfy their expectations. The consumer is always right—even when they aren't. Winners admit defeat before defeat overtakes them. Admit failure. Take responsibility. No excuses.

Below are several characteristics of a CEO or business leader. Please choose the one that you most respect in a CEO or corporate leader.*

	Total
Never makes excuses. Takes responsibility for failures and gives credit to others for successes	57%
The ability to see the challenge, and the solution, from every angle	36%
The willingness to fail and the fortitude to get back up and try again. Always finds a way to get things done.	28%
The ability to connect with others and create an enduring team chemistry	27%
The ability to move forward when everyone around you is retrenching or slipping backward	24%
The ability to see what doesn't yet exist and bring it to life	21%
The ability to grasp the human dimension of every situation	21%
The ability to distinguish the essential from the important	20%
The ability and the drive to do more and do it better	20%
The ability to communicate their vision passionately and persuasively	17%
The ability to know what questions to ask and when to ask them	15%
A curiosity about the future and the unknown	5%
A love of life itself	5%
A passion for life's adventures	5%

*   Source: The Word Doctors, 2010

In *Words That Work*, I wrote briefly about Steve Wynn, saying that, at the time, fully 30 percent of Americans recognized his name and knew it stood for certified, guaranteed quality. I can guarantee you today that number would be higher. The reason? Here's a better explanation than I could write, from an article in *BusinessWeek* a full two weeks *before* Wynn Las Vegas ever even opened its doors (and well before the ground had been broken for Encore):

Wynn's reputation is that of a man obsessed with details. Daniel R. Lee, who served as chief financial officer at Wynn's Mirage Resorts and who [ran] Pinnacle Entertainment Inc., remembers Wynn criticizing what Lee thought had been a well-executed annual report. "He told me there was a split infinitive on page 23," recalls Lee, who immediately corrected the *error at a cost of $9,000. After Lee told his boss, Wynn replied: "When you're close to perfect, why wouldn't you try for perfect?"*[36]

The man's reputation for perfection precedes him. The name Wynn means quality, sophistication, and detail. It comes as close to perfection as a mortal can get in this world. So by affixing his name to the side of his flagship hotel, and making sure the Encore upholds the same standards as the original, Steve Wynn builds intangible value into his product with the use of four simple letters.

PERFECTION: LEADING BY EXAMPLE

Of all the mistakes I've watched CEOs and business leaders make over the years, failing to lead by example is often one of the most egregious and damaging. Unlike a financial misstatement or other acts of malfeasance from the top, saying one thing while doing another is one of the quickest ways to kill morale and vaporize any respect your employees have for you. After all, when employees know their manager, director, or even CEO demands nothing but the absolute best—always—over time that mindset seeps in. For the ones who care, as well as for the employees who are vested in the company and the cause, your commitment to perfection will eventually become their commitment to perfection. You must lead by example.

Whether you're the leader of a dozen people or 120,000 people worldwide, it is your job to set the strategic vision for your division, your campaign, or your constituents. The journey toward perfection forces you to create this vision, setting standards and expectations. It allows you to define what your organization stands for and what you expect everyone on the payroll to help you deliver. For Virgin Airlines, it means developing and maintaining a team of flight attendants who not only understand, but bring to life, the company's mission to offer the most unique, distinctive, and pampering service in the industry. Let's be honest, having an open bar on an airplane should be reason enough to follow Virgin's founder, Richard Branson, to the ends of the Earth.

There's another, more subtle, power of perfection that galvanizes employees around doing what's best for the company, even if it means so many late nights they forget what eight p.m. looks like (not that this is how you should want your employees to work or live). First let me explain how this method works. There's a commercial you may have seen in the past year or two from Liberty Mutual, the third largest property and casualty insurance company in America in 2009.[37] I'll keep the summary as brief as possible, but I want you to understand what's happening in the commercial to appreciate the message. This is true advertising perfection.

It starts with a man walking down a sidewalk and noticing a woman's child has dropped a teddy bear from her stroller.

The man bends down, picks up the bear, and puts it back in the stroller.

The mother, busy on her cell phone, thanks him and goes on her way.

In the next scene, the same mother is in a coffee shop when she notices a man's cup of coffee dangerously close to the edge of the table, so she scoots it over to keep him from accidentally knocking it off the table. The man smiles and is clearly appreciative.

Outside the coffee shop window, a man sees her move the cup—he witnesses her act of kindness. As he's later walking down the street in pouring rain, he helps a man who has slipped and fallen on the wet pavement.

Another onlooker sees this act of generosity, which later prompts him to hold the door for a lady sprinting toward the elevator in their office building.

In the next scene, a stranger who had been in the elevator taps on a car's rear window, letting the driver know he's about to hit a motorcycle.

A woman walking by with groceries sees this and is later shown in her office catching a coworker about to flip over backward in his chair while he talks on the phone.

Another of their coworkers witnesses this and is later inspired by the random act of kindness to push a man out of the way of a stack of boxes about to fall.

A passerby notices her act of bravery and is later moved to let a fellow driver pull out of a parking lot and into a road of barely moving traffic.

The final person to witness kindness in action finds himself jogging one day past another little girl who has dropped her teddy bear out of her stroller.

The jogger stops, picks up the bear, puts it back in the stroller, and goes on his way.

The girl's father turns out to be the man at the beginning of the commercial who picked up the teddy bear for the mother on the phone.

End.

So, besides the need for someone to start putting Velcro on children's teddy bears, what do you notice about this commercial? What's the recurring theme? Kindness is contagious. In every scene, someone's random act of kindness and responsibility inspires someone else to "pay it forward." It's a virtuous circle.

The same is true for perfection and how you embed it into your culture. The more your employees, partners, and associates see your own dedication to perfection come to life, the more willing they will be to embrace it. Like kindness, drive and passion for what you do are contagious.

When I sat down with Marc Cherry, the creator and executive producer of the hit TV show *Desperate Housewives*, I found him to be a passionate leader who practices exactly what he preaches. I wanted him to teach me when it's OK to compromise, when good enough . . . is good enough. *"You have to listen to the little voice in your gut that says, 'If you give on this one, you will live to regret it,'"* he told me.

You also have to listen to your gut when it goes "On this one, I think you can probably live with this compromise." But to me it's all about listening to that inner voice telling you. Because there are times where I have compromised when I knew I shouldn't. But I did it because I was tired, or I did it because of expediency's sake. And then I'll be in that editing room kicking myself, because I'll see the result of my compromise up on the screen, and I was right, and they were wrong, and yet, I have no one to blame but myself because I let it happen.

The more you're able to demonstrate your commitment to excellence and perfection the way Marc Cherry has done, the more you'll instill a sense of attainable perfection in the people who work for you. There simply isn't a winner, a champion, or a great success story that didn't put in the time, the effort, and the persistence in the pursuit of perfection.

PERFECT WORDS

Here, then, are the ten words and terms to communicate the pursuit of perfection:

PROVING PERFECTION

1. No excuses
2. Extraordinary/exceptional
3. Continuous improvement
4. No surprises
5. Hassle-free
6. No worries
7. Unparalleled flexibility
8. Real-time
9. Lasting solutions
10. Total satisfaction

I start with *"no excuses"* because it symbolizes the pursuit of perfection better than any other phrase. Of all the language I have tested to address the decline in trust and confidence in business, politics, the media, and the other institutions that run America, no two words better capture what Americans really want from their various leaders. "No excuses" does not guarantee perfection, or even success, but it does communicate good intentions and maximum effort. Of course, if you say "no excuses," you have to mean it.

"Extraordinary/exceptional" are the words that best explain products and services that go above and beyond the usual. Descriptions of the winners in this book, and the way they describe what they do, frequently include these words because they vividly demonstrate the difference between their efforts and a more ordinary, traditional approach.

"Continuous improvement" rates higher than *"best in class"* because it articulates effort and intention as well as result. Winners focus on the future, not the past or even the present. To them, having success this year is no indication that next year will be better or even as good. *"Best in class"* is static. Consumers don't want you to rest on your laurels—even if you're currently the best. They want to know that whatever they buy this year is better than last year's product, and they're prepared to buy again next year if the improvement is measurable.

"No surprises" is, once again, a more negative approach for a negative population, but it communicates exactly what Americans want in their products and services. It is similar to *"We stand behind our [fill in the product]"* in delivering a level of confidence that things will work exactly as promised. Candidly, almost none of the winners interviewed for this book used *"no surprises"* to describe what they do or how they do it, but because it is such a highly desired attribute among consumers, it deserves its place in this list.

"Hassle-free" has taken its place in the lexicon of corporate America over the past half decade as more and more companies realize that their consumers are prepared to pay a little bit more (as much as 15 percent) to avoid life's daily annoyances. *"Hassle-free"* is *"no assembly required"* and an instruction book that is a page or two long rather than book-length. It means you turn the thing on, whatever it is, and just go. In fact, a growing percentage of Americans now consider a *"hassle-free lifestyle"* to be one of their highest priorities.

"No worries" was originally Australian slang used to end a conversation, much the way Americans say *"Have a nice day."* But *"no worries"* has taken on an even greater meaning in recent years as a way to communicate the overall dependability of a product or service for the long haul. If *"hassle-free"* is about day-to-day concerns, *"no worries"* is about the bigger picture. *"No worries"* says the car will start regardless of the temperature, the TV will turn on regardless of its age, and the refrigerator won't break even if the kids slam the door or leave it open.

"Unparalleled flexibility" takes two essential attributes and combines them into one highly desirable characteristic. If *"customized"* is the way you buy a perfect product, *"unparalleled flexibility"* is the way you use it.

"Real-time" is the new way to describe what we used to call *"almost in-*

stantaneous," and it is how an increasing number of us live our lives and what we expect from what we use. The definition of perfection is *"what we want, when we want it,"* and *"real-time"* is the best description of when we want it. The Nielsen Company, which at its core is a polling and measurement company, has become the best practitioner of real-time research on

LUNTZ LESSONS

THE RULES FOR YOUR OWN RELENTLESS PURSUIT OF PERFECTION

1. **Perfection = Every experience, every time, is better than the last.**
   You don't need Gordon Ramsay's on-screen flair for the dramatic as part of your pursuit of perfection. But you do need his behind-the-scenes, in-the-kitchen dedication to products that always pursue perfection.

2. **Every winner pursues perfection *differently*; what matters more than the nature of the action is the depth of the drive.**
   Your passion might manifest itself in quiet intensity or bold activity. What matters more is that you understand how to channel it, and never stop doing so.

3. **Good enough . . . isn't.**
   It doesn't matter who you sell to or what you sell; if you want to win over your competitors, you must pursue perfection. Relentlessly. If you don't, they will.

4. **Perfection sets you apart.**
   Consumers know the pursuit of perfection when they see it. And even when they can't see it, they can *feel* it . . . in how the car door feels when it slams shut. Or the sense of peaceful bliss they get in that five-star hotel. Pay attention to all the details, and you will get the attention you deserve.

5. ***Lead* the way to perfection by example.**
   At a minimum, employees expect you to practice what you preach. If you're not in the trenches with them, they won't follow you into battle. But this isn't about just doing the minimum; perfection never is, and winners never do. This is about the *highest and best* reason to lead by example: you inspire others to be their greatest too.

the globe, developing the technology to provide instant knowledge (not just numbers) to thousands of clients, including most of the people interviewed for this book.

"Lasting solutions" is how winners define the result of their work. They don't want to make or do things that work for a while. They don't want Band-Aids to fix a broken system. They want to do things that last for the long haul. Success is about creating something that people want, that lasts. A winner not only creates that product, but perfects a system of production. That's why *"lasting solutions"* and *"scalable"* are so often heard in the same conversation.

"Total satisfaction" has replaced *"satisfaction guaranteed or your money back"* as the desired outcome among consumers. Why? If you need your money back, it's clear that something went wrong. Boasting about your quality repair service is telling them straight out that your product is going to fail. Conversely, *"total satisfaction"* means you won't have to worry about refunds or repairs because you will be completely happy throughout the life of the product—and that's exactly what winners aspire to provide.

7

PARTNERSHIP
Creating alignment in words and actions

If I have seen farther than others, it is because I was standing on the shoulders of giants.

—SIR ISAAC NEWTON

Coming together is a beginning; keeping together is progress; working together is success.

—HENRY FORD

Watch, listen, and learn. You can't know it all yourself. Anyone who thinks they do is destined for mediocrity.

—DONALD TRUMP

A long, long time ago—in the year 1624 to be exact—an English writer by the name of John Donne was recovering from a serious illness. Donne used his time recovering to contemplate the sickness from which he suffered. He put pen to paper, and twenty-three chapters later the world was given *Devotions upon Emergent Occasions*. Each chapter was broken up into three parts: a meditation, an expostulation, and a prayer.[38] Of these, his most famous work was Meditation 17. You may have read it in high school or college, and you've definitely heard parts of it quoted:

No man is an island, entire of itself; every man is a piece of the conti-
nent, a part of the main. If a clod be washed away by the sea, Europe is
the less, as well as if a promontory were, as well as if a manor of thy
friend's or of thine own were: any man's death diminishes me, because I
am involved in mankind, and therefore never send to know for whom the
bell tolls; it tolls for thee.[39]

It's amazing how often we can simply look back at the thinkers of the past to have a better idea for how to approach the future. The 2011, Twitter version would probably be something more along these lines:

@DonneFan92: Don't go it alone. U need people to get u there. We r all
in this 2gether. #belltolls.

(The only thing I will give Twitter credit for is forcing people to be concise—even at the expense of clarity. It may be tough fitting profound thoughts into 140 characters or less, but at least it puts a premium on efficiency.)

In his most recent book, *War,* famed journalist Sebastian Junger makes an updated version of Donne's argument through the lens of modern combat. "Combat is a series of quick decisions and rather precise actions . . . much more like football than, say, like a gang fight," he writes. "The unit that choreographs their actions best usually wins. . . . The choreography always requires that each man make decisions based not on what's best for him, but on what's best for the group. If everyone does that, most of the group survives. If no one does, most of the group dies. That, in essence, is combat."

What John Donne wrote almost four hundred years ago is just as relevant as what Junger writes today. "In this new wave of technology, you can't do it all yourself. You have to form alliances." So said the biggest winner of 2010, Carlos Slim Helú, the richest man on the planet. Winners understand they need other people to get where they want to go. They understand they don't know everything. They understand, even if they'd never admit it, they're probably not the smartest person in every room. But, most important, they understand that a whole is often greater than the sum of its parts. And this is the driving force behind some of the most powerful and successful partnerships the world has ever seen.

The best companies are governed by leaders who understand that they exist because of a partnership with their customers, their employees, and the communities in which they operate. It is a four-legged stool that cannot function any other way. Destroy any leg of that partnership and you destroy the entire enterprise. Winners always remember one thing—they do not offend the people they most need on their side.

Someone should have told that to the top brass at British Petroleum. On April 20, 2010, eleven men died in a massive explosion on BP's Deepwater Horizon oil rig in the Gulf of Mexico. A month later, then-CEO Tony Hayward apologized to the American people for the damage the company had caused. Not willing to leave good enough alone, however, he decided to stick his foot in his mouth . . . and chew. "There's no one who wants this thing over more than I do," he explained in a wistful, almost somber tone. "You know, I'd like my life back."[40]

In a nanosecond, Tony Hayward became America's Public Enemy Number One, the most hated CEO on the globe, and a living, breathing symbol of what's wrong in corporate America. On the heels of the worst environmental disaster in American history, caused by a foreign oil company (evil incarnate to many), where countless animals died, jobs were lost, economies were crippled, and lives were ruined, BP's over-paid CEO sniffed—on camera—about wanting *his* life back? You can't make this stuff up.

Not to be outdone by Hayward's raw display of puerile whining, BP Chairman Carl-Henric Svanberg said just two weeks later, "I hear comments sometimes that large oil companies are greedy companies or don't care. But that is not the case indeed. We care about the small people."[41] That was a great morning to have purchased stock in Lowe's, where I'm told you can get a great deal on pitchforks.

In Svanberg's defense, he's Swedish. English clearly isn't his first language. And he probably didn't mean to insult everyone alive in the Gulf region—in fact, I'm sure he didn't mean to. The point is, it doesn't matter. Remember, it's not what you say, it's what people hear—and see. BP's senior executives seemed to be put out by all of this anger and frustration over a "small" oil spill. Tony Hayward had yacht parties to attend, and all the hubbub about cleanup was putting a crimp in his social calendar. Didn't the Louisiana fishermen understand that?

The lesson here is simple: When you're communicating to people (which you always are), remember that you're communicating *with people*. Especially when you've done something wrong, like destroy an entire body of water and all the surrounding ecosystems, don't make the issue about you. In fact, you don't exist. Your only job is to make the problem right. Whether you've sold some defective widgets or kept a plane full of passengers waiting on the tarmac for five hours, as far as your communications are concerned, your own life becomes meaningless. The customer—or the injured/angered party—is the only thing that matters. Put yourself in their shoes. Making the communication about you, unless you're talking about how you are going to help *them*, only serves to undermine any shred of true sincerity or credibility you may have.

Consider this exchange between Hayward and Florida congressman Cliff Stearns during Congressional testimony in the wake of the BP oil spill:

REP. CLIFF STEARNS: The people of Florida, when I talk to them and they say there's oil spilling on the coast, would it be appropriate to say that it's because of BP's reckless behavior? Yes or no?

TONY HAYWARD: It is a consequence of a big accident.

REP. CLIFF STEARNS: No, yes or no? Reckless behavior or not?

TONY HAYWARD: There is no evidence of reckless behavior.

REP. CLIFF STEARNS: So, you're standing here, you're saying here today that BP had no reckless behavior? That's your position. Yes?

TONY HAYWARD: There is no evidence of reckless behavior.

REP. CLIFF STEARNS: No, yes or no? You're saying BP has had no reckless behavior, is what you're saying to us.

TONY HAYWARD: I have seen no evidence of reckless behavior.

REP. CLIFF STEARNS: OK. So you're on record saying there's been no reckless behavior. Has anyone in BP been fired because of this incident? Anybody?

TONY HAYWARD: Not—

REP. CLIFF STEARNS: Yes or no?

TONY HAYWARD: No, so far.

REP. CLIFF STEARNS: No people have been fired. So, your captain of the ship runs into New Orleans, spews all this oil, causes all this damage, from Alabama, Mississippi, Florida, Louisiana, and no one's been fired?

TONY HAYWARD: Our investigation is ongoing.

REP. CLIFF STEARNS: So, let's say the investigation goes for three years. Does that mean you wouldn't fire anybody?

TONY HAYWARD: As the investigation draws conclusions, we will take the necessary action.[42]

You can see this exchange on YouTube—but be prepared to cringe. In Hayward's defense, a position I'm loath to take, there was a team of lawyers who told him what he could and couldn't admit to, comment on, and talk about. If he had answered directly, he would have conceded BP's legal culpability for everything stemming from the explosion—even if a faulty part manufactured by someone else was the cause. But regardless of any actual reckless behavior on BP's part, an oil rig explosion that kills eleven men and unleashes untold millions of gallons of oil into the Gulf waters is reckless behavior in most people's book, especially if the beach in your backyard is about to be destroyed by an oily Armageddon. His weasel words didn't work.

Generally speaking, people don't particularly like or relate well to CEOs. Especially foreign CEOs. Especially foreign oil-company CEOs. Because of this preexisting condition in the American psyche, Hayward chose to speak like a lawyered-up suspect at his (and BP's) peril. He was stonewalling. He refused to answer those tough questions because he knew the congressman was trying to give him enough rope to hang himself. And while he didn't take the bait, he still managed to slip the noose around his neck and tip over the chair. He could have said, "If reckless is being indifferent to the consequences facing the people and the region, no, we have not been reckless. We care very deeply . . ." But he didn't. To make matters worse, every time he spoke, whether in front of Congress or in a national TV ad, he sounded aloof. Distant. Caught at the center of a human drama, complete with death, devastation, and an angry mob, Hayward divorced himself from the ability and willingness to communicate like a human. He became robotic, dogmatic, and worst of all, arrogant.

On a more practical level, ignoring the human aspect of communication in cases like these gives your competitors and critics a line of attack they wouldn't otherwise have. By making such patently foolish, out-of-touch public remarks, the two BP chiefs exposed themselves, even more than they already were, to critics attempting to paint the company as indifferent to the human suffering in the Gulf. For the most part, BP eventually responded well, took full responsibility, and made clear it was going to put the resources in place to fix the problem, no matter how long it would take. They partnered with the local community, and they were saying and doing the right things. But all it took was a couple of memorable gaffes before the vultures swooped in for the kill. Without these remarks—and with the addition of a shred of feeling or compassion in the executives' public statements—the media stories about BP might have been far less negative. BP's reputation in the United States might have been spared complete annihilation. And Tony Hayward might still have his job.

I believe that the business world has a lot to learn from the sports world, and that's why you see numerous references to great athletes of modern times on these pages. The principles of winning that sports stars take for granted the rest of us need to learn. Sportscaster Jim Gray has been an astute observer of athlete behavior for three decades. For him, it's the partnership, the teamwork, that turns great players into winners. Says Gray:

> You're only as good as your weakest link. Michael Jordan didn't just show up at a game. He can't inbound the ball to himself. He has to throw it to somebody so they'll throw it back to him. He understood that if it weren't for Phil Jackson, Frank Hamblen and Tex Winter and Jim Cleamons putting all of the right people in the right places defensively and offensively, if he didn't have the trainer to tape his ankles, if he didn't have the travel secretary to make sure that plane got him there on time, if he didn't have the whole confluence of events that it takes to win, then he wouldn't win. Would he be great? Yes. But he can't do it alone.
>
> LeBron James is great, but has LeBron James won a championship?

No. Why not? Because all the people around him are not fulfilling the expectations that he has, and they're not able to lift him to where he has to be because they all aren't doing their job as well as they need to be.

You have to trust people, you have to allow them to do their jobs, and you have to put the best people in their jobs so that you can succeed as a leader. If you don't have good people around you and you think it's all about you, you'll be the first to hit the door. A lot of people who get near the top don't understand that it's not just because of them, it's because of everything that everyone has done for them that's put them there.

Sports celebrities began lending their popularity to products almost a century ago, but business partnerships between sports and brands rarely endured and often involved nothing more than free travel and free stuff. Television made the relationship a lot more valuable for both sides, but few consumer brands were willing to shell out the big bucks for the popular stars of the day or to stick with a marketing campaign for more than a few months. But all that changed when a beaten and battered "Mean Joe" Greene tossed his dirty football jersey to a starstruck kid before chugging a Coca-Cola. Still regarded as one of the best ads of all time, it changed the image of the player and product and jump-started sports-product partnerships. Several years later, Miller beer took its Miller Lite brand to a new level by highlighting the player-product partnership. More than a dozen sports legends, including John Madden, Red Auerbach, and Yogi Berra appeared on television to declare either "tastes great" or "less filling." The verbal tug of war went on for years, even launching the entertainment careers of relatively unknown sports personalities Bob Uecker and "Marvelous" Marv Thorneberry. It clearly put Miller Lite on the map.

Yet no company has done it better than Nike. Watch any sporting event across the globe and you'll immediately notice a similarity in all of them. From cricket in Asia (official outfitters of the Indian national team) to European soccer (Nike sponsors nearly all of the top club teams and players) to basketball in the United States (Kobe Bryant, anyone?) to Tiger Woods, the Swoosh is there. It's no coincidence people all around the world want to wear Nike; it's everywhere they look. But thirty years ago partnerships like these were far from the norm. All of these have been built on the mother of all relationships, that between Nike and a skinny, cocky North Carolina basketball player named Michael Jeffrey Jordan.

Founded in 1964, it took the athletic shoe manufacturer only sixteen years to capture half of the American market. But that wasn't enough for founder Phil Knight. He took the company public in 1980, and started national television advertising in 1982—but he wanted more. Several years earlier, the Nike team had signed a deal with ill-tempered tennis star Ilie Nastase (a sign of Nike's quirky tastes) but now the company was looking to go mainstream and Main Street—and the twenty-one-year-old Michael Jordan was the sports star they wanted. There was a problem, however. Converse was Jordan's first choice, Adidas his second. But because Converse already had the league's two best players (Larry Bird and Magic Johnson), and Adidas was inexplicably uninterested, the window was open for Nike. After signing Jordan to what was one of the most lucrative endorsement deals in the league, Nike went on a campaign to build their brand around the budding superstar.

You know the rest of this story, right? Jordan becomes the greatest athlete on the planet, and Nike sells tens of millions of sneakers. But wait. Something you may not know is that in 1986, just two years into the five-year deal, Jordan wanted out. To everyone's surprise, the Air Jordan series was not selling, despite Jordan's on-court success. The lack of sales was partially due to their exorbitantly high retail price, but there was something else, something missing in their design process. What they had ignored is something that all of today's modern sports-entertainment mini-moguls take for granted—collaboration between designers and the stars themselves.

Prior to Jordan, footwear companies designed their athletic shoes based on what they believed would sell, and the athletes gladly wore them, happy for the extra income and free shoes. Jordan and Nike changed this dynamic. Designer Tinker Hatfield, newly in charge of the Jordan Nike line, brought Michael into their Portland headquarters to ask him for design ideas. For Jordan this was the ultimate sign of respect and loyalty, and it convinced him to remain with the company. For Nike, this was the start of something great. From that point onward, Jordan played a role in the design for all products bearing his name, and every shoe "his Airness" has created has sold like Evian in the Sahara. Long after his playing career ended, Air Jordans still rank among the highest price tags in the sneaker world, sometimes upward of $170, not to mention what the insane "sneaker-heads" will pay for vintage pairs of the originals.

Today almost all promising athletes are signed to a major shoe deal almost immediately after turning pro, and the best, like LeBron James and Tiger Woods, are highly involved in the development of their own personal brands. These kinds of hands-on partnerships between Nike and their athletes have helped them become the first and often only stop for all up-and-coming superstars, and have left their competitors playing catch-up for decades.

But Nike has not confined its partnerships to individual sponsorships. In fact, some of its shrewdest business moves have been in acquiring iconoclastic brands like Converse, Umbro, upscale footwear company Cole Haan (who have transformed the term *comfortable high heels* from oxymoron to reality thanks to Nike Air cushioning), and the Hurley surfboard company. In doing so, they have developed a fashion partnership portfolio that can offer customers nearly anything they want. To make their dominance even more explicit, when Nike's main rivals Reebok and Adidas merged in 2005, they combined for just 20 percent of the U.S. shoe market. Nike controls 33 percent.

When it comes to partnerships in the sportswear industry, Nike set the standard. Their ability to see the importance of collaboration before anyone else has played an integral part in their rise to dominance. Without Michael Jordan, Nike would not have become one of the most recognizable brands on the planet. Without Nike, Michael Jordan would probably still be considered the greatest basketball player ever, but probably not a global icon. By working together, Nike and Jordan have made billions of dollars and created billions of loyal customers.

CHEMISTRY

An effective partnership is one where the combined result of the individual parts is something markedly better than the individual parts themselves. Some familiar examples might include: macaroni and cheese, Lennon and McCartney, Procter & Gamble, *Will & Grace*, and Siskel & Ebert. You may think I'm kidding, but I'm not. Together, what they accomplished was far greater than what they would have done individually. In a positive partnership, each side works to complement, support, and gain from the strengths of the other. It's called chemistry, and winners know how much it really matters to their eventual success.

For example, it was clear during my interview with Mort Zuckerman that he had great respect for his business partner, Edward Linde, with whom he worked for over forty years, which surely had something to do with their immense success. Their company, Boston Properties, survived several real estate downturns to become one of the largest owners and developers of Class A office space in the United States. *Both my partner and I had a wonderful time in the real estate business because both of us were irreverent,"* he said with a reminiscing smile. *"I think it helped that neither he nor I took ourselves too seriously. We had fun doing it, and people sense that, somehow or other, it added to the credibility of what we were saying. We had a great time. We teased each other; we teased everybody else. We'd make fun of what we were doing and had fun with what we were doing. So there was a joyous quality to it.*

The problem with chemistry is that it's tough to define and even more difficult to manufacture. Allow me to use a television icon as an example. Bob Newhart had not one but two top-ten series, two bestselling comedy albums, and he continues to pack concert halls across the country after fifty years performing because, well, he has chemistry. I asked him to explain why he was able to survive at the top of his game for so long. I loved his answer (partially because, in typical Bob Newhart style, it took him about three minutes to say it):

> Chemistry is about liking each other. What happened on both shows [The Bob Newhart Show and Newhart] is that we liked each other. We had a good time. We had a lot of laughs. We went to work and we just

---

* Once again, that word *fun* appears. It is almost impossible to find a winner who doesn't regard the seventy-hour workweeks and the ups and downs of business life any other way. If you're not having fun, you're probably not in the right situation to be a winner.

laughed, and somehow that comes through the camera into people's homes. Audiences have the right to say who they want to be in their home and who they don't want to be in their home, and that's what they do. Twice they decided, "Yeah, OK, I like him. He can be in my house."

I wasn't always successful. I did a show in the 1961–62 season that won an Emmy, a Peabody, and a pink slip from NBC. From that point on, in the back of my mind, I'd think, Is this going to work? When I did Newhart, I told Mary [Frann], "You're going to have the toughest job in the world playing my wife, because Suzie [Suzanne Pleshette] and I had chemistry and people are going to compare you to Suzie. It's not going to be easy." It was just there. We had mutual respect for each other, and it showed. I guess people like me. I don't make people nervous. Jerry Seinfeld had that quality, whatever that quality is, and I wish I could have bought stock in Jerry Seinfeld.

Chemistry is really about balance. If one partner is creative and excessive, the other partner needs to be organized and disciplined. You can't have one partner who is a complete disorganized mess without someone there who has everything lined up, listed, and ready to go. That's how things get done. Winners get this. *"The one thing I realized was that I was not a good manager from a details sense. So as soon as I could, I hired someone to manage the business,"* John Sperling billionaire, founder of the University of Phoenix, told me when I asked him about the value of the right partnerships.

I thought of myself as the outside guy. I was the one responsible for the macro conditions—the social, economic, and political. I was the one who did the politicking, the lobbying, and the negotiating. The managers stayed at home and didn't worry about those things. I said, "I'll take care of those outside problems. You just focus on the inside." They got used to that, and I said, "I'll protect you." So they felt protected from all the slings and arrows about for-profit education, and they were able to concentrate on their jobs. But I'm not a great creator of partnerships unless they're immediately of use. Most CEOs are managers. They come up from the managerial chain, and ingratiating themselves here and there is what they do. When you come up as an entrepreneur, you don't have time for that. You are struggling constantly, so making nice with people, unless you need them immediately, you just don't have time to do. So partnerships, when I have them, are ephemeral.

Balance creates synergies; imbalance leads to failure. If you don't have that balance, you're not in the right partnership. When the scales tip too far in either direction on a particular attribute (for example, aggression, stubbornness, confidence, or kindness) you will end up at odds with each other and, ultimately, with your customers.

THE POWER OF PARTNERSHIP

Like a great pinot matched with just the right Reblochon cheese, the right pairing can be both delicate and divine. Partnerships take on a variety of forms, but can be grouped into three main categories: personal partnerships, institutional relationships, and third-party endorsements.

Personal partnerships are, as you might have guessed, between two or more people. The Clinton Bush Haiti Fund, for example, came together shortly after the devastating earthquake in Port-au-Prince, Haiti, in early 2010. Its goal was to unite people of all political persuasions to donate money, clothing, food—you name it—to the people of Haiti, who were suffering extreme hardship in the wake of the worst calamity in their tumultuous national history. Former presidents Clinton and Bush joined reputations and forces in a nonpartisan effort to bring humanitarian relief when and where it was needed most. President Clinton would have had immense success alone—among a wide but not as universal a segment of the American people. President Bush, the same. But by *combining* their reputations and appeals, they *more than doubled* their impact. When political archrivals set aside their differences to help mankind, it opens the door to a *wholly separate* set of donors who would not have contributed to *either* president individually. In this way, personal partnerships are the best to achieve the "whole is greater than the sum of its parts" objective mentioned earlier.

A good example of an institutional partnership is that between Apple and Nike. Apple and Nike forged a partnership in an attempt to increase sales of their iPods and Nike+ line, respectively. The partnership has been relatively successful, as people continue integrating more technology into their lives. The partnership was founded on a simple premise: People like to listen to music while they exercise. So Nike and Apple worked to integrate the music-listening experience and the fitness experience. The result was Nike+ technology, which digitally tracks your workout progress. You can sync up your Nike+ equipment with your iPod, and as you jog it can generate playlists based on your speed and distance. By the time you've hit the showers, the device has already posted your results online for you to see and to compare with others. The partnership brought two of the largest and most successful companies in the world together to achieve a common goal. Not surprisingly, Nike and Apple both reported increased product sales on Nike+ products thanks to the success of their collaboration.

Effective partnerships motivate both partners to achieve more than they could on their own. It's rare to hear the CEO of a global communications conglomerate openly admit to having a twenty-two-year-old teaching him how to improve the business, but that's exactly what Tom Harrison, chairman and CEO of Diversified Agency Services—the largest single component of global marketing giant Omnicom—does. In fact, he boasts about it. It is refreshing to hear someone that successful speak so candidly about the need for great partnerships, no matter who the partner may be.

> I've got a guy who is twenty-two years old who beats the crap out of me. "Why are you doing it that way? Take the shortcut," he'll tell me. What these geeks are doing for us—Geek Squad is a great name, actually— what they are really doing for us is showing us, based on what they are and their pursuit of the digital environment, where we're going to have to evolve to. Because they are the forefront. They're out there. They are innovators. The CEO of one of the great marketing companies on the globe is being mentored by a twenty-two-year-old.

And at the same time this young man is gaining invaluable knowledge and experience from one of the giants in the business. This is an example of a near perfect partnership, because it helps both sides do more. When you find the right match, the results can be exponential.

There are few issues Americans are as vocal and concerned about as personal security. One of the very few powers given explicitly to our government in the Constitution is the power to "provide for the common defense." Our government, as originally intended, wasn't asked to do too many things, but keeping us alive and safe was clearly at the top of that list. Today, that debate takes two forms: the more widely discussed issue of national security and the relatively ignored problem of domestic security, the latter having to do primarily with prison-control issues like funding, overcrowding, and safety. One recent partnership that has helped solve our domestic security program combines both private- and public-sector strengths to offer the best of both worlds. It is also a good case study in effective messaging.

First, the statistics: According to the *New York Times*, "the number of federal prisoners in private prisons in the United States has more than doubled, to 32,712 in 2008 from 15,524 in 2000. The number of state prisoners in privately run prisons has increased to 93,500 from 75,000 in that time."[43] Many of those private prisons belong to CCA, the Corrections Corporation of America. CCA is the "fourth-largest corrections system in the nation, behind only the federal government and two states."[44] They were also a client of mine.

CCA founded the private corrections management industry more than twenty-five years ago. They specialize in the design, construction, expansion, and management of prisons, jails, and detention facilities. Simply put, when bad guys need to be put away for far less than governments spend doing the same thing, CCA is the company you call. When you visit CCA's Web site today, you'll notice something interesting. Their tagline is "America's Leader in Partnership Corrections." Partnership corrections? That's new. It's also very effective, because they figured out what the rest of corporate America has still not learned: the concept of "private" anything isn't always positive.

That's right. Just one word can transform the national discussion. To some, *private* is just another word for *profit*. To others, *private* means exclusive, privileged, and oftentimes unaccountable. The current debate on prisons—and in so many areas where the government and business intersect—pits those who put their faith in the marketplace against those who put their faith in government. In America today, that is a fifty-fifty divide (we hate them both). Nobody trusts private business to police itself and serve the public interest. And nobody believes the government is capable of operating efficiently or spending taxpayer dollars wisely. That's where the concept of partnership comes in. What CCA offers is the best of both worlds.

By "partnering" with government, CCA provides the public with the advantages of each approach and minimizes the disadvantages of each. If you're taking notes or underlining sections, the next line from CCA is a language lesson for all business: *"We offer the oversight and account-ability of government with the efficiency and cost-effectiveness of a business."* That's a message people get—and it resonates now more than ever. Today, family, state, and national budgets are stretched to the limit, government waste is out of control, and many believe the free market has let us down. Ensuring safety and efficiency should not be an either/or proposition. CCA has found credible and convincing language, and we're no longer stuck with a false choice between efficient, private prisons and safe, public prisons. Partnership prisons can be both efficient and safe.

CCA's current use of the phrase *public-private partnerships* works so well because it embodies collaboration, cooperation, and inclusiveness. It takes the sharp edge off *private* while lending a sense of efficiency and effectiveness to *public*. That combination is a winner because it appeals across the political spectrum.

BUILDING CREDIBILITY

Partnerships are often an exercise in credibility-building. When you go to a Web site with a search bar that reads "Powered by Google," you know what you're getting. Moreover, you're probably not afraid to use it. The Google name gives the site's search function credibility. In return, Google gets a share of the revenue generated when the user takes advantage of the search bar. Similarly, when you see one of those "Intel Inside" stickers on your laptop or PC, you know it's powered by an Intel processor, the most reliable name in computing. In fact, in June 2005 at the Apple Worldwide Developers Conference, Steve Jobs announced that Apple would be transitioning their computers from their chips to Intel chips because:

> When we look at Intel, they've got great performance, yes, but they've got something else that's very important to us. Just as important as performance, is power consumption. And the way we look at it is performance per watt. For one watt of power how much performance do you get? And when we look at the future road maps projected out in mid-2006 and beyond, what we see is the PowerPC gives us sort of 15 units of performance per watt, but the Intel road map in the future gives us 70, and so this tells us what we have to do.[45]

Jobs swallowed his pride and admitted that Intel was superior.* This move allowed Apple to focus on creating their own groundbreaking technologies instead of being held back by their own processors. For Intel, it meant having their chips associated with one of the strongest, most-admired brands in the world. Apple benefited, Intel benefited, and, most important, customers benefited. Win-win-win.

One company that talks a lot about sustainability, namely of the environmental sort, is eBay. The Web site has become more than a place to score vintage Pez dispensers or the source of oddball anecdotes, such as the Arkansas mother who auctioned legal rights to name her unborn child, or the British man who listed his wife, claiming she had an affair. The Web site's first sale (it was then known as AuctionWeb) on September 3, 1995, was a broken laser pointer that sold for $14.83. Pierre Omidyar, founder of eBay, contacted the buyer to remind him that the laser pointer did not work. The buyer responded, "I'm a collector of broken laser pointers."[46]

Today, eBay has fifteen thousand employees and claims $8.7 billion in revenue. And as their reach extended, so did their partnering efforts with organizations committed to social responsibility. For a few years now, they've touted their ability to help people reuse goods and reduce the amount of paper used in transactions, and highlighted their nonreliance

---

* I'd like to see that on YouTube. A CEO admitting that the competition is better happens about as often as Ozzy Osbourne strings together a coherent sentence.

on physical space or resources—their warehouses are people's houses and garages.

> At eBay, we think about sustainability a bit differently. From promoting the use of products that already exist, to paying without a paper check, all of our businesses empower people to do more with less. [. . .] One of the largest environmental impacts of our business model is the shipping that occurs between sellers and buyers. So, in 2007, we worked with the United States Postal Service to introduce new, environmentally friendly Priority Mail packaging. This co-branded packaging is Cradle-to-Cradle certified, and is available free through the USPS shipping hub on eBay .com.[47]

Sure, it sounds good on their Web site, but I couldn't really think of eBay as a company committed to environmental sustainability. It just seemed like a gimmick.

Then, not too long ago, I purchased something on eBay and noticed they had a partnership with Conservation International (CI), a nonprofit environmental advocacy group in Washington, D.C. That got my attention. Upon checkout, I was asked to donate $1 to help support CI and their efforts to sustain our planet and biodiversity around the world. Suddenly, with just that one little example of partnership, it all became real: eBay actually does care about the environment. More than just co-branding earth-friendly packaging, they're also helping a group like CI raise money to help clean up and protect the environment.

So why the change? Let's be honest, it's not a sacrifice for eBay to add the CI link. But for me it made them credible because I knew CI wouldn't have gotten involved with eBay if it wasn't serious. That's the power of the "certification" that comes through credible partnerships.

PARTNERSHIPS AND PEACE OF MIND

There are three organizations with whom a partnership means automatic peace of mind: the American Automobile Association (AAA), *Good Housekeeping,* and *Consumer Reports.* AAA says national and universal. *Consumer Reports* communicates the good, the bad, and the ugly of products and services. And the "Good Housekeeping Seal of Approval" is the very definition of "peace of mind." For AAA members, a yearly fee of approximately $50 to $60 for their basic service, depending on where you live, gets you several benefits, such as road maps, travel publications, hotel and restaurant ratings, and even discounts in places you didn't know discounts were possible. But if you ask most AAA members why they join, it's the peace of mind they get from having their Roadside Assistance service. All AAA members know that if their car battery dies, they get a flat tire, or they lock themselves out of the car, they're just a phone call away from help. So it makes perfect sense for companies to partner with AAA so they'll have access to their more than 50 million members in the United States and Canada.[48]

Founded in 1855 by Clark Bryan, *Good Housekeeping*'s purpose was to serve as a "family journal conducted in the interests of the higher life of the household." He also claimed the magazine had a "mission to fulfill composed of about equal portions of public duty and private enterprise . . . to produce and perpetuate perfection as may be obtained in the household."[49] By 1909, the magazine had opened the Good Housekeeping Institute in Springfield, Massachusetts, as a place to test and review consumer products that were of interest to the magazine's readers. In December of that same year, the publication introduced a list of products to carry the Good Housekeeping Seal of Approval, meaning they had met rigorous standards and fulfilled all of the claims made by the manufacturer. Twenty-one consumer products were listed in the issue and included various household appliances, such as a washing machine, refrigerator, gas range, and an electric iron. By the end of 1910, almost two hundred products were qualified to carry the Seal of Approval.[50] The Good Housekeeping Institute currently tests more than two thousand products a year and has awarded the Seal of Approval to five thousand products since its inception.[51]

Today, with a circulation of more than four and a half million, *Good Housekeeping* has more readers than *Martha Stewart Living* and *Family Circle* combined. Most of the magazine's readers are women in their mid- to late forties who live in mid-Atlantic, Midwest, and Southern states.[52] But what really makes the magazine so powerful is that Seal of Approval—the only one that comes with a two-year, limited warranty:

It has been our policy since 1909 to stand behind Seal products. Products that have earned the Good Housekeeping Seal or the Green Good Housekeeping Seal are backed by Good Housekeeping's *independent limited two-year warranty: If the product is found to be defective within two years of purchase,* Good Housekeeping *will refund the consumer, repair or replace the product. To the best of our knowledge, no other publication, website or third-party emblem will back products with their own warranty.*[53]

That's powerful language—but in this case, it's not about the word choice. It's about the strength of the partnership behind the words. It's putting *action* front and center.

The final member of the Peace of Mind Trifecta is *Consumer Reports,* which is actually a publication put out by the Consumers Union, "an expert, independent, nonprofit organization whose mission is to work for a fair, just, and safe marketplace for all consumers and to empower consumers to protect themselves."[54] The organization was created in 1936 when mass media advertising was just getting started and consumers had few sources of reliable information they could go to in order to separate commonplace wild claims from factual ones and good products from bad. Ever since, the Consumers Union has filled the role of objective examiner by offering a broad range of consumer information and product evaluations. To preserve independence and neutrality, the Consumers Union has never accepted outside advertising or free samples of the products it tests. In addition, it employs hundreds of "mystery shoppers" and technical experts to purchase and test the products it evaluates.[55]

Consumer Reports tests everything you can think of, from camcorders to cars. And each April, it releases its New Car Issue, which can almost single-handedly determine the fortunes of various models, depending on the ratings they receive. For millions of Americans, *Consumer Reports* is gospel; all else is merely apocryphal.

Just as important, what *Consumer Reports doesn't* say means a lot. It's not good enough to simply avoid being criticized by *Consumer Reports . . .* if you want to be a winner, Americans expect you to win praise from *Consumer Reports.* If they don't recommend a washer, many people won't buy it. If they don't recommend a certain kind of oven, many people won't buy it.

But it gets worse. Toyota, the most popular automotive brand globally, halted production and issued a recall on a model that had been rated "do not buy" by *Consumer Reports*. It's very rare for *Consumer Reports* to issue that rating—but when it does, it's like the kiss of death. On the flip side, if they do recommend a new TV or computer, the sales of those items can experience a substantial increase. But, just like the copy of *Good Housekeeping* in your doctor's waiting room or that AAA membership card in your wallet, the most valuable thing *Consumer Reports* offers is peace of mind. And, in today's world, that reassurance is priceless.

WORDS TO USE

If the language of perfection is about the product, the language of partnerships is primarily about people. Here are ten words and phrases that the winners in this book most commonly used to describe what they did, how they did it, and the relationships they built while doing it:

THE LANGUAGE OF PARTNERSHIP

1. Fully aligned
2. Inclusion (rather than diversity)
3. United
4. A fresh approach (rather than reorganization)
5. Independent thinking
6. Independent certification
7. Peace of mind
8. Measurable results (rather than productivity or metrics)
9. Employee-focused
10. Personal responsibility

"Fully aligned" may have a business-school ring to it, but it's how the most successful people in business describe the management style of their companies. All winners tolerate disagreement, and some even encourage it, but winners enter into battle fully aligned.

"Inclusion" is how successful businesses should be describing their *"diversity"* programs, but most don't. Employees are generally proud when the companies they work for seek to expand the talent pool to the underserved communities. But problems arise when some people, particularly middle-aged white males, feel that *"diversity"* is being achieved at their expense. *"Inclusion"* is seen as an addition, bringing more people to an expanding table, while diversity is perceived by some to represent the promotion of some at the expense of others.

In companies undergoing significant management turnover, **"united"** is what rank-and-file employees want from their leadership team. Employees know that divisions within leadership often lead to chaos in the ranks below. To know that the board of directors is *"united"* in their choice of new CEO or that senior management is *"united"* in their vision for the future helps instill a sense of peace of mind among employees.

"A fresh approach" is what winners often use to describe what they did that led to a great strategic advantage or product breakthrough, yet very few use this language in day-to-day communication with employees or customers. Investors and shareholders appreciate the language because it suggests "new" and "different" without being alarmingly radical. Conversely, the word *reorganization* is seen either as correcting a bureaucratic mistake or an excuse to fire people—neither with a particularly endearing result.

"Independent thinking" is an essential attribute in the people winners hire. The people profiled in this book are certainly strong willed, and all are relentless, determined, and single-minded (three words that work) in their pursuit of excellence, but they value and surround themselves with people who provide alternative viewpoints. Selling yourself as an independent thinker is a good way to get hired by a winner.

"Independent certification" is the best term to build trust and confidence among employees and customers. We no longer take businesspeople or politicians at their word. We want and demand verification from independent sources that whatever is claimed is real: *"Don't take my word for it. Just ask the people at [fill in the blank]."* Magazines like *Consumer Reports* and *Good Housekeeping*, organizations like AARP and AAA, and companies like Amazon.com, FedEx, and Intel are universally known and have universal appeal. They are the ideal independent certifiers.

"Peace of mind" is what partnerships are meant to provide. While this phrase works on so many levels, I have applied it here because of the value it brings to any business relationship. The best illustration is the charitable partnerships between Bill Gates and Warren Buffett. When those two announced a joint effort, people sat up and took notice. It signified that whatever they set out to do would get done with minimum waste and maximum results—and that donors would have the peace of mind of knowing that these two titans of business were directly involved.

"Measurable results" is what investors and shareholders, as well as consumers and employees, expect from a partnership. You've heard the phrase *"the proof is in the pudding,"* which dates back to the early 1600s. *"Measurable results"* is the twenty-first-century equivalent, demonstrating with evidence, not assertions, that an effort is working. In fact, the best way to demonstrate *"measurable results"* is with either *"evidence-based"* or *"fact-based"* statistics. Sure, people expect effective partnerships to lead to greater *"productivity,"* but that word makes people think of profits at the expense of people, while measurable results conveys a benefit to everyone. The oft-used *"metrics"* is perceived as cold and void of the human component.

"Employee-focused" describes almost every winner profiled in this book. In fact, one of the single most important traits of all winners is their attention to and support of the people who work for them and with them. It is almost impossible to reach the top heights of success without the ability to build a strong team of senior executives and middle-level management. If your language and efforts are *"employee-focused,"* you have what it takes to win.

"Personal responsibility" is what everyone expects from the people in charge. The challenge is to communicate the need for personal responsibility down to the most entry-level people. There isn't a person I interviewed who doesn't take personal responsibility for what they do, but their success depends on others being equally committed to accountability.

8

PASSION

The power of intensity

There is no passion to be found playing small—in settling for a life that is less than the one you are capable of living.

—NELSON MANDELA

If you can dream it, you can do it. It's kind of fun to do the impossible.

—WALT DISNEY

Did you know that Walt Disney mortgaged everything he owned, including his own personal insurance, to fund the $17 million construction of Disneyland? Or that Oprah Winfrey, the child of a single teenage mom, was sexually assaulted at the age of nine? Or that Steve Wynn took over his father's bingo company while still in college because of his father's sudden death? Or that Stan O'Neal, the former CEO of Merrill Lynch, was born into abject poverty and picked cotton as a young boy to help his family survive?

What do these and most other winners have in common? First, they all faced enormous obstacles. Second, they all failed multiple times. And third, no matter how bad it got—and it did get horrifically bad for some of the people in this book—they never gave up. Never. So why didn't they? What made them want to start at the bottom, work sixteen hours a day, and spend most of their lives with their necks on the line? With enough money, you can buy almost anything—information and influence, access and acclaim. Yet without passion, you will not win no matter how much of anything else you have.

The people I interviewed for this book see everything. They notice dust in corners, a burnt-out lightbulb buried deep in the ceiling, an empty hanger in need of product. Mickey Drexler of J.Crew gave me a tour of their new two-story wedding store on Madison Avenue in Manhattan. The level of detail that goes into product and display placement is unimaginable. Nothing is out of place, and everything exists in its space for a reason. Drexler's attention to detail is impressive, but it's his passion and bold vision after almost forty years in the apparel industry that has made J.Crew the powerhouse in clothing.

You get inspiration from a lot of places. I got it from Benetton in Europe. I used to go in there to shop for my little boy, and it was so easy—pick the color, the size, and I was out in ten minutes. Small is beautiful in any business. You can control it. Don't just listen to the big company guys. Listen to the smaller guys with incredible track records, guys who are so creative and detailed and don't miss a thing. You can feel what they do and how they do it. They have an instinct, and they follow it.

Let me start by defining what passion is not. If you are like most Americans, you live within twenty miles of a Walmart store. In fact, if you live in a small town or rural community, it's possible Walmart is one of the largest—if not *the* largest—employers in your area. They are passionate about being the cheapest in town with the most stuff— shoes, Cheerios, contact lenses, motor oil, bananas, rifles (when you think about it, they sell everything a South American general might need to form a junta). But while they are surely passionate about pricing and profits, everything else about Walmart—the stores, the employees, the products—are truly passionless. Everything from its plastic footballs to its fabric softener is churned out like widgets from factories in Asia, devoid of personal significance, a craftsman's touch, or individual identity.

Now, walk into any Costco in the United States and there's a chance you'll see a seventy-four-year-old man strolling the aisles, taking a mental inventory, asking employees hundreds of questions about the store's prices and product lines, dressed in the very clothes he is milling over in the apparel section. This is not just a bargain-hunting senior citizen hoping to score a forty-pound bag of peanuts or a pair of designer slacks for less than half of department store prices. This is one of the most innovative and powerful men in the history of retail.

Jim Sinegal, cofounder and CEO of Costco, visits nearly all of the four-hundred-plus stores every year so that every employee, at least in theory, has the chance to meet the CEO. Twenty-seven years ago Sinegal and his partner Jeff Brotman decided to start a big-box chain in order to offer patrons unbeatable prices. Literally unbeatable. Says Sinegal about their pricing, "We always look to see how much of a gulf we can create between ourselves and the competition. So that the competitors eventually say, f--k 'em, these guys are crazy. We'll compete somewhere else.'"[56]

Sinegal didn't learn the business of retail or his salty language in college classrooms. He got his professional education at the age of eighteen, unloading mattresses and bagging products at one of the original Southern California discount warehouse stores, Fed-Mart. He started Costco at the age of forty-seven, after working his way up to the top of the Fed-Mart corporate ladder. A passionate learner, he is eagerly engaged with his employees and personally involved in every aspect of the business. As he himself explains, "Retail is detail, show me a big-picture guy, and I'll show you a guy who's out of the picture." And he means it. His office is always open to staff who want to talk. He doesn't employ a single public relations person, often answers his own calls, and reads hundreds of consumer e-mails every day—not exactly the norm for the CEO of a multibillion-dollar retail giant.*

Sinegal is also light-years away from the status quo in the realm of customer satisfaction, which is why Costco enjoys an unparalleled reputation among retailers. "Many retailers look at an item and say, 'I'm selling this for ten bucks. How can I sell it for eleven?' We look at it and say, how can we get it to nine bucks? And then, how can we get it to eight? It is contrary to the thinking of a retailer, which is to see how much more profit you can get out of it."[57] Sinegal refuses to mark up any item more than 14 percent, a fact that can sometimes infuriate analysts and shareholders, but that ongoing policy has made his stores the king of the discount retail industry. Costco is consistently rated at or near the top of the American

---

* Lowe's CEO Robert Niblock posts his phone number and e-mail address online for anyone to use. Yes, you'll start with his secretary, but if you state your case well, you won't have a problem talking directly to the head of the company.

Customer Satisfaction Index, which comes in handy when your store relies almost completely on word of mouth as its sole source of advertising.

In fact, the only people more passionate about Costco than its CEO are its members. There are more than 55 million people paying between $45 and $100 per year just for the right to shop there. These same folks are willing—even expecting—to stand patiently in lines that can often take twenty minutes or more to get to the cash register. There is no impatience. Despite the wait, the value, service, and quality of the merchandise is really that good. Can you imagine that kind of patience and loyalty anywhere else?

Unlike effective communication or skill in the art of persuasion, passion is a difficult emotion to learn, to develop, and certainly to fake. Sure, you can pretend to care about something if you need to. And yes, you can sound passionate about your work if it's convenient (especially during annual reviews). But true passion is one of those rare human emotions that can't be manufactured. Passion just *is*.

This chapter will teach you how to express and harness the passion you have to put it to its best use. If you aspire to win, follow the simple directions in this chapter and you will inspire others to follow.

UNDERSTANDING THE ROLE OF PASSION

Winners eat, breathe, talk, sleep, and live passion. Their work is a *part* of them, and in some cases it completely defines who they are. Winners strive for perfection because they're driven by something deeper and more powerful than mere interest or curiosity. They never stop looking for ways to do things better and for where they can do more, where they can go that extra mile—and more—to blow away expectations and people.

The best advertisers understand passion. They manufacture it in thirty-second bites that capture not just our emotions but our memories. In fact, taglines that emphasize passion of some sort are among the most memorable. They stay with you long after the commercials that introduced them have hit the shelf. See how many of the examples that follow you still remember today.

Three elements separate real winners from those who merely play the game:

THE MOST PASSIONATE TAGLINES AND ADVERTISING SLOGANS

1. Nike: Just Do It
2. Lexus: The Relentless Pursuit of Perfection
3. Visa: It's Everywhere You Want to Be
4. BMW: The Ultimate Driving Machine
5. FedEx: When It Absolutely, Positively Has to Be There Overnight
6. *The New York Times*: All the News That's Fit to Print
7. Hallmark: When You Care Enough to Send the Very Best
8. U.S. Army: Be All You Can Be
9. Wheaties: Breakfast of Champions
10. De Beers: A Diamond Is Forever

Emotion without vision is just the heart's way of throwing a tantrum for no reason.

Vision without emotion won't get you anywhere because it lacks drive; it has no reason to keep fighting the good fight.

And *commitment* without vision is meaningless because without clear direction, there's no sense of achievement when you get there.

So much of corporate and political communication is devoid of passion because it lacks a connection to actual people. I've spent the better part of my life scolding CEOs, vice presidents of marketing, senators, and congressmen for their bland recitation of facts, figures, and statistics without any sense of the dynamism of human beings. It's what I'm most critical about in corporate America, and it distinguishes those who win from those who merely survive. Some CEOs get this, and they're hip to their contemporaries' lack of passion too. J.Crew's Mickey Drexler told me about one such CEO, who apparently suffered a dearth of passion in all parts of his being. *"He had been running that company for thirty years and if you met him, you wouldn't hire him to mow your lawn,"* he told me with a dismissive smirk. *"No passion at all. He was bored. You could see every day at work—he was bored. No creativity and no curiosity. If you aren't curious, you can't be successful—especially in a business where everything is obsolete every few months."* That pretty much sums it up.

It might surprise you to learn which companies are the most passionate in America. When Ben Cohen and Jerry Greenfield opened their first ice-cream shop in 1977 in an old gas station in Vermont, they wanted to create something different. They hoped to establish a profitable business, but, more important, they wanted to make a difference in the world. They wanted to give something back to their community. They started small by throwing a local festival and giving away free ice-cream cones. As their business grew, they expanded their efforts by donating an unheard-of percentage of profits to charity, forming partnerships with minority suppliers, and developing environment-friendly packaging.

Ben and Jerry's passion for social responsibility shaped all aspects of their business. From product development to marketing to human resources to operations, the social impact of their efforts guided Ben and Jerry's every move—even when those moves meant slimmer profit margins. The results were remarkable. The business that began in an old gas station in Vermont sold hundreds of millions of dollars' worth of ice cream every year, and *Forbes, Fortune,* and *The Wall Street Journal* all named it one of the most respected U.S. companies before Cohen and Greenfield sold it to Unilever in 2000.

PASSION AT 39,000 FEET

Would you be surprised to learn that airline passengers are the most dissatisfied, frustrated, irate consumers in America today? Probably not. The 2008 University of Michigan American Customer Satisfaction Index gives the industry a score of 62 out of a possible 100. To give you context for that rating, the Internal Revenue Service scored a 65.[58] For an industry to score lower than the IRS, something is wrong—very, very wrong.

According to the study, the lack of customer satisfaction is a result of "the same problems that have pulled airline passenger satisfaction down the past few years—disenchanted employees, increasing fuel costs, bankruptcy, and now also record levels of lost, delayed and damaged luggage." Keep in mind, this survey was done before some enterprising airline accountant came up with the bright idea of charging for bags. To add insult to injury, at least one airline is now contemplating charging for carry-on bags, too.*

There is an exception, an airline that exemplifies true passion (even at seven a.m., when most normal people are just waking up). Southwest Airlines. Year after year, they rank number one for industry satisfaction. In 2009, Southwest scored an 81—17 points higher than the industry average and considerably higher than other major competitors like USAir, my personal favorite for grumpy attendants and lost luggage. How do they do it? What makes Southwest better than the rest? The answer: the demand for change and the drive to win.

Rollin King and Herb Kelleher decided to make a different kind of airline—one for the common man. They started Southwest with a simple notion: Get passengers to their destinations when they want to get there, for the lowest price possible, and make sure passengers have a good time doing it. They would simplify and standardize operations, such as using just one plane configuration, allowing them to streamline costs, speed up flight turnaround times, and charge markedly lower fares. And they would hire energetic, self-confident, team-oriented younger staff with a sense of humor to offer friendly, fast, and reliable service. And for thirty-seven years, they have done just that. Southwest Airlines began operating in 1971 with four planes serving three cities (the Texas Triangle—Dallas, Houston, and San Antonio) and revenues of $2 million. Despite an onslaught of legal battles from their larger, more powerful competitors, Southwest prevailed and opened up the skies to millions of people who had previously considered air travel too expensive. The small-town Texas airline has grown to be one of America's largest carriers. Today, 100 million passengers a year fly Southwest to travel to sixty-six cities across the United States.

And it's not just the customers who are appreciative. In the process of doing a profile for CBS News, the correspondent observed the employees and found that something "unusual" was going on. "Everyone is happy. They all kiss and hug," even CEO Gary Kelly. Kelly says the

---

* One British airline is even contemplating charging for use of their restrooms. If they keep this up, pretty soon you'll have to bring your own toilet paper—and you'll be charged for the carry-on!

difference between his company and others is simple: "People working together, people lovin' each other, people respecting each other."[59] It's no surprise that Southwest's branding logos include a heart. In fact, it's smart. For them, flying really is a matter of the heart. Of love. Of passion. And you can tell that from every employee you meet. Libby Sartain, vice president of Southwest's People Department, looks for an employee whose commitment to the customer and the company is "a sense of mission, a sense that 'the cause' comes before their own needs."[60] Everyone from senior executives to baggage handlers has the freedom to make on-the-spot decisions. Employees are encouraged to be creative and "color outside the lines" in their work. They make improvements on their own initiative, serve customers in their own unique ways—singing, dancing, and cracking jokes—overtly shunning the rigid formality of their competitors. You can see it in their eyes and in their smiles. They truly *want* to be there, and they make *you* want to be there—or at least there versus on another airline. At other airlines, they *have* to be there.

Passion starts at the top—and it started from day one. Kelleher, part P. T. Barnum and part Warren Buffett, openly rejected the stuffy corporate style that had existed since the Wright brothers. They brought an outrageous sense of fun to the job that flows throughout the company. In 1972, his flight attendants wore tight pants instead of military-style uniforms to get attention. In 1992, rather than going to court over the rights to the airline slogan "Just Plane Smart," Kelleher agreed to settle the matter over a highly publicized and closely followed charity arm-wrestling match. He lost the match, but he was given rights to the slogan anyway—along with the goodwill of his employees, customers, and the flying public, which cannot be quantified in dollars and cents. Only on a Southwest Airlines flight will you hear attendants rapping the safety features of the plane to passengers. If country music is more your thing, there are flight attendants whose home-strung country songs describe the benefits of Southwest right before takeoff. No other company has employee-produced videos that routinely get hundreds of thousands of hits on YouTube.

But behind the free-spirit nature of the company and its leader is a smart, innovative business executive who is even willing to make personal sacrifices to see the company move forward. Southwest was the first airline to simplify its frequent-flyer program to credit you by the trip, not the amount of miles flown. It was also the first to offer ticket-less travel and senior discounts, Fun Fares, Fun Packs, and same-day airfreight delivery service. And when Southwest needed its pilots' union to agree to a five-year pay freeze, Kelleher took a five-year pay freeze too—earning his employees' respect by not asking them to do any-thing he wasn't willing to do himself. He figured it cost him $75 million to $100 million in compensation, but it bought him trust and five years of labor peace. And while the rest of the industry continues to figure out ways to nickel and dime consumers, Southwest's adver-tising campaign is based on what used to be a given—free luggage on every Southwest flight. Southwest put decals with the slogan "Free Bags Fly Here" on more than fifty airplanes. As someone who flies more than 250,000 miles a year, every year, I can tell you . . . passengers notice the difference.

There is something else different at Southwest besides being the fun, affordable, and reliable airline. They are profitable. For thirty-seven consecutive years, Southwest has posted an annual profit. Even with oil prices soaring and the market for air travel constricted, Southwest turns a profit while its competitors do not. Year after year, Southwest is rolling in the green while competitors bleed red. The passion derived from em-ployee respect, smart business acumen, and customer satisfaction has made Southwest Airlines an industry leader and an example for thou-sands of other companies looking to increase worker productivity and profitability.

As Southwest has proven, passion can be contagious, but you have to see and feel it in order to live it. No amount of coercion will inspire others to follow. Making passion contagious requires translating your emotion, your vision, and your commitment into a language they under-stand and want to hear.

SLEEP IS FOR THE DEAD

Meet Stephen Cloobeck, the personification of passion. Five years ago, he was the CEO of a vacation-ownership company that had one lo-cation: Las Vegas. Today, he heads the second-largest privately owned vacation-ownership company in the world—Diamond Resorts. He is so committed, so dedicated, so passionate about what he does that his business cards (with his personal e-mail address) are prominently placed at the front desks of all one hundred–plus resorts he owns around the world. At times, his BlackBerry rattles on the table for ten minutes straight with comments, requests, and demands—and he takes the time to respond to every last one.

Cloobeck's passion for customer satisfaction and service, supported by his boundless energy, drives him to surprise his staff by visiting all of his resorts unannounced. He makes a point to have face-to-face conversations with owners and members, and his late-night telephone conversations can last hours. He'll show up at the front desk unexpectedly and ask for ten keys, then personally inspect each room for cleanliness, sanitation, and decor to make sure housekeeping and maintenance are at their best at all times. He'll pitch in anywhere and do anything, from folding towels to modifying sales scripts. He attacks the day according to time zones, beginning before dawn with calls to Europe and winding up after midnight on the phone to Hawaii. He takes the time to know his staff by their first names, and they understand what he expects from them. As he says, "I can sleep when I'm dead."

Cloobeck clearly loves what he does. As he puts it, *"I'm like a kid in a candy store!"** His instinctive drive, coupled with a loving family, a firm workout schedule, and the ability to go full-tilt without much sleep, give him the energy to be a forceful leader.

Best of all, his passion is contagious. In fact, it's infectious.

As we go through the branding process, we are seeking to build a highly motivated group of individuals with one primary mandate—customer care—and I expect everyone fully on board We're in the business of providing consumers with effortless vacation experiences that get even better year after year. No matter how good we are now, we want to be even better tomorrow. I refuse to stand still. I want to know what else I can do for you.

---

* Several of the people interviewed for this book used the "kid in a candy store" analogy to describe just how much they enjoyed what they did. Almost no one talked about "work," or his "job," or even a "career."

Cloobeck has developed a management theory that will soon revolutionize the hospitality industry. He calls it "the meaning of yes," and it's predicated on the principle that the customer should be affirmed and respected—always. He's writing a book on it and I don't want to steal its message, but the meaning of yes" is passion at its very best.

If you own a company with offices in nearly every time zone around the globe, and you believe every e-mail and telephone call should be answered immediately, you have to be committed. That's what passion does. It turns a job into a joy. It turns work into wonder. And it's what keeps you going at two a.m. when others have given up.

So when you think about the *big* winners, people like Welch, Iacocca, Gates, Jobs, Dell, and Trump—success stories so big that they need no first name—ask yourself, what kept them going? Before they made it big and found themselves floating in enough money and power to make a king blush, what drove them to pursue a new vision, to make a new commitment? Of all of them, probably Donald Trump said it best: *"Without passion you don't have energy, without energy you have nothing."* One thing is for certain: it's not just the money that drives these success stories forward.

While this book has focused primarily on Washington and Wall Street, some of the most passionate people live and work in Hollywood. Even though it debuted more than thirty years ago, *Apocalypse Now*, the 1979 American epic war film set during the Vietnam War, is a perfect illustration of what people are prepared to do when they feel passionate about a project. In particular, Francis Ford Coppola's passion and persistence to see the dream he had hatched almost a decade earlier paid off in the end, but not without losing his mind, his body, and (almost) his life.

It wasn't supposed to be that way. In fact, with Coppola coming off back-to-back smash hits (*The Godfather* and *The Godfather: Part II*), *Apocalypse Now* was supposed to be a piece of cake. Still, warning signs were evident right from the start, beginning with casting. Steve McQueen was Coppola's first choice to play Captain Benjamin L. Willard, the lead role, a veteran officer who had been serving in Vietnam for three years. But McQueen wouldn't accept because he didn't want to leave America for seventeen weeks. Al Pacino was also offered the role but he, too, didn't want to be away for such a long time and was afraid of falling ill in the jungle, as he had in the Dominican Republic during the shooting of *The Godfather: Part II*. Jack Nicholson, Robert Redford, and James Caan were all approached to play either Colonel Walter Kurtz (eventually played by Marlon Brando) or Captain Willard. Finally, a young Harvey Keitel was pegged for the part, but within a few days of filming, Coppola flew back to Los Angeles and replaced him with Martin Sheen.

You're probably thinking, "Come on. How hard can it really be to make millions of dollars and star in a movie?" In this case, the work was insanely stressful. Here are just a few issues Coppola had to push through to make this film the masterpiece it is:

- Halfway through filming, a massive typhoon hit the Philippines, wrecked the sets, closed down production, and stranded the cast and crew in separate locations.
- Despite 24/7 surveillance by bodyguards, one day the entire payroll was stolen.
- Martin Sheen had a heart attack and struggled for a quarter of a mile to reach help.
- The Ferdinand Marcos–run Filipino government was fighting rebels in the area where filming was taking place and seized the film's helicopters and pilots just when they were needed to film the battle scenes.
- Brando showed up on set extremely overweight, which led Coppola to admit that he had no ending because Brando was, in Coppola's words, "too fat to play the scenes as written in the original script."

What was supposed to take seventeen weeks lasted sixteen months in the harsh Philippine jungle, not to mention three solid years of editing. The $14 million film ended up costing more than double ($31 million—think what *Avatar* would've cost in the 1970s), putting the director and the studio in serious financial jeopardy. And Coppola himself lost one hundred pounds thanks to the sweat and strain of the entire process (which may not have been such a bad thing—at least for the first eighty pounds or so). But he wouldn't give up, and he wouldn't give in.

Despite all of those setbacks, *Apocalypse Now* won the Cannes Palme d'Or, was nominated for the Academy Award for Best Picture, won the Golden Globe Award for Best Motion Picture Drama, and is on dozens of "Best Movie" lists of the century. It was even the first film released in the United States to play on Dolby Stereo 70 mm film with surround sound, which would later revolutionize the film industry. Without Coppola's endless drive to overcome mounting odds and unimaginable setbacks, he never would have achieved his vision for the story he wanted to tell: This epic tale would just have been another epic Hollywood failure.

VISUAL PASSION

Conveying your passion is just as much visual as it is verbal. What you're doing while you're talking is just as important as the words you're saying. The wrong visuals can completely undermine your message because they contradict your words or inhibit people from paying attention to you altogether.

When I was an adjunct professor at the University of Pennsylvania, I never used speeches or even notes when I taught a class. I wanted to make eye contact with every student at every moment. I never taught from the lectern. I preferred to wander up and down the rows so that people in the back of the class could feel connected and engaged. I still do, because part of the passion you bring to something is in getting listeners to move to the front of the room, and to the edges of their seats, either literally or figuratively. We all know the people who sit at the front of classes or presentations are the most engaged—and therefore the ones really doing most of the learning. It's hard to be passionate with three hundred students— especially if they're one hundred feet away from you. But if you're thrown into the mix—if you're right on top of them, or if they're right next to you—your proximity and intimacy become their own amplifiers.

My presentations to Congress are no different. I'm always moving around the room, walking back and forth, deliberately. I don't want to give members of Congress a chance to zone out, which they often do if there's an e-mail waiting for a response or a phone call waiting to be answered. Once they zone out, they may still be hearing, but they're not actually *listening*, which means they're not learning. This is the fault of the teacher, not the student. Passion is an obligation of any effective communicator. Frankly, that's why I'm a big fan of the Socratic method. When I'm making a presentation, a part of me wants the audience to be following me out of fear, afraid that I'm going to get right in front of them and challenge them. That's how I know they're hanging on every word. In order to accomplish this, I make eye contact with various audience members to connect with them in a meaningful way. You'll rarely see a truly impassioned speech delivered straight from a script. You can't really evoke strong emotions—the kind that genuinely rouse others' spirits—when you're busy turning pages.

Shortly after September 11, 2001, George W. Bush climbed up on a pile of smoldering rubble at Ground Zero. He had a bullhorn in one hand and his arm around the shoulders of a rescue worker who had been clearing debris looking for survivors. He addressed the crowd that had gathered around him to give them support and encouragement in a time of unimaginable suffering and loss. As he started to speak, a man yelled from the crowd, "We can't hear you!" President Bush paused a moment and said, "I can hear you; the rest of the world hears you. And the people who knocked these buildings down will hear all of us soon."[61]

Regardless of what you thought of President Bush at the time, or what you think of him now, you probably remember that moment favorably. He captured what Americans wanted to feel and hear at that critical moment. It was one of those rare examples in American life when our commander in chief was able to inspire us—to take his passion and emotion and transform it into words that genuinely moved us. If he had delivered that line as part of prepared remarks, it would have come off as contrived. It had to be off-the-cuff, spontaneous, and completely unexpected. It caught everyone off guard and allowed us to connect with him in a way we hadn't been able to before—or since. It was a powerful, passionate moment that still resonates with us today.

Body language is another key visual component of passion. The way you move your arms and hands, the way you walk around the room, and the way you stand all contribute to the passion in your message—and the amount of passion you evoke in others. You cannot be passionate with your hands in your pockets or with your arms folded across your chest. Those poses create walls, pushing people away from you when you want them to draw near and listen.

This is particularly problematic in the business community. Many CEOs have horrible body language that they use to make it clear that they own you, not the other way around; they think they're demonstrating control. What they don't realize is that they're undermining their credibility with the audience by putting barriers between themselves and everyone in the room. This disconnect often comes during the question-and-answer sessions of meetings, which typically is the best time to demonstrate passion, because that's their chance for spontaneous one-on-one communication. But the minute you fold your arms, the receptivity of your audience dies. It's defensive. This body language says "Don't you dare challenge me." GM's former CEO Fritz Henderson was a solid leader and communicator, but every time he crossed his arms, people saw a man who didn't care what others thought. He turned people off without even realizing it. When he closed himself off and looked away, many people actually thought that he was lying—when he wasn't.

Another visual no-no is the finger wag. Next time you turn on the TV and see a politician speaking at a podium, see how often he or she wags a finger at the camera. That's not passion; that's lecturing. Passionate people—people who truly care about and believe in what they're saying—don't just use their fingers to tell a story. They use their hands in a full field of motion to help tell the story. They talk with their arms fully outstretched, palms pointing upward because it's embracing, uplifting, and authoritative. They create a compelling visual that draws you in and makes you pay attention.

When using images in your messaging, the most essential element you can have is the single-shot visual—a picture so visceral that it immediately conjures such an intense emotional reaction that you cannot look away. Think of the images you saw of the people in New Orleans after Hurricane Katrina and in Haiti after the earthquake—the suffering, the misery, the hardship—all told from one camera, one lens, one angle, one person. Those images made you want to take action. My publisher, Hyperion, crafted a book cover for a book about Darfur that featured the haunting face of a girl with bright green eyes across the entire front jacket. The visual was so mesmerizing to me that I picked up the book and began to take it table to table to ask people whether the book title, *Not on Our Watch: The Mission to End Genocide in Darfur and*

LUNTZ LESSONS

THE PERFECT PASSIONATE VISUAL

1. Less is more. One photo can be better than a montage.
2. You can't look away. It is so compelling that it demands focus and concentration.
3. Connect emotionally as well as intellectually.
4. The picture alone communicates a message without any words necessary.
5. What minimal words are used make you want to learn more and do more.
6. Black-and-white images are just as powerful as those in full color.

Beyond, or the book jacket intrigued them more. Unanimously, they chose the book jacket. It evoked a passion among those who saw the picture that made them want to help her and others like her. It connected on an emotional level and was a call to action. A picture is really worth ten thousand words.

Conversely, those who show the least visual passion are the organizations that run ads containing lists of people who have endorsed some statement, commitment, or cause. You've seen them—the so-called phone book ads—with dozens of faceless names that no one ever reads except the people whose names are listed. Let me be clear: a laundry list of names is not passion.

PASSION PERSONIFIED

The biggest difference between winners and everyone else is in how they communicate their passion to the people around them. Since I began working with and talking to America's most successful politicians, CEOs, business leaders, and entertainment moguls nearly twenty years ago, the only thing as consistent as their passion is their ability to inspire a passion in the people around them.

One of my most passionate clients is Lowe's Home Improvement. In

2008, I was invited to attend the annual store manager meeting at the swank Mandalay Bay in Las Vegas (and really, who can turn down a trip to Vegas?). All the top executives were in attendance, along with regional and district managers, as well as their 1,500-plus store managers. The energy in the room was palpable. It was spellbinding. Every session began with the Lowe's cheer (which begins the day at every Lowe's store—get there early enough and you'll hear it through the doors), and that was the low point of the day! Imagine the emotional impact of hearing more than two thousand people shout out the store letters, including an "oomphhh" as they drive a clenched fist and raised elbow down, representing the apostrophe in Lowe's. It felt more like a Dallas Cowboys tailgate party than a corporate seminar. Then, as the meeting went on, they invited people to the stage and gave them awards for their achievements. Managers received awards for the most sales, the greatest store improvements, the best customer satisfaction, the most store savings, and so on. The reason the energy became so infectious was because as one person won, everyone won. It really was that powerful. You could feel it lifting the room.

Lowe's makes passion contagious. By singling out a few dozen winners and lauding them for their achievements, they turned the entire room of three thousand participants into winners by creating a shared experience to which everyone in the room could connect. And unlike many companies that might have their annual meetings in a place like Las Vegas just to play, the people at Lowe's worked for it. They were there early in the morning and didn't leave until late at night. There was no gambling, no late-night partying, no messing around. They were there for a purpose: to build up their team, foster their communal passion, and empower everyone there to help keep the company—and one another—growing and achieving.

What makes Lowe's and companies like it so good at communicating their passion is that they're powerful storytellers. They don't just tell you that what you're doing is important. They don't just ask you to work as hard as you can, or issue the infuriating challenge to do "more with less." And they don't just ask you to trust that they will change the way people remodel homes. The reason they don't do those things is because simply *telling* people doesn't work. In order to really motivate your workforce to care about what you care about, you have to give them reasons that connect with *them*, not just with you. They have to feel an emotional response to what you say, not just a rational one.

Another company that has mastered the art of passion is Amway. In fact, you could say that without a mixture of passion and patriotism, Amway might not even exist today. Founder Richard DeVos told me this story, which sums up how to use passion to rally your people. He explains:

> In 1959, Castro took over Cuba. So Castro just celebrated his fiftieth year, as did we, and at that time the same mood was in this country that we have today. Freedom and enterprise are dead, capitalism is gone, and socialism is the wave of the future. Remember, this was the early 1960s. It was just a time of change. And we decided that we didn't agree with that; we didn't like that. So we began to make Amway a campaigning point for freedom and free enterprise. All my speeches in those days were about America and why our American system was better. I would say to our distributors when I went on the road to speak, "Do you want me to talk about Amway?" and they would say, "No, talk about why we have got to fight for freedom and a free enterprise system." So all of my speeches were about why free enterprise works because that's what motivated them, that they were a part of something to preserve and protect America.
>
> And I think it worked because people want to be part of a cause. I have always said that a business is only as good as what it represents. You need something to stand for. If it's going to be a great company it's got to have a reason to exist beyond profit making. Our passion came from the desire to fight for freedom. But you also get passion when you put people together. It's hard to be passionate alone, but when you get people in a big room and everybody is cheering, and everybody feels like you do, your passion gets aroused. It's like being in a football stadium; you don't cheer quite that loud at home watching TV, but when you get into a stadium, somehow it captures you.

That's the kind of passion that turns ordinary businesspeople into extraordinary fighters for a better future.

Passion sustains us. Logic, as powerful as it is, can take people only so far. Eventually all rational people will go through a basic cost-benefit analysis in their heads. They will inevitably ask themselves, "How does this directly benefit me?" You might ask them to give up large chunks of their personal time, family time, and even financial stability . . . for what? For some crazy vision you have about reinventing the personal computer or getting one million people to sign a petition?

Few people are willing to say to themselves, "Consequences be damned." But those that do can literally change the world. If you don't believe me, just ask Rupert Murdoch. *"We put a lot of passion into getting The Wall Street Journal on the iPad and making it look better than anybody else,"* he recounted. *"We had seven or eight technical people who worked eighteen hours a day. They moved into town, into a cheap hotel, didn't shave, didn't shower, just worked for three weeks, eighteen hours a day, and the result was beautiful. It was certainly better than anybody else."* I don't care what anyone says, no one works on something for eighteen hours a day for three weeks straight just for the money.

Quitting—and losing—are part of our nature and ingrained in our genetic makeup. When faced with a stressful or dangerous situation, we're biologically programmed for "fight or flight," to either stand tall and handle the threat, or to turn tail and run like the wind.[62] We choose one of those responses based on a quick calculation of the risks and rewards involved—can I take this guy or will he take me? The same is true when it comes to situations that start to overwhelm or threaten us professionally—am I going to lose everything I've worked so hard for on someone else's big bet? If the answer is yes, get ready for letters of resignation and U-Haul trucks speeding out of town.

That's why being able to tell the story that's inside you, the story of what's driving you to believe so strongly in what you're doing, is critical to turning others into true believers. Without a story to establish a new frame of reference, there's nothing to hold on to. There's no vision, no emotion, and no commitment driving them toward a "big win." As any hopeless romantic can tell you, the heart is often stronger than the brain, which leads to the late-night driveway sonnets any person in their right mind wouldn't be caught dead performing. The same holds true when it comes to passion and logic, business and politics.

But again, don't just take my word for it. I had the chance to interview

Arnold Schwarzenegger for this book, and of course I seized the opportunity. Truth is, I followed him into a small restaurant in Brentwood, the elite section of Los Angeles, and begged him for five minutes. He gave me a lot more—not just in time but in wisdom. You know you've made it when people start talking about amending the U.S. Constitution so you can run for president one day. In what was one of my most intriguing and engaging interviews, he really opened up about how passion had helped him achieve so much and get to where he is today. I have included much of it here, unedited, because I think there's a lot to learn both from his challenges and his accomplishments:

Passion is something that comes from your gut. It's something that you say, "I love it, I need it, I want it, and I can't be without it." I knew that if I wanted to be a champion, that the potential was more in lifting because when I lifted, my body responded very quickly. I knew that I had the potential to become a world champion. So I was passionate about it, and I loved going to the gym. I loved lifting weights, I loved the way my body responded, and I loved learning about lifting.

Then I started to get passionate about acting, and I started going to acting school. I took private lessons. I took accent removal classes. People were scared of my accent because it sounded kind of evil. So I had to take voice lessons, and all of those things to get rid of the accent; not as much to get rid of it as to tone it down and to be more understandable.

I worked my way up in the acting profession. I had a very clear vision that I wanted to be who Clint Eastwood was, Charles Bronson was, I wanted to be on top. I felt the ladder is empty on top, and full on the bottom. Why compete on the bottom when the top of the ladder is much emptier? And there was much more room for another person there.

I put 100 percent of my marketing skills into promoting my body building and promoting my movies so people would buy into it. I knew that it's one thing to get Joe Namath into a movie—he already had a huge name. I had to create a name for me first, even though I was a world champion body builder. So this is why I did Pumping Iron, Stay Hungry, *and those kinds of movies that relied on the body. And even the Conan movie,* The Villain, *all of those movies relied on my body. But then eventually, I bridged over, through substance, to make the body become secondary, like Terminator, Commando—movies that did not rely on the body that much anymore. They relied much more on the acting skill. So that's how I bridged from one career to another. I felt very passionate, very determined, and failure was not an option.*

My third career was in politics. I felt I had run my course in acting. I wanted to take on another challenge. That's why, when the recall came up, I said, "This is a perfect moment." So I decided to go on the Tonight Show to announce that I was going to run for governor of California. We didn't have a team together or anything, but this was my new goal. And I jumped into that again with the same passion, not so much for being governor, but passion for public service.

The thing that made me a success is passion and loving what I'm doing. Never looking at it as, "Oh my God, it's a job." It was always a pleasure to do it, whatever I was doing. It was always a fire in the belly, which comes from growing up in poverty, and growing up with nothing, and wanting something out of my life, of wanting more than nothing.

I know what you're thinking: Arnold had his accent *toned down?* Who knew? But what's more important is to know that his is a life that is defined by passion—at every phase and before every challenge. Learn from his example. Fight the urge to give up. At some point, mere mortals would have thrown in the towel. To quote Jimmy Dugan in *A League of Their Own:* "It's supposed to be hard. If it wasn't hard, everyone would do it. The hard . . . is what makes it great."

WHEN PASSION BACKFIRES

I've spent much of this chapter explaining why passion is so important to winners and how they're able to spread their passion to others. But passion (like success, or an all-you-can-eat buffet) is a double-edged sword. When passion's leash is taken off and it's allowed to go too far, bad things happen. That's the kind of passion that can completely undermine your efforts and, in some cases, destroy your career.

On January 19, 2004, Howard Dean's presidential campaign suffered a staggering blow when a last-minute surge by rivals John Kerry and John Edwards led to a disappointing third-place finish for Dean in the 2004 Iowa Democratic caucuses. Dean, who had been suffering from a severe bout of the flu for several days, attended a caucus night rally for his volunteers at the Val Air Ballroom in West Des Moines, Iowa. He delivered a rousing concession speech aimed at cheering up those in attendance—but got a lot more than he bargained for. Dean was shouting over the cheers of his enthusiastic audience, but the crowd noise was being filtered out by his microphone, leaving only his full-throated exhortations audible to the television viewers. To those at home, he seemed to raise his voice out of sheer (and unwarranted) emotion. It was a visual nightmare as well. He began his speech with a flushed-red face, clenching his teeth as he rolled up his sleeves and started belting out why the night was not a total loss.

And then came the so-called scream that was aired repeatedly in the days and weeks following the caucus:

> *Not only are we going to New Hampshire, Tom Harkin, we're going to South Carolina and Oklahoma and Arizona and North Dakota and New Mexico, and we're going to California and Texas and New York. . . . And we're going to South Dakota and Oregon and Washington and Michigan, and then we're going to Washington, D.C., to take back the White House! Yeah!!!*

That final "Yeah!" was shouted in an especially unusual tone, one Dean later said was due to the cracking of his hoarse voice. The incident is now known in American political jargon as the "Dean Scream" or the "I Have a Scream" speech. Dean conceded that the speech did not project the best image, jokingly referring to it as a "crazy, red-faced rant" on the *Late Show with David Letterman*. In an interview later that week with Diane Sawyer, he said he was "a little sheepish . . . but I'm not apologetic." (Big mistake: passionate people are allowed to cross the line occasionally, as long as an apology follows.) Sawyer and many others in the national broadcast news media later expressed some regret about how they covered the story. In fact, CNN issued a public apology, and admitted in a statement that they indeed may have "overplayed" the incident. The incessant replaying of the "Dean Scream" by the press launched a heated debate on the topic of whether Dean was the victim of media bias. The scream scene was shown more than six hundred times by cable and broadcast news networks in just four days following the incident, a number that does not include talk shows and local news broadcasts.

But here's the important part. Those who were in the actual audience that day insist that they were not aware of the infamous "scream" until they returned to their hotel rooms and saw it on TV. Dean said after the general election in 2004 that his high-tech noise-canceling microphone picked up only his voice and did not also capture the loud cheering he received from the audience as a result of the speech. But it was the television audience that mattered. While media pundits had a field day analyzing Dean's transformation into the Incredible Hulk on national television, what the American people saw was even worse. They saw passion explode into an uncomfortable display of apparent lunacy, and Dean's campaign was on life support from then on.

The "Dean Scream" is truly important because it exemplifies passion run amok. The mixture of the visual (red face, hair askew, crowds chanting, and so on) and the verbal was simply too much for too many people. Jump on YouTube and watch the video when you get a chance. It's a lesson of what not to do.

Passion is like fire—it can heat your home or burn it down. Keep it bottled up inside and you're finished. But capture it and channel it toward your goals and you can accomplish anything. Here's a checklist of what to say—and do—to help you win.

THE LEXICON OF PASSION

1. Imagine
2. Let me fight for you
3. Believe in better
4. Celebrate
5. Freedom
6. Life is an adventure. . . . Will you join me?
7. Nothing is more important than ___

WORDS THAT WORK

This is my favorite lexicon list because the words are so aspirational and inspirational. These words truly define the difference between ordinary and extraordinary.

"Imagine" allows the listener to consider life after the paradigm shift in their own terms, and allows the speaker to paint in vivid pictures how life will be different. When you ask someone to imagine something, you're halfway to getting them not only to want it, but also to embrace it.

"Let me fight for you" demonstrates that not only are you an advocate, but also an active participant in making something happen. It is the manifestation of an extraordinary personal commitment that creates an immediate and often unbreakable human bond. This phrase would have been too strong and, frankly, not credible just a few years ago. Today, however, we welcome those in business who are willing to put it all on the line for us.

"Believe in better" was a phrase created by James Murdoch, Chairman and CEO, Europe and Asia, News Corp., to describe the products and services provided by Sky, the world's most innovative satellite television provider. It is an overt rejection of the status quo in favor of guaranteed improvement—and it is one of the most powerful corporate slogans I have ever encountered.

"Celebrate" is a relatively new way to convey appreciation. It communicates a visual as well as verbal message of approval and gratitude. It is also a more innovative way to say that something is great. For example, "We celebrate inclusion" not only means we believe in it, but that we champion it.

"Freedom" is not just for politics anymore. Appealing to people's desire for more freedom, particularly as so many people now believe that their freedoms are being curtailed, is a powerful way to bring people to their feet and get them to demand something better. Freedom is more than just a core American value. It is part of who we are as individuals, and anything that promotes freedom—either in politics, business, or day-to-day life—will generate an impassioned response.

"Life is an adventure. . . . Will you join me?" is a good example of a specific call to action, an approach that nearly all winners employ. While

LUNTZ LESSONS

PASSION IN A PRESENTATION

1. **Explain why.**
   Start with a series of rhetorical questions designed to elicit an emotional response and explain why your mission in life should be their mission in life.

2. **The physical delivery is just as important as the verbal message.**
   Don't use podiums that create a visual barrier. Outstretch your arms to visually embrace and envelop the audience. Always keep your hands *out* of your pockets. Don't use a prepared text—just you and your audience connected by your voice and your presence.

3. **Voice volume variation is essential.**
   Passionate presentations can be unexpectedly quiet. Drop your voice when your message is most important, and then rise to a crescendo to indicate the end of an idea. Never shout—that is fake passion.

4. **Speech must have a cadence.**
   Whether it's words that rhyme or have the same number of syllables, or the repetition of a specific word three or more times, these are all rhetorically engaging and motivating ways to address an audience.

5. **Tell a story.**
   Passion requires more than just a beginning, a middle, and an end. It requires verbal illustration and metaphors. It needs human context.

some people prefer the word *discovery,* adventure generates a more favorable response because it conveys excitement as well as wonder. But it's the personal invitation to experience something new that makes this phrase so powerful in generating passion.

"Nothing is more important than ___" This is not a phrase that can be used capriciously or too often. But in the right context, it conveys the intensity of your passion for a subject.

9

PERSUASION

Building reputation and earning trust in politics and business

Tell me and I forget. Teach me and I remember. Involve me and I learn.
—BEN FRANKLIN

Thaw with her gentle persuasion is more powerful than Thor with his hammer. The one melts, the other breaks into pieces.
—HENRY DAVID THOREAU

Words have power. They can hit like a fist . . . especially if you write them on your fist.
—STEPHEN COLBERT

PERSUASION IS AN ART

I learned persuasion from my parents. More accurately, I learned how to persuade because of my parents.

My mom is the traditional Jewish mother in every sense. During my childhood, she worried about me every hour of every day: was I eating the right foods, was I doing my homework, were my friends a good influence, and was I getting enough sleep? No detail of my life was too small for her to obsess over, and nothing was beyond her control. A straight-A student in high school and college, she gave up what would have been a rewarding career in business to devote herself to making sure I would eventually become a successful adult. I would have never written books if it weren't for my mother. Writing doesn't come easily to me, and I have struggled over every page. But I pursued it because she instilled in me a passion not only to learn, but also to explain and educate.

My father was exactly the opposite. If my mother was serious, my father was humorous. If she was driven, he was relaxed. If she was all about knowledge and culture, he was all about having fun with his son. My desire to entertain comes from him, as does my penchant for mischief. I once told an ill-conceived joke live on Fox News to commemorate the anniversary of his death—because I knew that wherever he was, he'd be laughing.*

I have introduced you to my parents not because they best describe who I am, but because they are the reason for what I do. I discovered early in life that if I went to my mother for money to buy popcorn, candy, baseball cards, or anything fun, the answer would be no. Conversely, if I wanted to stay up late to watch something about politics or history, my father would tell me to ask my mother. The only way to get what I wanted was to know which parent to approach (never simultaneously) and which argument to make.

I wasn't the only person who learned the craft of persuasion from his parents. Says Steve Wynn:

> My father owned a bingo hall. That was his business. Every summer from when I was sixteen, my job was to help him. As I got older, I began to call the games. My father was a very good bingo announcer and a very good extemporaneous speaker. He taught me how to speak to a thousand people and how to have rhythm in my voice, because when people are playing bingo, they play to a rhythm. And if you don't have that rhythm, it upsets them.

---

* "If Hillary Clinton had won in 2008, she would not have been the first female president. Jimmy Carter was our first female president." That joke led to my only reprimand at Fox News—to date.

My father also taught me the importance of how to emphasize something. My dad said, "The only way that you can ever emphasize anything, Steve, is to pause before and after the important thing that you want to say. Never raise your voice. If something's really important, lower it, and leave space on either side." People listen more carefully when you talk softly. The louder you talk, the more they turn up their resistor.

That's also true in design. You have to leave space if you want something to be pretty and appreciated. If you want people to look at something, you have to give it room to breathe. These lessons that I learned as a kid calling numbers in a bingo hall are remarkably relevant in composition of images and in the way you talk to people, the way you communicate.

It may be counterintuitive, but Steve Wynn's three rules of verbal and visual persuasion are right on:

1. Silence says more than noise.
2. Rhythm is more effective than random.
3. Open space allows you to see more than clutter.

In his obituary, Roger Ailes will be celebrated for creating and running the most successful cable news network in television history, but he also wrote the seminal book on public communication: *You Are the Message.* A media savant, he guided three candidates to the presidency, starting at the tender age of twenty-six. He is notoriously critical of the elites in American society for their inability to talk or lead, and he isn't shy in his explanation:

There are some good CEO communicators, but they're frightened. They don't get paid to talk. They get paid to think and make money, and so they have never focused on speech as a requirement for their paycheck or their bonus. They have to hit a set of numbers. And if they hit it, they win, and if they don't hit it, they don't. Good words can't hide bad performance.

The most successful people don't set out to communicate. They set out to motivate. They don't want to change your opinion. They want to change your life. They don't want supporters. They want disciples. Nowhere is this more evident than in the world of retail, and no company better reflects passion and intensity than Amway. With 13,000 employees, three million independent business owners (IBOs) operating in dozens of countries, Amway is a retail juggernaut. Founder Rich DeVos explains that the secret to the enduring success of the company, created more than a half-century ago, is their ability to *"teach"* its universal appeal:

> *You're not going to achieve anything if you don't learn how to explain what you do. That's how everybody learns, that's how you move people, and it's the only way you get anything done. We tried to build our business so that anybody can do it and anybody can teach it. It isn't until you teach it that you learn it.*
>
> *When you bring somebody else in is when you come to know it the best. Now you have someone that you're responsible for, they look up to you, you're a leader, and suddenly you have more responsibilities in your life. That's always it—training up. The person who brings you in is responsible for you, he's your personal motivator, your personal counselor, and encourages you. I would always find somebody who stuttered, who didn't dress in the best suit, who didn't speak the best, and everybody would say, "If he can do it, I can do it." People are so doubtful of what they can do, so insecure in their lives. We build confidence.*

So how does perfection meet persuasion? Winners don't win by simply telling people "This is the way it is" or "This is how it's going to be." They convince us that what they're saying is true, that they can be trusted, so that we willingly follow their lead. Thanks to his powers of persuasion, Winston Churchill sold the British the stoicism and determination they needed to triumph over Nazi Germany. Even if they were scared as hell, they didn't show it. Don't underestimate how hard a "sell" this would have been for Churchill. It's easy to armchair quarterback this from the twenty-first century. We know how the war ended—the good guys won. But if you lived in 1940 Britain, with Hitler on the march, Europe in the hands of the Nazis, and tens of thousands of planes, warships, rockets, and more pointed at your tiny island . . . would you be inclined to believe a politician who said it was all going to be OK?

Churchill knew the power of language, and the determination of his people, and marshaled his best arguments and delivery to galvanize them. Britain was clearly overmatched, but he utilized Britain's greatest weakness—its size and vulnerability—to his persuasion advantage. The truth is, the British people long relished their ability to do great things of global consequence *in spite* of their relatively small homeland. It was that driving spirit that built an empire. So when it came time to defend that island, when public spirits were lowest, Churchill tapped into a deep-running national current and went on the offense:

> *We shall defend our island whatever the cost may be; we shall fight on beaches, landing grounds, in fields, in streets and on the hills. We shall never surrender and even if, which I do not for the moment believe, this island or a large part of it were subjugated and starving, then our empire beyond the seas, armed and guarded by the British Fleet, will carry on the struggle until in God's good time the New World with all its power and might, sets forth to the liberation and rescue of the Old.*

Churchill's use of anaphora—the repetition of words or phrases at the beginning of sentences—emphasized his commitment to winning the war no matter what. He repeats the words *we shall* ten times in the full speech. This is the linguistic equivalent of persistence. It demands you take notice. It forces you to keep reading, to keep listening until the very end. It carries you along in a way that ordinary speech cannot. Similarly, Dr. Martin Luther King's "I Have a Dream" speech repeats the titular phrase eight times to the same effect.

Two hundred and fifty years ago, America's founding fathers convinced us that life, liberty, and the pursuit of happiness were inalienable human rights. The nineteenth-century abolitionists convinced us that slavery was an affront to both human dignity and the will of God. Thomas Edison convinced us that electricity would fill our future with light and sound. Henry Ford convinced us that gas-powered automobiles would do away with the horse and buggy, while allowing us to move around more freely than ever before. In more recent times, people like Bill Gates (Microsoft), Steve Jobs (Apple), Larry Page and Sergey Brin (Google), Jeff Bezos (Amazon), and Mark Zuckerberg (Facebook) have convinced us that computers, technology, and the Internet will dramatically revolutionize the way people around the world shop, entertain themselves, find information, interact with one another, and conduct business. They listened to what was missing, paid attention to what we wanted, and came back to us with messages and products that resonated deep within our psyches. They connected with us, and because they were able to do so, we trusted them, we listened to them, and we eventually bought what they were selling.

Because they believed so strongly in what they were telling us, we were inclined to trust and believe in them as well. That's no small point. Trust is an integral part of communication and persuasion, and you can't really build trust if people don't think you actually believe in what you're saying. *"For me, the most important element in persuasion is that you really need to believe what you're trying to persuade people to share,"* real estate mogul Mort Zuckerman told me:

> I always liked urban life, so I went into real estate. I don't know how else to put it, but it just felt like, "Hey, I'm home. I love this world. I have a feel for it." Every urban center I had ever been in felt just right for me, and somehow that comfort level must have just come through. I actually believed what I was doing and in what I was saying. I wasn't phony. I wasn't acting. It was just who I was and how I genuinely felt.
>
> In the real estate world, you have to gain the confidence of people in the things you are going to do. You have to persuade the lender that you're going to complete the building, and you're going to lease the building. You have to persuade a tenant that the building will get done in time for them to move in on an appropriate schedule. And to some extent, I guess, language does convey that sense. It inspires confidence.

He's right; confidence is a critical component of persuasion. If people don't think you say what you mean or mean what you say, they have no reason whatsoever to listen to a word you say. Without confidence, you're not a leader. You're just someone standing at the front of the room who talks a lot.

I asked NBA commissioner David Stern why he thought confidence was so important when trying to persuade people to follow you. His answer demonstrates why building trust within your own team is so important:

The most important thing a coach can do, and different coaches do it in different ways, is to inspire confidence in their players, so that when he says to his team, "Do this and we will win," the players do it because they expect to win. And when they expect to win, they perform better. Some coaches do it by being disciplinarians, and others do it in a gentler manner. But what I think all of them are doing is inspiring confidence in their leadership. When it gets down to crunch time and the game is on the line, the coach says, "OK, we're going to run this play," or "We're going to have this kind of defense," the team that says, "Coach knows what he's doing—if we do it, we're going to win," invariably does better than a team that says, "What are we doing? Why is he playing this? Let's change the play." It's about the inspiration of confidence whether you're leading troops into battle, or a basketball team, or a corporate industry.

PERSUASION GONE WRONG

The line between what constitutes a winning and losing sports team and a successful or failing corporation is remarkably thin. In both cases, you're trying to put up the numbers playing within a set of someone else's rules against opponents trying to win at your expense. That's another reason I've spent so much time using parallels from all different facets of life—sports, entertainment, politics, business, and so on—because these are all human creations which are governed by the same laws of human nature. What works in one field will often work in another, not by coincidence but by design.

People who fail will give you ten reasons why. Successful people will give you one or two reasons why they succeeded. But winners, they'll tell you how lucky they were. Almost without exception, every person in this book attributed at least some of their success to luck. Says Sheryl Sandberg of Facebook, *"If you start to think you have all the answers or misinterpret your luck for skill, you'll stop learning."*

But what happens when your luck runs out?

You can't write a book about winners without a conversation with New York mayor and multi-billionaire Mike Bloomberg. While I'd like to report that he has a set of clearly defined rules for success, Bloomberg credits *"luck"* and *"being in the right place at the right time"* more than any particular life lesson. Confident and irreverent, he even downplays the role of language in the race to the top. But while Bloomberg isn't particularly driven by communication, he does quickly identify the political pitfalls when good words go horribly wrong.

> *When you start out, you don't always recognize the code words that different groups in the population may have. You just can't know the entire history of a particular word or phrase. There are things you can say, a word or phrase that already has a life of its own. We had a fire commissioner who was a major union leader who had famously said "suck it up." It had been unpopular when he said it, and it was unpopular when I repeated it. If I had known that, I never would have used it. When governing, words matter more because the actual product is harder to define. In business, it's easier because you're selling something people can see.*

Financial crisis? Worst recession in decades? Americans losing their homes? Don't blame me! I'm just a humble banker "doing God's work," Goldman Sachs CEO Lloyd Blankfein seemed to say in an interview with the British newspaper the *Sunday Times* in November 2009.[63] If it weren't so incomprehensibly repugnant, it might almost be amusing.

In late 2008, as the Bush presidency was winding down and the Obamas were picking out White House china patterns, Wall Street's Goldman Sachs bellied up to the federal trough for a $10 billion taxpayer-funded feast to stay afloat. Basically, the boys at Goldman were caught unprepared to handle the financial consequences of their AIG-insured credit default swaps. Consumers were overleveraged. Banks were overleveraged. The seams came undone, the economy fell apart, and the venerable Goldman was in trouble.

From a communication and perception perspective, the way Goldman has handled itself since its halcyon days came to an end in 2008 is instructive. Showing at least a shred of respect for the way average Americans felt about the financial sector bailout, Goldman (and many other banks) effectively scrapped executive-level bonuses that year, including Mr. Blankfein's, and drastically slashed everyone else's. Smart. Total compensation for Goldman Sachs employees in 2008 averaged $364,000 per person, down 54 percent from the year prior. Goldman's CFO, David

Viniar, told reporters that the firm would pay more of its people with stock so employees would be more invested in the company's long-term growth and success.[64]

By summer of 2009, Goldman had already paid back the $10 billion loan from the government, with interest—23 percent, in fact.[65] Things seemed to be looking up for the investment firm. Then, somewhat unexpectedly, Goldman was plagued by an embarrassment of riches—literally. According to the *New York Times,* "Goldman posted the richest quarterly profit in its 140-year history [in July 2009] and, to the envy of its rivals, announced that it had earmarked $11.4 billion so far [that] year to compensate its workers."[66] Talk about bad timing.

Normally, record profits would be good news. Remember, people only went ballistic on the record oil-company profits in 2008 because gas prices were at all-time highs. Had Americans not been getting hit so hard at the pump, few would have complained. Corporate profits are really only a perception problem when they can be tied back to some form of "harm" imposed on the larger society. Whether that harm is real is immaterial. Record earnings announcements when the public is already angry at your company or industry is like dumping a bucket of chum into shark-infested waters: the sharks, or senators in this case, will soon be circling.

And circle they did. "People all over this country feel an incredible frustration that they are seeing their neighbors lose their jobs and the government is helping companies like AIG and Goldman Sachs, and then the next thing, they are reporting huge profits and huge compensation," howled Ohio Democratic senator Sherrod Brown. "I think people are incredulous that this system is working this way." In response, not to the senator directly but to the situation, Goldman's CFO said, "We understand that we are living in a very uncertain world where a lot of people are out of work, but pay increases were justified."[67]

That's the sound of public anger striking a tin ear. To the vast majority of the American people, we are in an "uncertain world where a lot of people are out of work" because companies like Goldman Sachs played fast and loose with other people's money, in a promiscuous display of reckless abandon. Not surprisingly, that makes for a less-than-ideal canvas upon which to paint a portrait of faux contrition. And while no one begrudges a company that pays its employees for doing their jobs well, outlandish bonuses worth more than most people will earn in their entire lives were never going to sit well with a public that just bailed out the industry responsible for our economic smackdown. No one at Goldman, or any other Wall Street titan, should have been surprised when congressmen like Dennis Kucinich proposed heavy taxes on such bonuses upon hearing the "good news." They were lucky not to have been tarred and feathered.

To no one's surprise, Goldman Sachs went on to have a banner year. By early 2010, it was widely reported that the company earned a princely $13.4 billion in profit. Clearly they missed the memo re: the Great Recession. Compensation was back up, only slightly below the record levels set in 2007. Again sent to face the wolves, in January 2010, Goldman CFO David Viniar said, "We tried to strike the right balance, and we think the message that we'll be able to send to our people with the compensation is that they had a great year and they're being paid well and fairly, but within the context of what's going on in the world."[68]

Only to a Wall Street executive could an average salary of $498,000 per employee be in "context of what's going on in the world," at a time when the national unemployment rate stood at 9.7 percent and a third of Americans were working more hours but bringing home no additional income. Speaking to Charlie Rose just a few months later, Goldman Sachs CEO Lloyd Blankfein delivered this gem when asked why the American public was so outraged:

> I think the financial system failed the American people. I think people on Wall Street did well, and carried themselves in a very proud way. Some might say a haughty way when things were going well. [They] talked about the contributions they were making to the wider society, and to the economy, and to the country and to the world.[69]

It's as if Mr. Blankfein had no clue why average, everyday Americans were so angry with an industry that spent money like gambling addicts trapped in a casino, then came begging for a handout when the tab arrived. Perhaps buying another house in the Hamptons with what looked like taxpayer money while Lisa in Kansas was working nights to keep food on the table could have had something to do with it.

If it seems like I'm angry with these big financial firms and their messaging, I am. I've worked with some of these leaders. In private, they are among the most charitable people I know, but in public they act like they just don't care about what the rest of the country thinks unless it threatens their seven-figure bonuses. And as a communication professional and a businessman myself, I find this infuriating. Profit is profit, and you shouldn't be ashamed of it. Profit made America the strongest economy on the globe. But you have to remember your audience and their day-to-day experience with home values plummeting and stock values at 20 percent less than just a few years ago. No matter how well-intentioned you are, ignoring the impact of your words only hurts your own reputation and credibility.

Goldman Sachs did a particularly handsome job of bungling their communication about bonuses, profits, and bailouts. To hear Mr. Blankfein tell it, the real problem was that the Wall Street crowd simply bragged too much. In fact, his remarks almost made you feel as if he chalked up America's anger at the financial industry to envy.

The biggest problem with claiming to do *"God's work"* is that man is not God. And for many, bankers are barely man. A statement like Mr. Blankfein's will, more often than not, become an albatross around the speaker's neck. It epitomizes arrogance, avarice, and wanton disregard for the millions of Americans whose hard-earned tax dollars kept Mr. Blankfein's golden ship afloat. Communication that disrespects, disregards, and degrades honest, hard-working Americans is tantamount to giving them the finger from your limo as you're driven to your private jet. In the end, however, the people will prevail. Just ask Marie Antoinette.

THE THIRD TIME'S THE CHARM

Persuasion requires disciplined persistence. It never, ever happens in a sentence, or a sound-bite, or a flip of the switch. It requires repetition.

Steve Jobs is an example of a winner who persuades us, year after year, that we need to buy yet another Apple gadget we don't *really* need. You can see from the way he dresses to the commercials his company airs, one idea prevails in his world: *simplicity.* Apple's products, from the most basic MP3 player to its most expensive computers, are simple and easy to use. Jobs knows how to persuade customers that researching, buying, and using yet another Apple product will actually make their lives *simpler and better* in the long run.

Jobs has been able to keep Apple on top because he knows how to talk to consumers. His Apple Events, the technological equivalent of the Super Bowl, are legendary. He struts out in less-than-fashionable blue jeans, sneakers, and a black mock turtleneck. He doesn't try to project a corporate persona or be something he isn't. He is genuine, and he is sincere. He's as simple and accessible as his product. No tie, no podium, nothing that instills a feeling of space between him (or his product) and the person watching. He's not afraid to get excited and emotional over what he is talking about. Even after more than two decades of these chats, when he thanks the families of Apple employees at the end, you can hear him getting choked up about the commitment and dedication they bring to work each and every day. Maybe that's why they stick with him year after year even though he's known to be an incredibly demanding, uncompromising, unforgiving boss. They know they are working with history in the making.

Jobs focuses on the problem he's solving in endless detail. He doesn't even talk about his solution to the problem until he's told the audience no fewer than *three* times the criteria for a successful technology product. And then, of course, the product he introduces has *exactly* those attributes. It's not only an effective framing technique, but it creates drama and tension where there would be none otherwise. This is persuasion in action: Don't deliver the "you must buy the product" pitch until you have fully created the context of "why you need this in your life."

Let's go even deeper. Jobs always introduces new ideas first as a list, then he talks about each component of the list individually, and then he summarizes the list once again. He says everything three times—to make absolutely sure it's heard. And he always uses exactly the same words each time, creating a refrain that will stay with his people long after they hear it. He even gets the audience to chant the three items sequentially with him over and over. The result: even listeners who aren't paying attention get the message.

Explaining your goal of perfection, and how you approach it, builds customer support. Jobs uses comparisons to demonstrate features. When he has a feature he really wants people to remember, he always compares it to something else. He compared the iPhone to other smartphones. When he introduced the iPod nano, he compared it to other MP3 players. Comparisons allow him to emphasize the unique benefits of his products and frame the landscape of modern technology on his terms—terms you and I can understand. Few companies will effectively compete against Apple until they can convince consumers that their lives will be simpler, better, and more hassle-free when they use their products. Right now, Apple is the undisputed King of Simple Technology, and Steve Jobs is the King of Communication.

But for every business example of linguistic success, there are a dozen language failures. The winners who were interviewed for this book were not only generous with their time but also candid in their comments. Since this is primarily a book about effective communication, allow me an example from one of America's most focused, determined corporate leaders who admittedly used words that *don't* work—and paid a heavy price. Jim Murren, Chairman and CEO of MGM Resorts International, offers this example of what happens when language fails you:

After spending most of my professional life just saying whatever was on my mind without any thought, I realized that what I said has impact. I remember having a very flip answer to a serious question by a Wall Street Journal reporter that had serious consequences. I had joined in February 1998. Bellagio was being built, Mandalay Bay was on the way, and several other properties were soon to open. Her question was, "With all this new capacity coming online in early 2009, what would be the financial ramifications of all this capacity?" And I said, "It's going to be a bloodbath." It was in the Wall Street Journal the next day, and in the Review Journal the day after—with a blaring large-font headline, "BLOODBATH." The head of HR, and the then property president, came into my office and asked, "What the hell are you doing?" It was then that I realized that what I say matters, that I had to be more thoughtful. I don't change my opinions, but I had to be more aware of the import of my words.

GETTING FROM A TO B

LUNTZ LESSONS

THE PERSUASION SPECTRUM: UNDERSTANDING THE DEGREES OF PERSUASION

Persuasion is a process and a continuum, not a fixed point you must reach or you fail. The great misunderstanding about persuasion is the assumption that failing to energize enthusiasts equals failure. On the contrary, neutralizing opposition (which can be simple human resistance to change) is as important as winning support.*

Below are the five stages of persuasion that will help you to better understand how far you need to move your opposition to be successful. It may seem simple at first, but every day someone gets it wrong and risks irrevocable damage to their reputation as a result. For anyone who has to make public presentations or is preparing for a job interview, this chart is for you. Winners break every audience down into these five categories and prioritize their persuasive efforts accordingly.

1. **Rejection:**

    This is the most extreme form of opposition. Rejecters are the people hell-bent on making sure you fail—the ones who actively and gleefully work against you and do everything in their power to stop you dead in your tracks. They disagree with you in principle, many vehemently, and will never be won over—assuming you can even get them to listen. If you're an oil company executive, your rejecters are the heads of Greenpeace and the Sierra Club. If you are a union advocate, your rejecters are businesspeople from virtually everywhere.

    Convincing rejecters to support your cause is usually impossible. You're not trying to win them over—you can't. In fact, one of the biggest mistakes politicians, businesspeople, pundits, entertainers, and average Americans make every day is wasting time and effort on those who will

---

* I use the term *opposition* here not categorically, as if these people are decidedly against you, but rather to mean the people you must convince by overcoming resistance in order to move forward. For example, your employees, who certainly aren't your opposition, might very well oppose certain measures the company needs to take to stay competitive. So in this case they are your opposition generally speaking, even though they're part of your team and you can't succeed without them.

never agree with them. The more you talk, the angrier they get—and that leads to active opposition. A better approach is to simply acknowledge them, accept them, and offer them an olive branch if circumstance allows. You want them to go silent—that in itself is winning. So other than the obligatory recognition and respect due them, be silent with them.

2. **Disagreement:**

The next level on the persuasion scale is simple disagreement. These people don't want to defeat you. They see the world differently from you, but they're not so passionate as to actively stand in your way. It doesn't mean they won't try to stop you if it's easy or involves little effort (for example, signing a petition, joining a Facebook group that's critical of you, or choosing another product), but they won't actively organize themselves against your company or campaign because they just don't *care* that much.

The smart strategy here is to acknowledge their opposition and then give them three reasons to rethink it. Not two—that's not enough evidence to challenge the brain—or four—you're pushing way too hard. By acknowledging them, you are demonstrating respect. By giving them examples of *facts and evidence*, you are helping them to question their own judgment and building a bridge to your side. Remember, the goal is *not* to win converts on the spot—that takes time. But if you neutralize opponents now, you can win them over later.

3. **Neutrality:**

Sometimes called the moderate middle or the sensible center, these people can be just as hard to move as rejecters because often they simply don't care to engage. Some are ambivalent. Others are indifferent. In politics, they are not necessarily the independents who consciously reject both political parties. They are often unaffiliated, not caring enough to choose sides and not passionate enough to say no to everyone. In business, they don't care which product or service they use—they'll reach for whatever comes first. And in your life, these are the people to whom your existence is neither a benefit nor a liability. To them, you're just . . . there.

On a personal level, neutrality is my favorite audience position because it allows me to start having the conversation I want to have, not the one they want to have. If I can introduce an idea or concept to an audience that hasn't made up its mind, I know I'll win because I don't have to fight preconceived perceptions. The challenge is to make them care enough to pay attention. The ultimate goal of motivating neutrals is to find the messages and touch points that make them sit up and take note. Then you can start moving them to your side.

4. **Agreement:**

While people who are neutral about your cause aren't a threat like rejecters, they're about as useful as money sitting in a no-interest savings account. But supporters who are in agreement with your efforts aren't necessarily much better if they remain silent or inactive. The next step is to put them to work—to make them genuine advocates. You want them to weigh in on your behalf. You want them to seek out information and learn the facts so they can politely correct others when they misspeak. You want them out there doing the talking for you, changing hearts and minds along the way.

For them, the strongest motivations are the "consequences" of inaction. This may be counterintuitive but it is important: you need an "if/then" context to push them to action. If you don't watch this nightly news program, you will be uninformed and appear ignorant to your colleagues and supervisors. If you don't hire me, you'll miss out on my creativity, ingenuity, and loyalty—and I'll be working for your competition.

5. **Action:**

These are your advocates—the people who proudly speak up on your behalf, the ones who go around making your case for you without being asked. They don't sit on the sidelines waiting to see what happens—they're out there working hard each and every day to make sure your goal becomes the community's goal. Some might say they've drunk the Kool-Aid. I say these are the people you need by your side if you truly want to win.

All that action-oriented people need from you is affirmation. The three best at it are Jobs, Gates, and Buffett, whose shareholder meetings are standing-room-only affairs. In politics, Ted Kennedy was the best at it for the Democrats, and Ronald Reagan for the Republicans. A public pat on the back, a call to do even more, and hundreds, thousands, even millions of people are once again singing their praises and proudly displaying their corporate and political colors.

Persuasion is nothing more than the art of change. (For you business-wonk readers, it's about the "delta." The change from A to B. And promise me that you'll never use that econo-speak with your audience, who will think that you're talking about a river or a frat house.)

The key to successful persuasion is understanding the values, beliefs, opinions, experiences, traditions, cultures, points of view, hot buttons, and countless other aspects of human nature that make us who we are. Only by suspending your disbelief (and judgment) about others can you learn to listen to them—really listen to them—in a way that gives you the insights you need to communicate with them most effectively.

Think of it this way: Let's assume you've decided your company needs to hire an expert research firm to find out exactly what thirty-something mothers think about your new widget. Your business partner, on the other hand, is extremely skeptical of additional research on "widget moms" because you've done the same research already and it hasn't gotten you anywhere. So you bring in this new firm from Dallas to pitch for the project, they set up their boards in your conference room, run through a generic PowerPoint, and try to prove how great their research will be. You're sold, as you knew you would be. Your partner is not, as he knew he wouldn't be.

This is exactly what happens every day in corporate America because its leaders do not understand that persuasion is the art of change—not the art of acceptance. If you think you have to get them to be as enthusiastic about the presentation and the research project as you are so they'll be on board, then you're making the distance between points A and B much, much greater than it has to be. In essence, don't make B into Z. You're creating a chasm to jump over when it could be a mere gap. Rather than trying to move them from rejection to action, instead try moving them from rejection to neutrality. This is a much lighter and more realistic lift and, in the end, neutrality allows you to do what you wanted anyway.

Going into any presentation or campaign, be prepared to address these five strategic imperatives in order to move disagrees and neutrals one step in your direction:

1. **Answer objections.** Be direct. "Is there anything I've said with which you disagree? Let's talk about it."
2. **Allay fears to get buy-in.** Be empathetic. "Yes, I understand that concern and even anticipated it. So let me tell you about our plan to address it and get your feedback to see if we're heading in the right direction."
3. **Present facts.** As Reagan said, facts are stubborn things. They also move stubborn people better than any language could. "Let's look at what the data says and discuss how it applies to our objective."

4. **Present a compelling story.** Don't launch right into your pitch. Find some way of telling a compelling story about your own experience that has resonance and relevance among your audience. They are people, after all.

5. **Beg.** You read this correctly. You don't necessarily get your way just by making smart, rational arguments. That's what business books will tell you, but it's not real life. Sometimes you just have to push a little bit harder. Says billionaire mall developer Herb Simon, *"I don't mind begging. I don't mind doing what I have to do to make a deal, even if it isn't always necessity. I do what has to be done."*

There's no formula for leaping from one end of the persuasion spectrum to the other, and there is no standard measurement for success. It's all a matter of degrees.

HOW WINNERS PERSUADE

When you are listening to a business leader, what are some of the nonverbal cues that best indicate to you that you can believe what he or she is telling you?

	Total
They speak from the heart and make direct eye contact with the people to whom they are speaking rather than speaking from a text or teleprompter	35%
They say what they mean, mean what they say, and live by what they tell others	34%
They answer questions accurately, directly, and thoroughly	32%
They demonstrate a detailed knowledge of their products, company, and industry	26%
They show great intellectual capability and have thoroughly thought through the issues they are addressing	24%
They clearly demonstrate that they are listening to my questions, concerns, and advice	21%
They pause to think while they are speaking and before they respond to a question, showing they are putting thought into their words	19%
They talk to and relate to me on my level	10%

Source: The Word Doctors, 2010

TELLING VS. INFORMING VS. EDUCATING

Persuasion, at its most basic level, is about balancing emotion and reason. For every issue where there is a substantial divide in public opinion, whether it's about requiring kids to wear school uniforms, pursuing a merger that might cause temporary job dislocation, or determining how the country will deal with health-care reform, the division is often emotionally driven. If you think I'm wrong, ask any senior citizen drawing Social Security if we should cut their benefits because it's bankrupting the nation. Or ask a teacher whether they should be held to higher standards. Or ask a personal-injury lawyer if the losers of medical malpractice cases should be forced to pay all legal fees. Their reactions don't mean all persuasion should be driven by emotion. But they underscore the truth that we are driven at least as much by emotions as we are by logic and intellect.

There are right ways and wrong ways to go about any conversation. You can't just force-feed information and facts. You can't just assume the story tells itself. And you certainly can't assume that if you simply lay everything out there the way *you* see it, others will come to your conclusion too. Often our gut reactions to things we hear and issues we face determine how our brains process what we *learn* about the issue from that moment forward. That's why every act of persuasion should be seen as a moment for education, because education allows us to supplant emotion with thought. But educating should never be confused with telling or even informing. I will explain.

An informer aims to change you, a teller assumes he'll change you, and an educator aspires along with you to change you by empowering you. And a great educator will be open to letting you change him or her in the process. Most people fall into a single category and remain there for their entire careers, though on occasion I will come across someone who is actively transforming themselves from one category to another, probably because their situation in life has changed. In my two decades of message consulting, I have come across only a handful of people who transcend all three communication categories at the same time.

Former U.S. Secretary of Defense Donald Rumsfeld is a rare example

THE THREE TYPES OF PERSUADERS

1. Tellers:

This is the most basic form of information exchange. In fact, exchange isn't really the right word to use because exchange implies some sort of two-way process. If you exchange something, you must get something in return. Telling is the opposite. Telling is the dry recitation of information, facts, figures, statistics, and, yes, platitudes, that the teller assumes necessary to make his or her case. This is a "push" strategy—talking at your audience. You provide little if any context, no story, no vision, rarely even a hint of concern for what the audience hears, thinks, or believes. There is an undercurrent of arrogance in tellers; they assume they are right—and worse, they assume their audience *takes it on faith* that the teller is right. This sets you up for failure.

A majority of persuasion efforts consist of telling, because that's what we're most accustomed to. When you're young, your parents tell you what to do, what to wear, what to think, and what to believe, because they can. Once we grow up, however, the "because I said so" tactic doesn't work anymore, except in the office when it's your boss—and that is certainly not an indicator of long-term success. Not surprisingly, tellers tend to be extremely ineffective communicators because people usually don't like being told what to do. Telling is the most aggressive and least effective form of communicating because it's always on your terms, not the listener's. It's rarely interactive, which is necessary to keep many audiences engaged. Tellers generally tend to drone on and on for too long. They read their scripts, avoid eye contact, and speak with patronizing, monotone voices. Simply put, it's all about them—and that's why tellers are rarely winners.

2. Informers:

Informing is a more neutral attempt at persuasion that can eventually lead to a dialogue. The difference between informers and tellers is in the crafting of the argument. Informers *do* come at you with the assumption that they are correct, but they *do not* assume that you already think they are correct. They know they have some work to do . . . a responsibility to give you reasons to agree with them. This adds enough humility to the mix to help their case.

Informers are more engaging in their language and presentation, and they present evidence in making their case. They go beyond the dry recitation of facts and figures, but they stop short of the why—the deeper, more fundamental reason that what they're saying truly matters. Informers are often more technical and clinical than emotional and passionate. Unlike tellers, they try to make a case other than "because I say so." They don't just assume everyone else is wrong and they're right. But where they still come up short is that they lack empathy. They don't seek to understand or explain the topic from the perspective of the listener.

3. **Educators:**
Educators are winners because they understand the power and necessity of bringing others into the conversation beyond what they themselves know to be true. I consistently advise business and political leaders to stop calling their public talks *speeches* and to instead consider them *conversations*. Similarly, I tell corporations not to consider their marketing and public relations to be about *communication* but instead look at their efforts as *education*. By rewiring the mental process, the tone, delivery, and content are more likely to improve.

Educators are the best persuaders, and education is the most effective form of persuasion, because it promotes knowledge, wisdom, and ultimately empowerment, not just the dissemination of information. Education is achieved through listening, questioning, and engaging, and educators are motivated by their audiences, not themselves. The best educators do more than teach their audiences; they actually learn from them. Their presentations are multidirectional and interactive. They rarely read from a script, preferring eye contact with the audience instead. They want to know what people are thinking at every moment so they can recalibrate their message and address whatever doubts may linger.

of a leader who applied all three categories of persuasion with his innovative application of the English language. Democrats and even some Republicans reading this passage may still resent Rumsfeld for what he did or didn't do in Iraq, but this is a book about winning—and in the early months of the war, Rumsfeld did almost single-handedly win over the hearts and minds of most Americans. His press briefings, marked by a spirited back-and-forth with his media inquisitors, were satirized by late-night comics because they were so unusually entertaining and compelling. And while he was clearly confident in whatever he was addressing, his intense, dogmatic approach to policy was masked with an informal, humorous, and candid style with the public. His most famous example was in response to a question about U.S. military strategy in Iraq and his contingency planning:

As we know, there are known knowns. There are things we know we know. We also know there are known unknowns. That is to say, we know there are some things we do not know. But there are also unknown unknowns, the ones we don't know we don't know.[70]

There's a humility mixed in that lets the listener know that the educator understands he or she doesn't have all the answers, but also a purposefulness that lets the listener know the educator is committed to finding the right solution.

To be fair, the problem with a statement like the one above is that out of context it might sound a little silly. The media were quick to take on Secretary Rumsfeld for seeming to admit he didn't know what was going on. Yet he was merely acknowledging a fact that was as clear as day: There are some things we don't know, and we need to expect the unexpected. When I had the chance to ask him about this now famous quote, he responded with his usual candor: *"One thing I try to do all the time is I try to put myself in other people's shoes, particularly when you're negotiating or you're trying to persuade someone to do something. Most people don't do enough of that. Force yourself to ask, 'What does it look like from their perspective?' . . . So it was really an exercise in understanding where the other side—in this case the media—was coming from and trying to address their concerns."* And yet when I asked him about the press corps' negative reaction to his candid response, Rumsfeld told me, *"If I got up every morning worried about what the press thought, I wouldn't be able to do much in life."* Interesting.

ELEMENTS OF SUCCESSFUL PERSUASION

It's Not What You Say, It's What They Hear

I learned this lesson the hard way. In October 2005, I had the rare honor of being able to address the entire Senate Republican and House Republican delegations on the same day—just minutes apart at either end of the U.S. Capitol. My theme at both presentations was exactly the same: Either change what you're doing and beg your constituents for forgiveness, or be prepared to be voted into the minority—and I came equipped with dozens of charts and graphs to prove it. I thought they would see me as the benevolent professor, but what the leadership heard was a disrespectful alarmist. My message so alienated the audience that it would be more than three years before I was invited back—after Republicans had in fact lost not just in 2006 but 2008 as well. It didn't matter that I was right—or that deep down, they knew I was right. What mattered was that I didn't tailor my tone and style to connect to a group of people more accustomed to demanding apologies than being asked to deliver them. I was so passionate—and so sure I was right—that I went there to "tell it like it was." I should have gone to "educate so they could make the right decision on their own." The facts were on my side. They were powerful enough to make the case for me. But I obscured them with my passion.

The lesson? Of all the winning *P*'s, remember to always make passion subordinate to persuasion.

A few years ago I was speaking to a packed room at the Milken Institute Global Conference, a gathering of the world's business, science, and academic leaders. My topic was the importance of language and messaging in helping businesses thrive. After I had finished my remarks, several people came up to ask me to sign one of my books and grill me about the upcoming elections. As I was getting ready to leave, an older man wearing a baseball cap—which was odd for a gathering of this wealthy demographic—pushed his way forward and challenged me (rather loudly) to explain exactly what I meant when I said, "It's not what you say that matters, it's what they hear." I was somewhat taken aback because I'd specifically addressed the phrase and its meaning in my presentation earlier and it's not even close to the most controversial thing I'd said that evening. He then went on to tell me he didn't care much for what I had to say, or my philosophy of communication, because it was all about using language as propaganda to scare people and manipulate them into doing what I wanted them to do. He even said angrily that my line about "It's not what you say that matters, it's what they hear" gave me away—I was a "snake" whose mission in life was to deceive people.

I share this anecdote to illustrate several essential principles of language. I work for some powerful and controversial clients, so I've become accustomed to getting called lots of really bad things. For example, *The Daily Show*'s Samantha Bee once called me an "amoral Yoda" after

I explained to her the intricate science of visual stagecraft at political events.[71] And Stephen Colbert did an entire segment that began with "Thank God for Frank Luntz," which in true Shakespearean style positioned him as Marc Antony and turned me into the Brutus of our time because of my use of the phrase "nuclear option" to describe the congressional procedure known as reconciliation. (". . . Now I'm sure Frank would have a more positive name for actual nuclear bombs—instant suntan.")

Returning to the Milken critic, what I realized after talking to this older gentleman was just how true my saying "It's not what you say that matters, it's what people hear" really is. I had just spent a solid hour explaining how using language to your advantage in business isn't propaganda, it's simply maximizing the effectiveness of one of your most valuable resources—communication. Every business, at least every *successful* business, does that every single day. There is always a right and wrong way to tell the truth. But that's not what he heard. He heard, "Tell them what they want to hear, knowing full well you don't really give a damn." If someone leaves one of my speeches thinking that's what I'm recommending, I haven't done my job at all.

Too many business and political leaders fail to achieve greatness simply because they do not comprehend why others don't see the world the way they do. They just don't get it—how can my employees not realize this is the way for us to move forward? How can the voters not understand the importance of this legislation? Why? Why? Why?

Persuasion is all about recognizing *other* people's realities. You can't get them to accept your story until you understand and appreciate theirs.

The Role of Listening

As NBA commissioner David Stern told me, *"Listen, Listen. Listen. Listen far more than you talk. Talk ten percent of the time, listen ninety percent of the time."* Without question, one of the most important components of being persuasive is knowing how to listen.

Simon and Garfunkel's classic "The Sound of Silence" is instructional to those in both politics and business: "People talking without speaking. People hearing without listening." Many people, especially busy people who have organizations to run, often mistake hearing for listening. They are not the same. I repeat, listening is more than hearing. Listening requires genuine understanding. Tellers *talk*; persuaders *speak*. Tellers, at best, are heard. But persuaders earn the right for you to listen. Are you, really and truly, on the right side of these equations?

Listening is active. When we listen to people the right way, we think about and process every word they say. We listen for the tone and cadence of their voices, the words they use, the words they omit, the gestures they make and the way they focus their eyes or look away. Listening is hearing plus analysis. It requires us to really pay attention and focus on who's talking and what they're saying. It involves strategic questioning, not challenging, to achieve full understanding. Good listening involves effort, because you can't really understand the way a person feels about an issue until you take the time to listen carefully to what they're saying. Often you'll realize more is learned from what is not said than from what is. For example, if you know your people care deeply about environmental issues because you've spent time talking to them about it and listening to what they've said, you'd know to frame your new energy-reducing lightbulb project in terms of its long-term green benefits rather than its cost savings. Winners understand the importance of focusing on what matters most, and they live by it. They know that persuasion depends upon understanding people and what motivates them.

SHARED PRINCIPLES

Just as important as making sure your first sentence sets the right tone for what you're about to say, you must also recognize there is a natural flow—an order—to persuasive speech. First among its elements are shared principles. Shared principles are the big, umbrellalike statements that most people agree with. A few examples:

- No child should ever have to go without food, clothing, or shelter . . .
- Every American should have the right to determine his or her own future . . .
- Businesses should not be allowed to put their profit ahead of our safety . . .

- All Americans should have access to quality, affordable health care . . .
- The American Dream should be accessible for everyone . . .

You'll often hear very persuasive people—the kind of people who win arguments without their opponents even knowing it—start their conversations with these kinds of statements. The communicative power of principle-based statements lies in their universality. No matter what you believe, these are the kinds of statements you'll agree with. Or, if you want to look at it another way, these are the kinds of statements that stem from the very heart of what it means to be an American. The ideals of equality and democracy, freedom and fairness, are so fundamental to the American experience that many of these statements are simply taken as a given.

There will be times when you disagree with your audience, and they with you. The point is simply, why turn them off (and be tuned out) first? Why not make an honest attempt at finding common ground before staking out turf to defend? You lose nothing by making this first attempt . . . but what you gain can be immense.

By establishing shared principles, you stop the skepticism that blocks audiences from hearing you. These shared principles disarm your audience so that you can start a real *conversation*, slowly applying the techniques of persuasion to your language. And make no mistake; if you're going to be a winner, you're going to cause controversy. Bill Gates and Steve Jobs didn't get where they are by playing nicely and marching in lockstep with conventional wisdom. They pissed people off. They said things others absolutely did not want to hear. To become a winner, you have to make passionate persuasion your best friend. The most persuasive people don't go to war against their audiences. They court them verbally. The key is in using universal ideas, concepts, and principles that validate all sides and help foster unanimous agreement. Once you've built a rudimentary consensus—a structure—you can start building your more advanced ideas on top of it.

POLITICAL PERSUASION: SAY WHAT YOU MEAN AND MEAN WHAT YOU SAY

Democracy is the art and science of running the circus
from the monkey cage.

H. L. MENCKEN

President Barack Obama has proven that even a twenty-four-hour day can be a lifetime. The day he was sworn into office, he had a remarkable 68 percent job approval and a 70 percent personal favorability rating— higher than all but two presidents since FDR. Since then, it has all turned upside down. As this book goes to press, his personal favorability rating still hovers around 60 percent, but his job approval is in the mid-40s, and less than 40 percent support his policies. Not good. Another age-old adage in politics has come true for him: Pleasing people while governing is a lot harder than doing it as a candidate.

Obama's successful push for a national health-care plan after decades of failure transformed the president's image in ways he did not expect. His campaign for president promised to bridge our country's deep partisan divide; instead, the American people believe he is forcing it wider. He pledged to govern from the middle, but is now increasingly labeled as "liberal," left-wing," or worse, *"socialist."*

Sure, he has his supporters, and Americans still want him to succeed so that America succeeds. But they are worried about what he has done— and worse yet, what he might do next. The faith and confidence in his presidency cratered faster than for any president in the past half century except for Gerald Ford, and Ford was an accidental president. With the loss of Democratic governorships in Virginia and New Jersey, the defeat of the Kennedy legacy in Massachusetts, and the rise of the Tea Party activists, Americans sent a clear message to those in Washington: STOP.

But they didn't stop. Finally, the American people put their foot down and applied the brakes, yielding a Republican majority in the House and the third straight "Rubber Band" election. In 2006, 2008, and now 2010, Americans have had their patience stretched to the breaking point, firing a Washington run amok, and are demanding their new leaders to snap back to attention. For years now, the political elite has overpromised and underdelivered, which is why they keep losing elections. The reality looking forward is simple: If the Republicans don't deliver on their promises, they're finished. If the Democrats simply continue doing what they're doing, they're finished.

Both sides are promising to fulfill the will of the people, but people aren't asking for promises. They're asking for new priorities—*their* priorities.

The agenda of America is simple. In broad terms, Americans want the government to spur job growth, but not by subsidizing more government jobs with taxpayer dollars. They want Washington to balance the budget and reverse the growing government influence over our lives. They want government to encourage success, allow failure, punish those who break the law—and then get out of the way. And above all, they want politicians to follow through on their promises, even if that means tempering those promises in the first place.

It's not all about policy; it's also about personal accountability. House Majority Leader Eric Cantor, the creator of the YouCut spending reduction program that puts the congressional budget knife in the hands of taxpayers, is linguistically visual, talking about his commitment to *"drain the swamp rather than learning to swim with the alligators."* Clearly he gets it. Voters want their representatives home in their districts holding monthly town hall sessions. The single worst strategic mistake House Democrats made in 2010 was canceling scores of public meetings, denying their constituents the chance to be heard. Hell hath no fury like a voter scorned; their voices were silenced during the health-care debate, so they spoke in unison on Election Day.

The last time Republicans gained control of the House of Representatives, in 1994, they achieved more in the first hundred days than some congresses in two years. From welfare reform to tax cuts, from a balanced budget amendment to term limits, they successfully passed every one of their ten Contract with America items. Some of it stalled in the Senate, and much of it was vetoed by President Clinton, but they held on to their majority for a dozen years because of all they did in those first hundred days. They worked with the president when they could, opposed him when they couldn't—and the American people were satisfied with the result.

The national political narrative today is most accurately defined not by red states versus blue states . . . Republicans versus Democrats . . . or even Tea Partiers versus Progressives. The battle in America is between the people (us) versus Washington (Obama/Pelosi/Reid) and Wall Street (insert name of big bank here). It's the overworked, overtaxed, over-hassled American versus those who create the rules and always seem to win. The chasm to be bridged is not between political parties or philosophical ideologies, but between the *results* Americans demand and the *excuses* they receive from whoever is in charge.

Americans today are more informed about decisions made by their elected representatives than ever before. In the past, sneaking isolated provisions pushed by lobbyists or special interests into thousand-page legislation was commonplace, and elected officials could do it without fingerprints or fear of voter reprisals. It was often weeks after a bill was signed into law, if at all, before someone discovered the offending clause. Now, fortunately, all legislation is posted online, allowing regular citizens and activist bloggers to cull through it page by page, looking for the most egregious add-ons. But the awareness of how crafting legislation really works—and how laws are actually passed—has heightened public frustration. A major component of the perception that Washington cannot do anything right is the belief (often valid) that lobbyists write many of the bills. But thanks to advances in technology, communication, and twenty-four-hour cable television, it makes it a lot harder for politicians to hide their add-ons, earmarks, backroom deals, and lobbyist-written loopholes.

Take for example the "Cornhusker Kickback" and how it affected the politician fortunes of Senator Ben Nelson (D-NE). By trading his vote on health care for a preferential Medicare deal exclusively for his home state, the once universally popular politician became a political punching bag. Nelson's favorability dropped more than 20 percent in a single month—the fastest public opinion collapse of any sitting senator not facing an impending election or corruption charges. But for the power of the Internet and the American people's demand for accountability, his deal would have been considered politics as usual. Perhaps that is what makes it even more outrageous.

So what do Americans really want from America's political elite? The ten statements on the next page would be a very good start. More than 80 percent of Americans say they would vote for a candidate who made these ten commitments.

THE TEN RULES FOR 2012:

WHAT AMERICANS REALLY WANT TO

HEAR FROM THEIR REPRESENTATIVES

1. **I will never accept the status quo.** I believe there is room for improvement in everything we do, that we can and must do better. We owe it to our children to give them a better America than what we inherited.

2. **I will never apologize for America.** This country is a beacon of hope for the oppressed and a force for good across the globe. No nation is perfect, but when help is needed, America is usually there.

3. **I will find at least one penny of waste to cut from every dollar in spending.** It's time to hold government accountable for how they spend your money. It's time for them to stop talking about ending waste, fraud, and abuse, and get it done.

4. **I will never raise taxes in a recession.** You don't create jobs by making life more difficult for job creators. You don't alleviate the pain of economic hardship by making it harder for people to make ends meet.

5. **You don't work for me. I work for you.** It's time for government to remember that it serves the American people, not the other way around.

6. **I will fight for the public's right to know the cost and consequences of every piece of legislation and regulation.** It's your government. It's your life. It's your future. No government entity should deny you that right.

7. **I will always prioritize American rights over the rights of those who wish to do us harm.** I will do whatever it takes to keep American soil safe and secure. We should be hunting terrorists down, not lawyering them up.

8. **I will work with anyone who will work with me.** No one has a monopoly on solutions. Good ideas should be applauded and supported wherever they come from.

9. **I will always support freedom.** Our economic system has created more prosperity for more people than any other system anywhere at any time. It should be protected, not destroyed. Our political system is broken, but with genuine accountability and responsibility, it can and must be restored.

10. **I still believe in the American principle: of the people, by the people, for the people.** It's time for the people's voice to be heard, and I'm listening.

After years of research and literally millions of interviews, I finally believe people when they tell me they don't want to hear negative attacks— not from politicians, not from corporations, not from anyone. The best way around the negative attack is by neutralizing the competition or opposition in the very beginning. Rather than starting off by saying how bad Bank X is or how awful Company Y is or how out of touch Candidate Z is, you start instead by talking about how consumers have the right to expect more. If customer service is what matters, acknowledge its importance. If quality is your most important attribute, promote it. If the public wants someone of unassailable character and ethics to lead them, say so. You've all heard the phrase "give the people what they want." By preempting disagreement and highlighting these shared understandings, you show that you get it. Most important, it allows you to start the conversation affirmatively and graciously, and only then to steer it in your direction toward an agreed-upon outcome.

Again, I go to Steve Jobs. He knows better than most how to quietly and captivatingly disarm his audience. At the 1997 MacWorld Expo trade show, Jobs made the announcement that Microsoft was going to invest $150 million in Apple and would develop future versions of certain programs for Macintosh computers. Not surprisingly, Apple loyalists were dismayed and many jeered at the announcement. But Steve Jobs, unwilling to throw any red meat to the crowd, gave a thoughtful and somewhat surprising response. "We have to let go of a few things here. We have to let go of the notion that for Apple to win, Microsoft has to lose," he said.[72] And just like that, Jobs changed the playing field. He neutralized not just the Microsoft threat—but the bigger threat posed by a revolt of Apple's supporters. No longer was Apple locked in an epic struggle with Microsoft, where only one could be the winner. Jobs painted a picture of a future where Apple could thrive alongside Microsoft. He set new rules for victory with which no person could in good conscience disagree. Our political elite can learn a lot from this win-win approach.

SIMPLE, NOT SIMPLISTIC

Have you ever tried reading a global corporation's annual report? How about a 10-K filing? A House resolution amendment? An article in a professional academic journal? Furniture assembly instructions from IKEA? (OK, so technically that last one has no words because it's not efficient to print the same "Expedit" how-to manual in forty-six different languages, but you get the idea.) Some of the least effective communication you've ever come across was also very likely the most complicated and complex, right? If you really pay attention, you'll notice one of the hallmarks of persuasive communication is just how simple it actually is.

No matter how many times I read the First Amendment to our Constitution, I can never get over just how powerful and, yes, persuasive, those scant few words are:

Congress shall make no law respecting an establishment of religion, or prohibiting the free exercise thereof; or abridging the freedom of speech, or of the press; or the right of the people peaceably to assemble, and to petition the Government for a redress of grievances.

In just forty-five words, the founders were able to articulate the bedrock principles of democracy. To give some context, that's only thirty more words than McDonald's uses to describe the ingredients in a Big Mac—and 2,700 pages less than the 2008–2009 health-care reform legislation that Washington engineered over a yearlong process.

People don't have time or energy to process complexity. Now more than ever, we have countless other whosits and whatsits competing for our attention. Turn on the TV or the radio, or open your physical or virtual mailbox, and there are more messages flying at you from all directions than you can ever possibly fully analyze and consider. But the ones that break through, and the ones that ultimately end up persuading you to do anything, are the ones that are clear, concise, to the point, and memorable. And the key to all of those things is simplicity. But one thing you have to understand is that simplicity is not the same thing as dumbing down.

Think about the way winners communicate. President Franklin Delano Roosevelt gave an impassioned and powerful inaugural address on March 4, 1933, intended to help break the American spirit free from the nadir of the Depression. And in that speech, one line stands out among them all: "the only thing we have to fear is fear itself."[73] Again, ten words. In just ten simple (mostly), monosyllabic words, President Roosevelt gave the American people hope, courage, and a reason to keep fighting for tomorrow. His prose was simple, but the idea behind it was anything but. When you look at the entirety of that particular inaugural address, you'll notice that President Roosevelt spoke to the American people like adults. He didn't feel the need to dumb anything down, because he knew that by keeping his message simple, clear, and direct it would resonate, persuade, and fortify a despairing nation. By all accounts, it did exactly that.

"The first thing about words that are meaningless is that there are too many of them," Fox News chief Roger Ailes likes to say. *"Whenever you're trying to obfuscate the fact that you don't know what you are talking about, you add words."* I see it all the time. People try to dress up a bad idea with a bunch of ten-cent words. It never works. There's no reason to use twenty words when twelve will suffice, and there's no reason to use twelve when six will do. In every piece of communication you create, cut out at least one-third of the text. If you can do so without losing any meaning, you will have made it stronger, clearer, and more persuasive.

Another example of simplicity in persuasive communication is Google's unofficial mantra, "Don't Be Evil." You won't find these words on the Web site, but you will definitely hear employees refer to them when they debate public policy from a Google perspective. The beauty of the statement is its simple appeal to common sense. People's frustration with corporate America is that too often it operates way too far out of line. Americans believe corporate America's moral code resides squarely on the dark side of the ethical equation . . . for the simple fact that *all* they care about is their *bottom line*. So a company that clearly differentiates itself from the rest of corporate America is going to win big.

Google is consistently rated one of the best places to work, is known for giving its employees more perks and freedom than many heads of state enjoy, and aside from issues around privacy and its digital book ventures, the company is still highly regarded by both business leaders and the general public. There's power in Google's mantra because it is so simple and straightforward. Its mantra is not "We're going to try to be a company that does good things when we think we can but that will, of course, depend on the external realities we face at the time in conjunction with our larger expectations among shareholders and the financial community."

It's hard to argue that any of the men and women I've talked about aren't winners. They win because they understood the power and me-chanics of persuasion and were able to demonstrate the superior nature of their products, services, and ideas. They used language to overcome deep-seated skepticism, fear, confusion, and plain old human inertia so they could advance their ideas in the marketplaces of human thought and commerce. They also used word of mouth, effective advertising, social networks, and every possible means to inform and spread the word. And each of them, through persistence and a keen ear, was not only able to make it to the top, but to completely redefine what it meant to get there in the first place.

When it comes to persuasion, women have a communication advan-tage in many areas—healthcare, education, consumer goods, to name a few—because they are seen as more candid, more caring, and more compassionate than their male counterparts. Whereas a fair number of top male CEOs take great pride in using $10 words that are strung to-gether in sentences that never seem to end, women prefer more com-mon language and stories that illustrate. Men talk. Women paint a picture. In an era of deep-seated cynicism and distrust, a woman's per-spective is seen as uniquely refreshing and honest—provided she uses the words that work.

THE LANGUAGE OF PERSUASION

The words most likely to persuade all revolve around what people want most in their day-to-day lives. Of all the chapters of this book, these words and phrases are most likely to change because their effectiveness depends on answering human needs that are constantly changing. However, al-though the words might change, pay close attention to the principles behind them. Here are the nine words that currently matter most:

"**Stability.**" There was a time when *renewal* was one of the most pow-erful words that work because it suggested a return to something better. Then *change* became the *in* word. Now, it's *"stability"* that we are all seeking. We've had enough change, thank you. What we want now is an end to the ups and downs, the boom and bust. We will gladly give up the highs if it means preventing the lows.

Similarly, *"predictability"* has emerged as a significant priority. With dollars tight and no room for error, we can't afford to take chances on

PERSUASION WORDS THAT WORK

1. Stability
2. Predictability
3. Insight
4. Specialist (rather than expert)
5. Performance-driven (rather than profit)
6. Common sense
7. Reliable/reliability
8. Convenience
9. Consequences

the untried and untested. We want to know that we are getting exactly what we paid for, and nothing less. The linguistic challenge for paradigm-breakers is that what they're offering is often brand-new, and occasionally the kinks have not quite been worked out. But as long as those issues are minor and predictable, we'll tolerate them.

"**Insight.**" The best definition I have heard for *"insight"* comes from my interview with Donald Rumsfeld about that infamous *"known knowns"* comment. When I told him I probably would have edited his quote if I was working for him, he responded, "There are a lot of people who can review something and make it better, but there are very few people who can identify what is missing." That's the definition of *insight—the ability to identify what's missing and bring it to life.* When your audience hears about how "insightful" a company is or that you bring "insight" to a particular problem or issue, your audience thinks they are getting a unique and valued product, service, or information.

"Specialist" has become more powerful than *"expert"* simply because there has been an explosion in so-called experts, thanks to talk radio and cable news. Everyone in the media claims to be an expert in their field, and therefore we trust no one. Conversely, a *"specialist"* is still considered special because there are fewer of them, and we are still willing to assume that they have added training or education to deserve the title.

"Performance-driven" works on so many levels. If pay and bonuses are "performance-driven," we assume that they are based on merit. If the product is *"performance-driven,"* we assume it's going to work as promised.

If the corporate culture is *"performance-driven,"* we assume that people are rewarded for success.

"Common sense" is one of the most desired attributes that the American people believe is lacking in their political and business leaders. Defining common sense is impossible—it has 300 million definitions for 300 million Americans. But what makes this term so powerful in a persuasive sense is the way that it works convincing people that an assertion is so obvious that it just makes sense. Saying *"It's so obvious"* is insulting; saying *"It's common sense"* has lasting impact.

"Reliability." Ask people what they want most from anything technology-related—a car, television, computer, etc.—and they'll tell you *"reliability."* In fact, reliability is the combination of two other powerful phrases—*"no hassles"* and *"no worries"*—something that works 100 percent of the time and never fails. But that only scratches the surface. *"Reliable"* is what people want most from marketing and advertising, and that translates into being told the truth. The most persuasive people are those who think carefully about the construction of their assertions, always building *"reliability checks"* (facts, data, proof points, etc.) into their presentations.

"Convenience" should be specifically targeted to working moms, and it is the sister word to *"value."* The combination of convenience and value is a powerful motivator for people without the money to afford what they really want and the time to find it cheaper someplace else. Some of the most powerful innovative brands of the past two decades, from eBay to Amazon.com, were built specifically on convenience.

"Consequences" is last on this list because it's the only negative attribute in your persuasive arsenal. Notice that all the words on this list are about improving confidence. This is the exception. While the word is technically neutral, and it is certainly possible that some actions will have positive consequences, the real power is in the concern it creates in the listener. When you end your speech with *"the consequences of failure,"* they individualize and personalize it to their own lives. You have been given nine words or phrases to promote success. *Consequences* is the one word that will help you communicate the reasons not to fail.

10

PERSISTENCE
Learning from failure

*The trouble in America is not that we are making too many mistakes,
but that we are making too few.*

—**PHILIP KNIGHT,**
FOUNDER AND CEO, NIKE

*The most rewarding things you do in life are often the ones that look like
they cannot be done.*

—**ARNOLD PALMER**

*I have missed more than nine thousand shots in my career. I have lost
almost three hundred games. On twenty-six occasions, I have been
entrusted to take the game-winning shot . . . and missed. And I have failed
over and over and over again in my life. And that is why I succeed.*

—**MICHAEL JORDAN**

PERSISTENCE ISN'T JUST EFFORT

Of all the attributes it takes to win, persistence is the most important,
because without it, winning is impossible.

Just ask Jimmy Connors. Unquestionably one of the greatest tennis
players of all time, Connors held the world Number One ranking for
five straight years, winning 109 official tournaments along the way, a
modern-day record for men, including the prestigious U.S. Open five

times. But the match Connors will always be most respected for was when he reached the semifinals of the U.S. Open in 1991 at the seasoned age of 39—the oldest player ever to advance that far in the most brutal of the Grand Slam tournaments.* The bad boy of tennis had staged a career comeback of monstrous proportions, winning the respect and admiration of the same crowds that had booed him fifteen years before because of his on-court antics. Today, Connors is surprisingly quiet and reserved, not at all what I expected when I sat down to interview him, but there isn't a hint of remorse in his relentless persistence to be the best:

> I played crazy, and that's the only way I knew how to play. I wasn't worried about making friends out there. I'm here to win, and winning was the only thing that mattered to me. I didn't care what it took. I played five six-hour matches. It didn't bother me. Hundred-ten-degree heat, that didn't bother me. I'd rather play in the middle in the day because I knew I was in better shape than my opponent. I didn't want them to breathe, ever. I won half my matches or more before I even stepped out there, because no one wanted to go out there and face that for five hours. I wouldn't.

His words were very explicit, but his voice and tone were measured and careful. But when I asked Connors to give me an example of persistence in action, flashes of the old Connors came through:

> Bjorn Borg. I said I'll follow that son of a bitch to the end of the Earth to play him again after I lost Wimbledon to Borg, and I meant that. I looked at his schedule and I said, "F—k, I'm here, he's over there, so I'm going over there." If you're going to be the best, you got to beat the best. From my standpoint, I wanted to beat Mac [McEnroe] every week. I wanted to beat Borg every week, and I hope they wanted to beat me, because that's where your legacy lies.

---

* I was fortunate to be in the stands that day, and I didn't see or hear a single person rooting against Connors. For the first and only time in his career, the fans were even more intent on his victory than he was.

Larry Bird was no less persistent, or Mike Richter, or any of the sports legends that remain in our memories long after they've retired from the game. They live what businesspeople and politicians need to learn.

I asked New York mayor Mike Bloomberg, who is on everyone's top ten list of most admired businesspeople, what he admired most in others. For him, adaptability and survival are the two essential characteristics of a winner:

> The business leaders that I really respect are people who are able to continue to do what they do in changing environments and for many years. Steve Jobs is in a business where you're only as good as your last product. He's gone from one business to another, he's mastered them all, and he's in a business where even before your product goes out the door there's a competitor ready with something better. The most successful people can see what's coming and reinvent themselves. They don't sit around. They know how to stay relevant.

I also turn to Larry Bird often in this book because his day-to-day routine is so instructive to the business and political profession in their daily grind. His intensity, passion, focus, and discipline are life lessons to anyone seeking to be the best at what they do:

> I love the game, and I want to get better every day and I challenge myself every day. I remember Robert Parish telling me, "I didn't touch a ball all summer." I said, "So what did you do?" He said, "I took yoga, lifted some weights, ran, but I never touched a ball." In my mind I think, "How in the hell can you not touch a basketball?" I had to touch one every day. Whether I was going to shoot it or not, I had to touch it. I always had one laying around. If I didn't pick it up, I didn't feel like I accomplished anything that day.
>
> I remember my first couple of years. Coach Fitch really worked us really hard every day. Every day. And when that whistle blew, a lot of players would run straight for the locker room. Done. But I always thought, "Jesus Christ, don't you want to work on your free throws? You're at seventy-eight or seventy-nine percent. Why not shoot eighty percent?" Ask any of my teammates to this day, "Did you ever beat Larry Bird to practice?

Did he ever leave before everyone else was gone?" And they will say no. In their mind, they also knew that if it got down near the end of the game, who would you throw the ball to, a guy who was in there practicing all the time, or somebody who walked in there cold about two minutes before practice? It is all in the preparation. Preparation to me is everything.

Persistence, unlike its weaker, less successful little brother, effort, is a way of life. It gnaws at you. It will wake you up at three a.m. so you can go over the numbers one more time. And make no mistake: it will laugh at you when you stub your toe on the coffee table as you fumble for the lightswitch. Everything about sports is preparation and persistence. *"I'm going to give you the greatest Bill Walton–ism ever, and I think he got it from Coach Wooden, 'Failing to prepare is preparing to fail,'"* says sportscaster Jim Gray. "Preparation is everything in sports. You've got to do the work to achieve greatness. I've seen a lot of guys who've had magnificent talent who were in and out of the league before they started. You can have all the talent in the world, and all the pride in the world, but none of it means anything without the ability to endure. You have to endure to be great, and to be great you have to be prepared."

Says Sherry Lansing, the first female CEO of a Hollywood studio, *"If the cause is bigger than you, you'll never be afraid of or hurt by rejection. Having been through a lot, I think you win by not giving up."*

What's the difference between persistence and effort? Isn't the former really just an extra helping of the latter? Unfortunately, it's not quite so simple. Rather than trying to explain, let's look at two straightforward statements made every day by managers that illustrate the main difference between the two:

Statement A: "Let's get to work, people, I don't want to be here all night."

Statement B: "We need to do whatever it takes to get it right."

If you work in any business in America, it's likely you've heard one or both of these phrases before. Whether it's that big account you hope to land or just a project you need to finish, these are the two ways people view the world at work. As someone who runs his own company and consults for the leaders of countless others, I can assure you that these really are the two attitudes under which everything else falls.

So which are the words of the winner and which are the words of the guy stuck in middle management?

This isn't rocket science. Statement B is a mind-set shared by about 5 percent of America. Statement B is more inclusive, it puts the boss in the same boat as his or her team, and it communicates a determination to get it right regardless of effort and cost. Statement A is the other 95 percent. It's about "I" rather than "we," and it's about one person's sacrifice rather than the team's success. It's about getting it done rather than getting it done right.

You're probably saying to yourself right now, "Well, that was too easy." And that's part of the point. There's nothing mysterious about what separates winners from the rest of us. Nine times out of ten, the benefit and rationale of what they're doing is as plain as day. Yet if achieving success is really that simple, then why aren't we all winners? If the answers are so clear, why do only a select few ever make it to the upper stratosphere of success?

Because *knowing* isn't *doing*.

Just ask Pierre Omidyar and Meg Whitman of eBay. By 1999, the fledgling four-year-old company was adding users so quickly that its computer servers were strained to the breaking point. Collectors and bargain hunters had flocked to the site in numbers entirely unexpected, and the company was struggling just to keep up. In an effort to prevent system-wide crashes, Omidyar attempted to hit the brakes by raising listing fees and capping the number of items that could be listed on a given day at ten thousand. But that had only the opposite effect—users began posting more items more quickly so as not to miss the ten-thousand-item deadline. On June 12, 1999, in what the *New York Times* called "one of the worst Internet outages," eBay crashed for twenty-two hours. The company's stock dropped drastically on the Nasdaq that day, and users expressed outrage over what they considered poor management.

"It humbled the company," said Meg Whitman, eBay's CEO at the time. "We were on a rocket ship. It was the bubble in Silicon Valley. And that really stopped any idea of, 'Gee, aren't we special,' which was really good culturally."[74] The company's leadership did not consider this setback a defeat. Instead, they persisted, addressing the problem head-on and using it as a lesson for the future. Whitman personally immersed herself in the technical causes of the breakdown and had the site quickly revamped and strengthened. And in a company-defining move, she enlisted the company's four hundred employees to personally call eBay users to apologize for the outage. Stop for a moment and think about the enormity of this effort and the message it sent to each employee about what matters and to whom it matters. This unprecedented personalized gesture earned eBay a lifetime of credibility and was the launching point for even greater expansion in the years to follow. It communicated the company's commitment to learning from its mistakes and a determination to improve at a time when other "surefire" Internet start-ups had begun to fail.

When it comes to a trait like persistence, it's all about action. No amount of IQ, cunning, or skill makes work finish itself, or inspires others to fight with you. You must be willing to put in the effort required to get the results that stand apart from—and miles above—everyone else's. And you must have the language that motivates people to join the effort.

I'm not just talking about the drive to get things done. I'm talking about doing them over and over again until you win. Effort may be an integral part of persistence, but it's only one part. You can't just spend twice as much time on something and, voilà, you have persistence. It's a mind-set. It's a way of life. It's a way of looking at your community, however you define it, as full of opportunities for you to achieve greatness. I agree with Tom Harrison from Diversified Agency Services:

> Persistence is about sticking to convictions and not understanding what the word no means. "No" actually means "not now." Because if you are persuasive enough and persistent enough, you will get the person who said no to say yes. And the reason he or she has not already said yes is because I haven't listened well enough to get them to the yes. But once I have really opened my ears and listened to what their needs are, I can marry what I'm doing to their needs, and I can get them to yes. So it's persistence and redefining the word no.*

One of the most important findings of this book is in those four words: "no" means "not now." I can't imbue you with persistence, but I can help you rethink the way you approach challenges so you can be more effective than you might otherwise be.

---

* For more on this essential philosophy, pick up *Instinct,* by Tom Harrison. It will change the way you think.

The story of Abraham Lincoln is remarkable as much for his failures as his successes because he simply would not give up despite a life of adversity and failure. In his own words, "I do the very best I know how— the very best I can; and I mean to keep on doing so until the end." We know him today not because of his failures, but because of his successes— and they were all due to his unrelenting persistence. Truth is, almost all notable figures in history had persistence as a primary characteristic. As a historian once noted, "If Columbus had turned back, no one would have blamed him. Of course, no one would have remembered him, either."

ABRAHAM LINCOLN: PERSISTENCE PERSONIFIED

1809	Born into poverty
1816	His family was forced from their home
1818	His mother died
1831	Failed in business
1832	Defeated for legislature
1832	Lost his job, wanted to go to law school, couldn't get in
1833	Again failed in business. Went bankrupt. Spent seventeen years paying off that debt.
1834	Elected to legislature
1835	Sweetheart died
1836	Had a nervous breakdown
1838	Defeated for speaker of the legislature
1840	Defeated for presidential elector
1843	Defeated for Congress
1846	Elected to Congress
1848	Defeated for Congress
1855	Defeated for Senate
1856	Defeated for vice president
1858	Defeated for Senate
1860	ELECTED PRESIDENT[75]

Nature essayist and conservationist John Burroughs once wrote, "A man can fail many times, but he isn't a failure until he begins to blame somebody else."[76] In the context of winning, I'd rewrite that quote to read, "A man can succeed many times, but he isn't a winner until he begins to take responsibility for everything he does—success and failure alike." This leads to another critical distinction between effort and persistence: the willingness to take responsibility for one's actions. I'm not suggesting that people who try hard to achieve blame others when they inevitably do happen to fail. But very often, the person who puts forth mere effort will find ways to point fingers at anyone but themselves as a justification for, in effect, giving up.

The excuses are endless, and none of them are words that work. Think of how many times you have heard or even spoken the following:

- "We were robbed."
- "They are just better than we are."
- "We can't compete with that."
- "It's not a fair fight."
- "This isn't a level playing field."
- "How can we be expected to go up against that?"
- "It's a lost cause."
- "No one is ever going to buy this."

And so on . . .

Any of those sound familiar? These are the attitudes, and this is the language, that snatches defeat from the jaws of victory. These are not, by any stretch of the imagination, the attitudes of winners. So I asked David Stern of the NBA what the right language of losing sounded like, since exactly half of his teams need to use it after every game.

If you grew up in Brooklyn, it was "Wait until next year," which was a way of saying, "We gave it our best, we busted our butts, and we're going to come back and do it again." The language of losing is something out of Shakespeare . . . "Better to have loved and lost, than not to have loved at all." It's "We fought our way in, we fought the good fight, we gave it our best, and we fell modestly short. But we're going to the gym and we're coming back next year." That's the most positive language of losing. Not "We were robbed," or "We'll get them."

Persistence doesn't care whose fault it is . . . it just drives you to keep going until you get it right. Too many people spend too much time looking for language to explain, justify, or excuse failure. Stop. Now.

That said, walking up to a wall and telling yourself it isn't there will not make the wall go away. What will help you is thinking about new ways to get above or around that wall—or break it down—or find a different route entirely. It will allow you to make the wall a challenge or a hidden opportunity, but not an insurmountable barrier you cannot overcome.

The result is language that is too soft, goals that are too easy, and a vision that is too gauzy to make anyone really care. You have to find your own Goldilocks approach—not too hot, not too cold, but just right. You have to find the middle ground between scaring the bejeezus out of them, which leads to paralysis, and making them think you're wasting their time with some kind of child's play, which leads to laziness. When in doubt, always err on the side of challenging people more than challenging them less. Most people are looking for ways to prove or improve themselves. Setting a high bar gives them the opportunity to do just that. Keeping expectations low, on the other hand, doesn't give them

---

LUNTZ LESSONS

MISSION VS. COMMITMENT

The two words that best communicate persistence are *mission* and *commitment*, but they have very different meanings.

A mission is the group or corporate articulation of persistence, while commitment is a more personalized, individualized approach. It explains why that group or business exists, and it communicates a purpose. Conversely, a "corporate commitment" is almost meaningless (or worse) because the listener immediately thinks, *"Well, who can I hold accountable if they don't deliver?"*

But when an individual makes a *commitment*, they are in essence putting their reputation on the line. Warning: don't make a commitment unless you're serious about the follow-through. If you fail, the damage can be permanent.

anything for which to aim. It doesn't force them to dig deep within themselves to pull out the fortitude you know is hiding beneath self-doubt. Focus on communicating the ecstasy of victory, the thrill of winning, and you'll motivate people to greatness. No matter the obstacle that comes their way, they always push back, fight on, and keep moving forward.

Mike Richter is one of the greatest hockey goalies of all time. He's best known for leading the New York Rangers to a Stanley Cup victory in 1994, as well as winning a hard-fought silver medal in the 2002 Winter Olympics. He was the first Ranger ever to win three hundred games, and he ended his career as their all-time leader in wins. A former teammate of Richter's, Brian Leetch, once said of him, "I have never seen anyone more focused than he was. As the game got tougher, he got better. If a goal was ever scored on him I was always surprised."[77] While he's a legend among many hockey fans, his success helps explain what it is about winners and their attitudes toward life and adversity that sets them apart. Says Richter:

> The number-one reason Lance Armstrong is so successful is because he's not afraid to fail. That releases him from expectations of what he's going to do. It allows him to focus on each mile for the entire race. Look at the best players in sports. Mark Messier won the Stanley Cup six times in a twenty-five-year career, but that means he failed three times as often. You have to learn to deal with adversity. That's what sports is, and that's what life is—a series of setbacks. It's how you handle those setbacks that determines whether or not you're a winner.

The sheer impact of constant microfailures is enough, over time, to cause system-wide, long-lasting failure. That's why you have to manage those countless, cumulative experiences in order to win. Richter continues:

> If you're going to be a leader, or a winner, or successful in anything in life, the most important thing to be in control of is yourself. You have to know what makes you successful and stick with that. Your approach has to be consistent. Adjust when things aren't working, but know what makes you click and stick with it.

Let's say I'm having a slump or I feel like crap or I'm just physically exhausted. I still need to win. The game—or life, for that matter—doesn't stop just because I'm not feeling my best. The truly great are able to marshal the inner strength and the perspective they need to excel no matter what the circumstances. To me, it's persistence. They get themselves to think in a way to make it happen. They stay in focus from the first moment to the last.

While mere mortals may accept a setback for what it is or make excuses so we feel less humiliated, winners take the defeat, flip it inside out, and figure out what it takes to win. Winners are truly unflappable, like the people in the old Yiddish proverb "upon whom you can spit, and they think it's raining."

Learning to handle negative publicity is an essential trait for those in the public eye. Even the most accomplished people stumble from time to time, and unbridled success still has its critics. The view at the top is stunning, but there are plenty of people trying to climb the same mountain and they will eagerly look for any excuse to knock you off.

Of all the people I have watched up close, none has a more different public image and private persona than Rupert Murdoch. Curious and affable, he is in person nothing like the tyrant his critics portray, and his generosity is legendary. Yet mention the name Murdoch on either side of the Atlantic and you get a steady stream of invectives usually reserved for brutal dictators. When I asked him how he developed his ability to deflect criticism, he offered a healthy dose of empathy even for those who wish him harm:

I don't read books about myself and I've got a pretty thick skin. We're painted in the publications as being big and therefore monopolistic or rich or whatever, so people get jealous. People get resentful. People hugely overestimate your power and resent that. I think that just goes with the territory. We've got a bunch of newspapers that aren't frightened of getting into controversies. We dish out criticism of others, so we have to take it ourselves. I was brought up in a family where my father ran newspapers. I remember at school I would be teased and criticized about my father and his newspapers, so I learned to live with it pretty early.

We're all bound to fail due to the sheer frequency with which failure likes to drop by unannounced. How, then, can you possibly keep moving forward to become successful if you assign them all equal value and let them each affect you the same way? You can't. That's why winners, knowingly or not, must find ways to downgrade defeat so that as each fresh batch of disappointment comes along, they can set it aside and keep blazing ahead, eyes firmly fixed on the prize. It's a continual process of making defeat something smaller, something less relevant and more incidental to everyday life, until it becomes so minuscule that it must be paid no mind.

Sportscaster Jim Gray and most of his colleagues consider Michael Jordan to be the greatest competitor they ever saw—on and off the court: *"It didn't matter if he was playing darts, tiddlywinks, blackjack, golf, you name it, he always wanted to win."* It's passion that drove Jordan to keep playing the game he loved. But it took persistence—the *action* that manifested his belief in his passion—to keep taking the shots that, one at a time, built the greatest career in basketball.

Larry Bird has a similar perspective:

You push yourself. You have to keep pushing and pushing and pushing. I had to shoot the extra four or five hundred shots after practice. That meant that every shot that I took during a game, I had shot a million times before. A lot of guys shoot just to shoot. I shot to score, and I never took a shot that I didn't think was going to go in. When it got about halfway there I could tell you if it wasn't going to go in. I also had to lead by example, which meant I had to be the first one at practice and the last one to leave every day. Not just once a week—every day.

Winners refuse to accept setbacks or failure for what they are. Instead, they redefine them as an opportunity, giving them new energy to attack the problem.

Let's think about motivational speaker Tony Robbins's "asking the right questions" philosophy (from p. 51) again. As a hypothetical example, imagine your firm is asked to pitch your services to a huge, global company. The project is a yearlong engagement worth much more than $1 million. You'll be competing against three other agencies, one of which is known to be the favorite. You prepare for weeks. You spend countless hours at the office, logging more late nights than you care to think about. You go in, present to the suits, and wait. You hear rumors that the favorite firm knocked it out of the park. You wait some more.

You don't get the business.

Welcome to defeat. Now, how you deal with that defeat is an indicator of whether you have the potential to become a winner. For many the knee-jerk reaction is to say, "Well, they were the favorite after all, so I never had a chance." Or "We're such a small firm compared to the rest, how could we possibly be expected to win?" Or my favorite (and the most detrimental by far): "We did the best we could."

But a winner looks at this experience differently, and so should you. Rather than sulking over the $1 million account you didn't win, take Tony Robbins's advice and ask yourself, "Why didn't we win it? What could we have done to make our pitch better? How can we use this experience to make sure we do win the next time? What did the other guys do that we didn't but could have? What has to change within us to make sure this never happens again?"

The only way you can recover from spectactular falls—as did Donald Trump twenty years ago when he found himself on the brink of financial ruin and daily humiliation in the press—is by refusing to quit. That's why he has built a respected, multi-industry dynasty even greater than his first and has made Trump a name his children are proud to carry.

Notice a pattern?

Redefining defeat as an essential ingredient to your ultimate victory is just as much about self-evaluation as it is about reframing and redefining the actual setback. You have to know what's going on inside you—what your own limitations, restrictions, and faults are—before you can fix the problem. The larger point to remember here is that it's not about them, it's about you.

MANUFACTURING MOTIVATION

It's easy to understand why Bill Gates, Oprah Winfrey, and Warren Buffett might work sixteen-hour days. The more work they do, the more successful they become and the more impact they have. The same cannot be said for the vast majority of their employees. Depending on where you are on the ladder at Microsoft, Harpo, or Berkshire Hathaway, the light from the executive suite may be so far away you never even see a shadow. So how on earth do you get your managers or colleagues, at every level, to care as much about your work and what your company stands for as you do? How do you get them to give their all when it's far less clear what the immediate benefit or eventual reward will be?

Persistence is the art of manufactured motivation. This may sound like a bad thing, but it's not. Anytime a manager speaks to her direct reports, a CEO addresses the company, or a president addresses the citizenry, the goal is usually to motivate—to get them excited, engaged, and ready to take on the grueling challenges that lie ahead. Political leaders do it, army generals do it, coaches do it, film directors do it, and parents do it. Motivating people is the key to progress no matter what you're trying to achieve. If you can't get people up off the couch, out of their chairs, and willing to run beside you all the way to the finish line, then what hope could you possibly have of succeeding? The winner has a natural reason to want to keep going—it's their "thing"—but persistence involves getting others to make it their thing as well.

When I asked Larry Bird how he would get motivated before a game, I have to admit the answer surprised me, mostly because I had never heard anything like it before. *"Mentally it's like somebody trying to take something away from you,"* he began to explain.

When I played a game I always felt that everyone on the floor was against me, even my teammates. That was my motivating factor. I always felt that people did not want me to succeed. They want me to lose. So I had to prove to everybody out there that I was going to overcome that, but not just individually, because I knew that I had my teammates who I really did depend on every night.

You hear athletes say it all the time—the great ones will use anything to motivate them. I always felt that I was a self-motivator. I didn't need a coach. I didn't need my teammates' "rah-rah." I just knew mentally right from the time that we left shoot-around that morning for the rest of the day that I was prepared to play right then. Once shoot-around was over, the rest of the day I spent my time finding whatever I could that motivated me for that night's game, whether it was positive or negative.

Winners know how to motivate people and create teams because they are people-centered. They know how to multiply the effect of their persistence and spread it throughout the entire organization. The most critical linguistic component is to see your ability to overcome adversity and translate it into a message that resonates deep within your team. You have to communicate that there is no barrier—that nothing can possibly stand in the way of you and victory. You have to reject, publicly, the idea that there are any external variables that could keep you from winning.

The language of motivation is the language of opportunity. When you communicate the need to "keep fighting the good fight," you should always look for ways to frame challenges, setbacks, and failures as anything but.

So another firm won the account? You now have the chance to completely rethink your pitch materials and make them better than ever.

So your new product has turned out to be a complete flop? You now have the opportunity to figure out what went wrong and make a new product that's actually superior.

So you made a bad investment decision and ended up losing a boatload of money? OK, not everything can be an opportunity in disguise. Sometimes mistakes just suck.

But that doesn't mean you can't learn from them. The people who cruise through life never facing a single bump in the road are often the ones who have no idea how to react when they hit an icy patch and go careening into the guardrails. The bumps teach us how to react so that when the really bad times come along, we at least know how to stay on the road and arrive in one piece.

Motivation is also about emotion. You have to take people to a "higher place" if you want them to believe in you. This is where persistence and persuasion meet. You will never galvanize the kind of support you're going to need from your people through a dry recitation of numbers, statistics, facts, and figures. You have to paint a picture of the future—a picture with them in it. You have to tell a story that is so compelling that they want to be a part of it. Visuals work, as does music, but language is how you best conjure emotion. And the ability to use language to motivate isn't some God-given skill you either have or you don't. It's one that can be learned through practice, study, and determination.

THE PROBLEM WITH BANKER'S HOURS

One of the things I've been legitimately accused of as an employer is my penchant for blurring the lines between personal and professional life. In the past, I often expected my employees to work well beyond the regular office hours published in our New Hire Manual. I've taken a lot of flack for it, and lost employees because of it. But I don't believe in banker's hours. Funnily enough, neither do bankers . . . or at least the ones at the top of the pyramid making all the money and enjoying the reward that comes with success—and bearing the responsibility for the economic mess they created. I promise you the last time the CEO or senior executives at a major, successful bank started work after nine a.m. and left before five p.m., it was on a federal holiday . . . when everyone else was off.

The phrase itself stems from the hours banks used to keep in the 1800s and early 1900s, when most banks were open from around ten a.m. until about two or three p.m. Since then, the saying has come to represent what is basically a short workday or an exceptionally easy job. When someone left my old office before seven p.m., you'd often hear people jokingly ask, "Since when did you start keeping banker's hours?"

The biggest problem with banker's hours is that they don't get you very far. More often than not, taking on any endeavor that has the possibility of making you wildly successful requires more work than most people are even willing to consider. For me, when a client needs a report from our research in the next twenty-four hours, that probably means I'm not going to sleep that night. While regular people light their midnight oil a little bit at a time, winners buy and burn theirs in bulk. If you've ever been to Manhattan at night, you've seen office lights on in many of the tall, elegant buildings that pierce the nighttime sky. There are countless hard working people in those offices doing whatever it takes to get the job done—right. They are the men and women who care so much about what they do that they strive for excellence every day. These are winners.

Another winner we've already met is *Desperate Housewives* creator and executive producer Marc Cherry. I asked him about how persistence had helped him achieve the success he has today:

I pitched Desperate Housewives *to about six different networks. No one wanted it. The last place I pitched it to was Lifetime Television Network. And that was my standard joke: "Lifetime Television for Women doesn't want* Desperate Housewives? *Lifetime? Really?" Once they turned it down, I was really devastated. And then I said, "Well, to heck with it. I'm going to write the script anyway."*

So I wrote the script thinking, This is such a unique vision, maybe they just don't understand, maybe I just have to put it down on paper. Sometimes when you pitch an idea, you know they just don't get it. You write it, hoping that your brilliance will gleam forth from the page, and that they'll understand. The hard thing for me is, I wrote the best script of my career, and then no one wanted to buy it. My agent called and said "The fifth network has now passed on this script," and I was a little sad. And then I get a call from my lawyer saying, "That agent, by the way, has just embezzled $79,000 from you."

So I got a new agent at Paradigm, and Paradigm looked at the Desperate Housewives *script and they said, "This is so good; we don't understand how this hasn't sold. How was your agent selling it?" And I said, "Well, we gave it to the comedy divisions of all the networks and all the studios, telling them it was a satire, a black comedy." And Paradigm said, "That's your problem. You've got to tell people that this is a soap opera, and it's got comedy in it." So we didn't change the script. It was just a change in the wrapping paper. The first place we gave it to with this new proviso was ABC, and they bought it.*

Marc Cherry would not give up, and his persistence paid off. In April 2007, it was reported that *Desperate Housewives* was the most watched show in its demographic, averaging 115 million viewers worldwide. That's what I call winning.

So do you have to work sixteen-hour days to make it to the top? Not always. Sometimes people actually *do* win the lottery. But again, this is a book about action, not gambling.

On a personal level, I learned the value of persistence at an early age— fourteen, to be exact. I wanted desperately to work in politics and had begged my parents to take me to volunteer for a presidential campaign. It was 1976 and my father called the chairman of the Democratic Party (you

read that right) for Hartford, Connecticut (Peter Kelly, later a senior partner in the powerhouse lobbying firm Black, Manafort, Stone and Kelly),
and arranged for me to be picked up outside a local shopping center to go
door-knocking in late February, when it was still bone-chillingly cold. So
I arrived at the appointed hour and waited to be picked up. And waited.
And waited. And waited. They never showed up, and this shivering, quiv-
ering fourteen-year-old was devastated. My mother used this as a lesson
to explain that politicians couldn't be trusted, but I refused to give up.
The next week, I made my parents drive me to the Republican headquarters, but all the organizers did was put me on the phones. I hated it.

For two years I would visit local Democratic and Republican headquarters and attend events, waiting for someone to put me to work. Then, at
sixteen, after more than a dozen failed attempts, I took my lunch money,
hopped on a bus, and went to the headquarters of a candidate for Connecticut governor, Lew Rome. I walked in and announced proudly to anyone who would listen, "My name is Frank Luntz. I am not a kid and I want
to help." There was dead silence, followed by howls of laughter from the
dozen or so people standing around. But fortunately, the local campaign
manager had her office door open, heard my declaration, and came out
and declared, "You're hired!" On that day, after two years of trying and failing, I became a loyal Republican and a political consultant—and the rest,
as they say, is history.

NEVER GIVE UP

If you've ever been to a casino, you'll always find a group of eager gamers
huddled around the roulette table. The bets are placed. The wheel spins.
The ball drops. The numbers flash. Red 12! Someone wins the big one,
everyone else lost. But on the next spin, you hear a lady say to her husband,
"Oh Jim, no, don't put anything on twelve. It just came up!" And every
time I hear someone say something like this, a little piece of my soul with-
ers and dies.

As anyone who's studied basic statistics knows, there's no relation between any two random mathematical events. Having the roulette ball hit
Red 12 every time you spin is just as likely as that number never coming
up after four hours of playing. In traditional American roulette, every

time the ball is dropped, there is a one-in-thirty-eight chance it will hit the number 12, or any number on the table. No matter how many times you play, the odds never change. Each and every spin is independent of the one before it and the one after it. No amount of luck or superstition will change that very basic fact.

So what does this have to do with communicating persistence and manufacturing motivation? Everything.

Persistence is about never giving up, no matter what. That means you must view every event, and every opportunity for communication, as a separate entity. The practical implication of that is approaching each day as something entirely brand-new. Even if you communicated one message the day before, you have to say it again the next day, and the next, and the next. Or if something failed yesterday, you must treat it as wholly independent from today, making it no more or less likely that you're going to fail tomorrow. One of the reasons Barack Obama's presidential campaign was so successful was because he and his team treated every day like the one before simply hadn't happened. No matter what setback they faced, or what victory they were given, each day was a new fight. A new campaign. A new chance to tell a new audience about their new message.

Think about the field of customer service. Imagine you're the head of a global corporation's customer service department. Your job is to make sure that the people on the ground—the men and women answering the calls and serving as the voice of the company—understand their duties and perform them with courtesy and professionalism. Now imagine you're the person who's just had fourteen people scream at and hang up on you. Today. You can easily see how someone in that situation could, in an extremely short window of time, become demoralized, depressed, and disgusted with his job. That's the challenge customer service managers and call center supervisors must face all the time. What are they supposed to do? How do you keep up morale faced with that kind of public anger?

The key is to remember these communication events are just like the roulette wheel—each one is entirely independent of the one before it and the one after it. Remind your people that every call is a new chance to make a customer's day better, to solve his or her problem, and to make the company you all proudly work for that much better. This is another way of redefining failure as an essential component of victory. By minimizing, or in this case negating, the collective importance/effect of each event, your employees are able to see beyond each "defeat." It won't make fielding fourteen angry calls in a row entirely painless, but it will help them keep their perspective, one of the most vital elements for success.

Sir David Frost had a wonderful story to tell about a time when he had to be persistent in questioning a British politician who desperately wanted to avoid giving a very simple answer:

> *I have found the technique of asking people the same question more than once to be quite enlightening. I remember interviewing all three candidates for Britian's prime minister in 1974. Harold Wilson for Labour, Edward Heath for the Conservatives, and Jeremy Thorpe for the Liberals. Usually, top politicians in Britain or America take pride that they get on pretty well together. But in Britain in 1974 Edward Heath, the prime minister, couldn't stand Harold Wilson, the leader of the opposition. And I thought it would be interesting to get on to this, because these two leaders of the parties really couldn't stand each other. So I thought I would ask Ted Heath a very casual question, "Do you like Harold Wilson?" A simple, gentle, easy question.*
>
> *I knew immediately that it was right on the money when Heath said, "Well, I don't know if it's a question of liking or disliking, my interests are getting the business of the country going, and proceeding efficiently, which I think I can do." And then I said, "But do you like him?" Pause. Nothing. And I ask for a third time, "But do you like him?" And he said, "Well, we will have to find out about that, won't we?" And that gave it all away in one perfect sentence.*

Frost could have quit after asking the first time and getting a typical nonanswer. But he didn't. He could have given up after the second attempt, but he refused. Frost got the answer he wanted—an answer that made headlines the next day.

I return to *Entertainment Tonight*'s Mary Hart because she created entertainment news and she's still the best at what she does after thirty years. For her, persistense is conversational, not confrontational.

Once I have looked at my notes and I know my questions, I put them away and I look at people straight in the eye. I have a conversation with them, not an interview. I look interested because I am interested, and I so believe in doing my homework. It makes all the difference in the world.

When I asked her for an example of how her conversational style allowed her to get more out of an interview, she offered up her October 2010 interview with Sarah Palin:

You can't start with a loaded question. Sarah Palin running is one of the biggest questions in America today, so I would never start the interview that way. It takes time to develop a comfort level. We were set to talk for twenty-five minutes, but we ended up talking for fifty-five minutes, and it was a delightful conversation. There were things I really wanted to know about her, and I think she could tell that.

Before I asked her about running in 2012, I asked her about other things. In fact, I actually asked her twice about running. We talked about her momentum, her two-week whirlwind trip, and I phrased it as, "Everyone wants to know, will you run?" she said she had to have a family meeting, but if there's no one else who is better, she will do it. And then we came back to it two minutes later. I said I knew Todd loves the outdoors, so could he stand the thought of being in D.C.? She said, "Oh yeah, Todd can do anything." So I said, "Are you ready?" and she said, "I'm ready."

PERSISTENCE PERSONIFIED

The key takeaway here is that you have to explain to your people why persistence matters. Don't just assume they share the same determination or ability to get up, dust themselves off, and jump back on the horse as you do. Remember, winning is much more in your direct interest than it is in theirs. You know what becoming number one in your industry will mean for *you*. The trouble is, they don't necessarily know what it will mean for *them*.

I've worked for two companies that do this very well: Lowe's and FedEx. Each have their own unique approach but both try to achieve the same goal: making sure every employee understands *why* the customer is so important and why they must treat them all with the utmost respect every time, no matter what. It's not enough to simply say the customer is important and then treat them otherwise. These are people-centered companies that teach their employees to elevate the role of the customer, to make the customer more than a random stranger who needs a package shipped or a new hammer. They stress that you will not succeed in pleasing every customer every time, but that you have to go back and try to do so over and over because that's what the company's service ethic demands. By underscoring the importance—and uniqueness—of each individual event, these companies help inoculate their employees against weariness and the inevitable impulse to throw in the towel, which nearly always accompanies a steady stream of daily defeat and customers who just want their damn money back.

One of the fundamental principles of winning is the ability to see what success looks like. To know what it is you're trying to achieve. To have a clear vision of where the finish line is and what's waiting on the other side. If you don't have those things, there's no way to focus and organize your resources around reaching that singular, most important goal.

In William Shakespeare's *Twelfth Night*, the character Malvolio reads aloud from a letter written by Maria: "Be not afraid of greatness: some men are born great, some achieve greatness, and some have greatness thrust upon them." For the 60,000 employees of MGM Resorts International, on March 27, 2009, Chairman and CEO Jim Murren represented all three. He had been in his job as Chairman and CEO for just four months, running the Las Vegas gaming powerhouse in the midst of the biggest economic collapse Vegas had ever experienced. The company was struggling under a $13-billion debt load, suffering a $1.15 billion loss in the previous quarter alone, forcing them to hire bankruptcy lawyers. And to top it off, their CityCenter development, the biggest construction project in Vegas history, was teetering on collapse just nine months prior to its opening. MGM was Nevada's single biggest employer, and for a month the entire state held its breath.

Almost exactly one year later to the day, I sat down with Jim Murren to ask him first about what he was thinking as his company, and his career, slid closer and closer to collapse. As he made very clear, winning is not just about the words you use. It's just as much about your thoughts, your beliefs, and your personal principles:

> *The overarching attribute that I think I brought to the table was unrelenting desire to succeed and a sense of determination that others did not have. There were moments of despair, candidly. There were moments of uncertainty. But what was going on inside me was just a stubborn determination to try to save thousands of jobs, save the shareholders from certain defeat and to preserve the legacy of Kirk [Kerkorian] and the other founders of the company.*
>
> *At the end of the day, it came down to faith. I'm a spiritual person. I'm not as religious a person as my mom would like me to be, but I am spiritual. I believe I live in Las Vegas for a reason. I believe my father died young for a reason. I believe my brother died unbelievably young for a reason. I believe that I'm the right person for this particular time, maybe not for another time, but for this time. I had faith that the board would intelligently and exhaustively examine all options and come to the same conclusion I did, even though the outcome was very unclear. I had faith that the banks, despite their own individual objectives, would collectively rally around CityCenter and MGM because it was the right thing financially. And I had faith that if we could live to fight another day I'd come up with some other solution for the next battle.*

I then asked Murren about the moment he realized that MGM would survive and that CityCenter would be built, the moment when he realized he saved his company and, in some ways, all of Las Vegas. To my surprise, it was not a moment of celebration. *"There was an understanding that Friday was just a pause, a calm before the next storm, so there was no euphoria. Frankly, I wish there was. We haven't been able to have any of those celebratory moments that we'd love to have. I remember I was just exhausted, but I went right back to work literally that day."* Winning is not always about the thrill of victory. Sometimes it's just the absence of the agony of defeat. And in those rare occasions, it's an all-or-nothing fight.

To build persistence and an unshakable "we don't quit" mentality in your people, you must help them see the light at the end of the tunnel. They have to know *exactly* what it is they're spending so much of their time and energy working toward if you expect their hard work to be sustainable and enduring. Absent a compelling vision, you're basically just saying, "Trust me." And while that may work for a few people, especially those in your inner circle, don't expect that approach to win over the countless other men and women you need who are far more concerned about spending time with their families than helping you sell 12 percent more widgets than the other guys.

These are the words to use to communicate persistence:

THE LANGUAGE OF PERSISTENCE

1. Relentless
2. Determined
3. Single-minded focus
4. A hands-on approach
5. Let's get it done
6. Let's get to work

"Relentless" conveys an uncompromising commitment to success better than any other word. When Lexus added *"relentless"* to its *"pursuit of perfection,"* they were telling customers that their cars were getting better and better . . . and better, and that no obstacle would stand in the way of the quest to be the best. It's hard to think of a word that more perfectly communicates persistence.

If *"relentless"* is about a company, *"determined"* is about the individual. It communicates a deep personal commitment to success. It connotes both deliberate intentions—setting your sights on a goal—and uncompromising pursuit of that goal.

"Single-minded focus" is about discipline, a trait common to all winners. Combining strength of mind with strength of will, winners have the innate ability to shut out everything else and focus on the task at hand—a skill rarely found in today's chaotic work environment. This has always been an unusual quality, but with the cacophony of elec-

tronic distractions now vying for our attention any given moment, it is a more valuable trait today than ever before.

"A hands-on approach" is what people want from winners. It's why they stay at a Steve Wynn hotel or buy products from Steve Jobs. It's the major reason Apple lost shareholder value and public confidence during the year of Jobs's absence. And it's why on his return, the stock price and public confidence were immediately restored. The assumption is that when the genius behind the company is missing in action, the company will falter. People admire and trust leaders who are willing to roll up their sleeves and participate in the "real" work.

"Let's get it done" clearly communicates your intention and your expectation of success. It's the call to action that audiences are waiting to hear, and it's a great way for a people-centered individual to end a presentation or pitch.

"Let's get to work" is the perfect ending to the perfect speech. Delivering a call to action is common to all winners, and this is the best call to action that I've tested, because the actual message communicated isn't about the work itself, but a focus on a successful outcome. It's an invitation to join together to accomplish a common goal.

11

CONCLUSION

PRINCIPLED ACTION
Winning the right way

From: Ken Lay <ken.lay@enron.com>
Sent: Tuesday, August 14, 2001 3:59 PM
To: All Enron Worldwide
Subject: Organizational Announcement

It is with regret that I have to announce that Jeff Skilling is leaving Enron. Today, the Board of Directors accepted his resignation as President and CEO of Enron. Jeff is resigning for personal reasons and his decision is voluntary. I regret his decision, but I accept and understand it. I have worked closely with Jeff for more than 15 years, including 11 here at Enron, and have had few, if any, professional relationships that I value more. I am pleased to say that he has agreed to enter into a consulting arrangement with the company to advise me and the Board of Directors.

Now it's time to look forward.

With Jeff leaving, the Board has asked me to resume the responsibilities of President and CEO in addition to my role as Chairman of the Board. I have agreed. I want to assure you that I have never felt better about the prospects for the company. All of you know that our stock price has suffered substantially over the last few months. One of my top priorities will be to restore a significant amount of the stock value we have lost as soon as possible. Our performance has never been stronger, our business model has never been more robust; our growth has never been more certain; and most importantly, we have never had a better nor deeper pool of talent throughout the company. We have the finest organization in American business today. Together, we will make Enron the world's leading company.

Winning without principle is like bricks without straw. Operating with a strong set of principles holds it all together, providing enduring strength. But leave them out and it's only a matter of time before everything comes crashing down.

For Enron, had to end this way. Enron was the stuff of legends. From 1996 to 2001, *Fortune* magazine named Enron "America's Most Innovative Company"—six consecutive years. During Ken Lay's fifteen years as the CEO of Enron from 1985 to 2000, he transformed the company from a regional natural-gas pipeline player into the largest energy-trading company on the planet, all with the help of Jeffrey Skilling, whom he was grooming to take his place. Under Lay's leadership, Enron's market capitalization increased from $2 billion to $70 billion, and Enron's shareholders enjoyed a return three times that of the S&P 500. With revenues of $101 billion in 2000, Enron had a hand in several diverse businesses— marketing electricity and natural gas, delivering goods through shipping and freight, and providing financial and risk-management services globally. The company also pioneered online business trading through Web-based services such as EnronOnline (commodity trading), which went live in 1999 as the world's first global commodity trading Web site. Other Web-based Enron trading tools included ClickPaper (transaction platform for pulp, paper, and wood products), Energy Desk (energy-related derivatives trading in Europe only), HotTap (customer interface for Enron's U.S. gas pipeline businesses), and even Enron Weather (weather derivatives).

Jeffrey Skilling worked at Enron as a consultant in the 1980s on behalf of McKinsey & Company, where he led the energy and chemical consulting practice. During that time, Ken Lay became so impressed with Skilling that he hired him as chairman and CEO of Enron Finance Corp. in 1990. He worked his way up the Enron ladder to become president and COO in late 1996. As his stature and credibility within the company grew, Skilling began convincing Enron's senior leadership that the company should move away from its traditional asset-based businesses and move toward the much more profitable world of contract trading—everything from energy and water to broadband and weather. Because of his innovative ideas, his passion for the business, and his ability to persuade Enron's leadership about the need for a new strategic vision, he was named CEO of Enron in February 2001. He would hold this position for less than three hundred days.

But the party had to end because the numbers were all bogus, as we now know. To say Enron's financials were a house of cards simply isn't correct. At least cards are real. Enron's success was the stuff of dreams, greed, and balance-sheet shenanigans. In the year 2000, you were more likely to stumble upon a rainbow-colored unicorn munching on four-leaf clovers than an Enron financial statement with even a whiff of reality.

Enron wasn't about winning. It was about lying. They blocked, obscured, and lied about their finances at every turn so they could keep employees busy, shareholders happy, and the Feds off their backs. To wit: here's how Enron described its "wholesale services" (trading) in their 2000 annual report: "Enron builds wholesale businesses through the creation of networks involving selective asset ownership, contractual access to third-party assets and market-making activities."[78]

I'll wait here while you pull up Google Translate.

Or I can save you the trouble. Roughly translated, the above means: "Bulls^%*&."

Winners work and live by principle. Losers do not. I sought out General Wesley Clark because I wanted a military perspective for this book. An intensely serious man, he raised a philosophical perspective I was not expecting: *"Democritus wrote that to be a good speaker, first you must be a good man. It's not just the words that have the power, but it's the person behind them that has the power."* While we've spoken at length about winners in this book, up to this point there has been only limited reference to life's losers. That's intentional. The purpose of this book is not to ridicule failure but to identify what distinguishes winning from mere success.

WHAT MATTERS MOST

Below are several characteristics of a CEO. Please choose the one that is the most important to you and would make you feel best about them.

	Total
Instills a standard of integrity in the company from top to bottom, starting with himself/herself	58%
Believes in better. Always seeking a better approach, a better product, a better service, a better answer to the challenges that face the company, the customer, and the community.	41%
Creates a positive work environment and a culture of respect for all employees	41%
Leads by example. Works just as hard as the hardest-working employee	37%
Communicates constantly, openly, and effectively with employees at all levels	26%
Listens actively, seeking good ideas wherever they might come from	21%
Committed to corporate social responsibility and is engaged and active in the community	18%
Has a can-do attitude. Doesn't make excuses. Always looking for ways to get things done.	17%
Prioritizes serving customers above all else	14%
Demonstrates passion and knowledge for the company's products and services	13%
Focused on the bottom line, profitability, and delivering for investors and shareholders	10%
Is voted one of the most respected CEOS in America by highly respected independent sources like *Forbes, Fortune,* and *The Wall Street Journal*	8%

Source: The Word Doctors, 2010

However, it would be incomplete without an analysis of those who by all of the other measurements *should* be winners . . . but in fact lost in life. They squandered their opportunities by failing on the final, and most important, requirement: act with principles.

WHAT WENT WRONG

Back to Enron. I got to know some of the people who had dedicated their lives to the company. I want to focus on the employees, not their corrupt leaders, because the people I met and talked to were good, decent, hard-working people who believed in their company and believed in the two men in charge. Now, remember, this is back in 2001, before the truth came out. Back then, Ken Lay was a father figure, beloved as well as respected. What he said, people believed—and they invested their personal fortunes as a result of his reassuring words.

When I asked the employees what they thought about Skilling—before the whole thing unraveled—they told me that he was driven, intense, and that he woke up trading and went to sleep trading. He was excruciatingly demanding, but they appreciated it because he led by example. He didn't say one thing and do another (he saved that for earnings calls). He worked hard and expected everyone else to do the same. Skilling believed that if he could work twenty hours a day, seven days a week, so could you. And if he succeeded, so would you. It had clearly escaped Skilling's attention that he was getting paid millions upon millions of dollars for his twenty-hour days while his employees most certainly were not.

Jeff Skilling is my worst nightmare. It's someone like Skilling who will read this book, learn the language and strategic lessons, and use them to manipulate good people into making bad decisions. They'll perfect the first eight *P*'s and ignore (or scoff at) this one. They'll achieve great heights. But they won't be winners. And, very likely, they'll fall from those great heights—eventually.

At the highest levels, Skilling invited people to share in the wealth and excitement of what Enron was "achieving." He got them on the magic carpet not to become rich, but to become truly wealthy. To become, in theory, winners—at least financially. Because he was so passionate, persuasive, and personable, people followed him to the edge of the cliff—and then jumped off. Every day was a new opportunity to break new ground, to conquer a new market, or to make more than they ever had before. What Enron did in a month was what most others did in a year. But it couldn't sustain itself. The cover-ups and the malfeasance, the lies and the trickery—it all came crashing down on itself, leaving a huge recess on the economy's surface. The fall of Enron was just as spectacular, if not more so, than the rise had ever been—what took years to build was destroyed in days. Yet it was destined to be that way, because one thing was missing: principles.

WHY PRINCIPLED ACTION MATTERS

Enron became the symbol for everything wrong with corporate America because the people running the show cared more about profits and quarterly earnings than any hint of a guiding ethos. Winning isn't the appearance of material success. It isn't the billion-dollar bank account or the private yacht. It isn't walking into a room and striking fear into employees' hearts. It's not about being profiled in *Forbes* or fawned over in the pages of *The Wall Street Journal*. Winning is about achievement, leadership, and doing what's right—even when it's not popular, and even when you are criticized for it. It's about using the skills and talents you have to make more of your life and do more for others than you ever thought was possible. It's about pushing yourself to always be better.

If Ken Lay and Jeff Skilling of Enron are poster children for how not to become winners, Ken Chenault, CEO of American Express, defines CEO excellence. He is a people-centered leader who fine-tunes his people skills on an ongoing basis for one of the world's most powerful people-centered companies. Consistently on everyone's most-admired list, American Express under Chenault has reinvigorated a genuine *customer-first* approach to its business—one reason it emerged from the Wall Street finance scandals relatively unscathed.

Chenault's self-description is as positive and principle-based as any I have heard. He has said publicly that leadership cannot only be learned, but "it is a responsibility and a privilege that must be cultivated."* A majority of CEOs talk about "earning" their position, and a few speak of it in terms of "sacrifice." All legitim`ate explanations, but the word privilege denotes respect, appreciation, and even a sense of indebtedness to others. Those are the CEOs that not only win for themselves but also for the people around them.

Chenault's finest hours came through his leadership and sensitivity to the needs of his community, his customers, and his employees in the wake of 9/11. American Express sat just across the street from the Twin Towers. More than 4,500 employees worked in the immediate area, including 250 who worked in Tower 7. Eleven employees were killed, dozens more injured, many lost family and friends, and thousands watched

---

* Alice Korngold, "American Express's Kenneth I. Chenault on Leadership," May 1, 2009.

helplessly as people jumped to their deaths before the tower collapse. Financially, the company suffered a $98 million loss as a direct result of that day.

During the attacks and in the hours, days, and weeks after, Chenault made innumerable decisions that would ease the impact both on his people and on the entire American Express customer family. Millions of dollars of cardmember late fees were forgiven, and credit limits were increased. But the emotional impact on his own employees—for whom 9/11 was up-close and far too personal—was even more profound. So Chenault invited five thousand employees to New York's Paramount Theater on September 20, 2001. In front of everyone, he confessed that his grief was so strong that he had seen a counselor, and he announced that AmEx would donate $1 million of the company's profits to the families of AmEx employees who had died on September 11. Charlene Barshefsky, a partner at Wilmer, Cutler & Pickering who viewed a video of the event, told *BusinessWeek*, "The manner in which he took command, the comfort and the direction he gave to what was obviously an audience in shock was of a caliber one rarely sees."[79]

In times of great economic stress, new millionaires are minted every day because they know how to spot opportunity amidst chaos. In times of great anxiety, new political leaders are born because they know how to relate and inspire. And in times when the country distrusts virtually everyone and everything, some businesses will thrive because they know to deliver more for less. That's surely success, but it still falls short of winning.

This is the era of integrity, of *voluntarily* going above and beyond federal guidelines, ethics codes, ground rules, and moral obligations. It is the era of continual improvement, and never settling for the status quo. No matter your past successes or failures, communicating that you're always striving to do more—and do it better—wins hearts, minds, and consumer dollars.

No one trusts the government to get anything right. So if all you're doing is complying with minimum standards, then you immediately wrap yourself up in the government's shroud of ineptitude. You must go higher.

No one expects companies to do anything except protect the bottom line. So if all you're doing is *selling* and *profiting*, you're telling people that your business is just like any other, and that it doesn't appreciate their plight. You must *demonstrate value* and *share in today's sacrifices.*

Over the past year, we have tested all sorts of themes, messages, and language to help companies earn back the trust and loyalty that was shattered with the economic collapse. Nothing—truly nothing—resonates as well as a *"company that consistently exceeds expectations."* That phrase reflects the demonstration, the measurable results of promises made and commitments given. The language, and the result, is both customer-

THE NEW BUSINESS LEXICON

	BEFORE THE RECESSION	TODAY
Brand Promise	The company is **devoted** to **opportunity.**	The **commitment** of the company is to **stability**, **predictability**, and **consumer protection.**
Product	Delivering **quality** products and services that are **guaranteed** to work.	Delivering **total satisfaction** that **exceeds expectations.**
Method	Based on **innovative thinking** and an **unparalleled grasp of issues** that are accomplished by **teaming** with the client.	Based on **listening** to you, the consumer, **understanding** and **delivering** exactly what you want, when you want it. **You're in control. You decide.**
Culture	The company can deliver these things because its culture is one of **excellence**, drawing upon the **talents and diversity** of its people, working across service lines and national borders.	**Believe in better.** The culture **respects** the people we serve, and every employee is held **accountable** to customers and each other. **No excuses.**
Company	The products, methods, and culture rely on the firm's **size and breadth** of services, and robust business knowledge.	Committed to the **pursuit of perfection**, with products and a culture that is in **total alignment** with our consumers.
Core Values	**Teamwork, excellence, leadership.**	**Accountability, strict standards, uncompromising integrity.**

friendly and the personification of value. Imagine getting everything you paid for—and then a bit more. As a consumer, if you believe it, you're buying it.

John Quincy Adams, our nation's sixth president, said, "If your actions inspire others to dream more, learn more, do more and become more, you are a leader."* *Win* is the story of principled victories, not pyrrhic ones. How you get there matters just as much as where you end up. In the world of business, sports, politics, and entertainment, we should never allow ourselves to slip into thinking the ends justify the means. You don't gain entry into the pantheon of winners—that fraction of a fraction of the top 5 percent of achievers—without winning, and winning requires you to do the right thing, even when no one is looking.

Chenault has all of the winning attributes described in this book. He is passionate, he is persistent, he builds strategic partnerships, and he is a perfectionist. All of these attributes have contributed to his success. But it is his people-centeredness that stands out in the minds of anyone who has ever worked for him. He is a role model for business; he is the best of corporate America today.

Another principled role model is Costco CEO James Sinegal. Despite his take-no-prisoners approach that enabled Costco to become the top warehouse-club retailer in America, Sinegal isn't a Gordon Gekko–esque corporate raider looking to increase the bottom line at any cost. In fact, he is almost the polar opposite—which makes him something of a hero among employees and an enigma among shareholders.

Like investing guru Warren Buffett, Sinegal has always taken the long view with his company. Wall Street analysts have repeatedly told him—publicly and privately—that his higher-than-average wages and unprecedented employee benefits for a retail company could lead to Costco's stock being downgraded, yet his approach has not changed one bit. In a 2005 *Houston Chronicle* interview, he made it clear that his two priorities were happy employees and satisfied customers, not shareholders. Investors may want higher earnings now, but Sinegal has a different mission: "We want to build a company that will still be here 50 and 60 years from now." When retail analysts criticized him for refusing to charge his

---

* thinkexist.com, John Quincy Adams Quotes.

consumers more, even though Costco would still have the lowest price on the market, he simply repeated his motto, "Doing the right thing is good for business."[80] He refuses to shortchange his employees in order to boost a quarterly stock report, offering them 90 percent company-paid health insurance and the best wages of any of his competitors. This strategy worked. Costco enjoys reduced theft costs and lower employee turnover rates than any of its rivals, saving them millions.

THE PRINCIPLES THAT MATTER MOST

WHAT AMERICANS WANT MOST FROM CEOS

	Total
Be accountable for their actions and their consequences	52%
Listen, listen, listen—to customers, employees, and the public	45%
Balance short-term objectives with long-term steady growth	23%
Innovate and continuously improve	21%
Become better corporate citizens, focusing on improving society as much as the bottom line	21%
Communicate more often and more effectively	14%
Deliver real bottom-line results	13%
A kick in the ass	11%

Source: The Word Doctors, 2010

Thinking honestly, what do you believe CEOs need most? Some choices might seem similar, but please choose the best.

We expect a lot from the people at the top. We expect them to be honest, reliable, candid, civil, visionary, understanding, compassionate, caring. Truth is, sometimes we expect and demand too much. We all make mistakes. Nevertheless, there are specific attributes and character traits of winners that matter more than others. Individuals and companies that reflect and replicate those at the top of the list will be forgiven should they occasionally stumble.

It's interesting to note what falls to the bottom of the list on page 275 of what people want from companies as a whole. Almost every Fortune 500 CEO cites his or her "vision" for the success of their company, yet it ranks at the bottom of the public priority list. Similarly, the media likes to play up new product "inspiration" and "imagination" that may be appreciated by the public but isn't particularly valued. My personal favorite linguistic faux pas, "transparency," appears in almost every annual report and corporate social responsibility document, yet it ranks far below its cousins "accountability" and "responsibility." And "measurable impact" is much less important than "measurable results."

But it is not enough to mouth the right words and deliver the right sentiment. These principles have to be authentic. They have to be lived on a day-in and day-out basis. And if they are ever betrayed, you will soon learn quite painfully that all glory is fleeting.

For over a thousand years, Roman conquerors returning from the wars enjoyed the honor of a triumph—a tumultuous parade. In the procession came trumpeters and musicians and strange animals from the conquered territories, together with carts laden with treasure and captured armaments. The conqueror rode in a triumphal chariot, the dazed prisoners walking in chains before him. Sometimes his children robed in white, stood with him in the chariot, or rode the trace horses. A slave stood behind the conqueror, holding a golden crown, and whispering in his ear a warning: that all glory is fleeting.
—PATTON (1970)

WHAT PRINCIPLE MATTERS MOST?*

When it comes to companies and how they behave, what do you want most?

Accountability	37%
Responsibility	32%
Measurable Results	22%
Effectiveness	20%
A Human Approach	20%
Moral Compass	18%
Leadership	14%
Measurable Impact	11%
Transparency	10%
Inspiration and Imagination	7%
A Creative Vision	6%

* Source: The Word Doctors, 2010

All glory is fleeting. But *doing the right thing* endures.

Glory is often the aspiration of those who pursue success; doing the right thing is the common quality of a winner. Time and time again, every winner I've studied does the *little* things the right way, even as they achieve bigger and better things than most of us can ever dream. They carry themselves differently because of a simple trait: they *care*.

Whether it's something as small as helping individuals in need, or something as grand as running a major corporation to perfection, winners share a commitment to doing everything they do the *right* way. To taking *responsibility*.

Winners understand that it's not about *them*; it's about you.

It should be no surprise that just about every winner functions on less than half as much sleep as most people. It's not because they have some genetic advantage that allows them to sleep less. It's because they just don't want to close their eyes and simply can't wait to wake up and return to their efforts to make a measurable difference.

Notice that I did not write that they wake up excited about *"going to work."* It's not work to them. I interviewed almost three dozen people for this book, and only five actually talked about "work" in the traditional sense. What is *work* to you is *life* to them. And they find life *exciting*. They spend their days soaking up everything around them, asking questions and looking for opportunities to learn, to create, and to innovate. To them, every day is another opportunity to excel. Winning is a lifestyle. It's a continual habit that isn't defined simply by what they do *"at work,"* but instead permeates who they are and what they want to achieve. They are constantly interacting with other people and learning from them, so that ultimately they can better serve those people by meeting their needs.

Throughout this book, I have explored the common traits that set winners apart, and the language they use to achieve extraordinary success. We've discussed *"what MAKES a winner."* But now we must ask . . . *"What do winners MAKE?"*

What is the common *product* among every winner?

What is their winning *in the name of*?

In short—*what is winning all about*?

Let's start with what it is not. Obviously it's not MP3 players, or opulent hotels, or people-centered airline services. There is something inside that tells us it must be bigger than some one *thing*. It's not something you can measure in dollars earned or widgets made. Make no mistake: those who seek to win as an end unto itself are setting themselves up for something less. They might achieve success, or wealth, or notoriety—or all three.

But those things are not winning. Winning transcends self. It is done in service to a higher calling: to improve the human condition.

Yes, winners achieve victory. However, true winners sail beyond the adage *"to the victors go the spoils."* For real winners, the truer maxim is *"from the victors come the spoils . . . for the enrichment of everyone."* To truly be a winner—to join the club of a fraction of a fraction of the world's greatest—you must be willing to do what they have done: to give even more than you get. And considering that every winner we have discussed has *"gotten"* a lot (yes, they're just plain rich), that means they've *given* a hell of a lot. This is the side of the story that few ever see, and fewer still report. But almost every winner I've ever known, interviewed, or worked for has a heart that knows no bounds. They have a passion for people— for meeting needs and improving lives—and a pride for their country that surpasses the rest of us.

From a distance, you see the results of their billions: their estates, their voluminous published profiles, or their earthshaking products. What you are seeing is their *success*. That's all well and good. But to judge whether they are truly *winners*, you have to evaluate the whole person and the entire record. And you have to judge that complete picture against a simple question: are they serving their fellow man, or simply serving themselves?

This is, at its core, about *applying the principles of winning in a principled way*. Winners leave an indelible imprint on society that lasts longer than their wealth, their trophies, or even their names. This is the final test of a winner. Even if you master every chapter up to this point . . . but just plain fail to do the right thing . . . it's just not enough. Think back over the other eight *P*'s, and you will see how they intersect with something greater than self.

Winners don't just break a *paradigm* to make a profit; they shatter expectations to move humankind light-years forward. After they're done, everything that comes next is superior to anything people previously thought possible.

Winners don't "practice" their *passion* in order to be powerful; they are innately driven to turn their dreams into realities that benefit thousands, or perhaps millions of people.

Winners aren't *people-centered* because they love to be loved; they're focused on identifying human needs and meeting them by doing whatever they do best.

Winners don't build *partnerships* simply to benefit from someone else's labor; they understand that the highest levels of victory only come when everyone shares in the benefits. And they recognize that there is moral value in sharing success.

You get the point. I haven't written this book so that a select few can achieve great wealth by using better words. I've written it so that the winners-to-be who might read it can spur all of us on to greater heights. I, and everyone else who shares this belief in betterment, am counting on you to improve our lives.

Few people can truly say, "I changed the world for the better." But that's the hallmark of a winner.

When I think of winners who have changed the world for the better—and refused to settle simply for self-interested success—I think of Mike Milken. Although I have spoken at his conferences and auctioned off items for his charities, he has continually declined to sit down and talk with me on the record about his efforts. It's just not his style. But even if he won't tell the story himself, it's a story that deserves to be told.

Milken is among the five hundred richest people on the planet, with a net worth estimated in the billions. Most of us would agree . . . that's success. I've seen him truly *work* the phones, sometimes three calls at once, connecting billionaires and making deals. But that's not what makes him a winner, and that's not why he's included in this book.

Rather than simply focusing on himself, Milken has used his resources, intellect, personal relationships, and passion to reach out and literally heal the pain of tens of millions of people by supporting and organizing groundbreaking cancer research. Never one to do things half-heartedly, Milken has used his Prostate Cancer Foundation to fund more than 1,500 programs at 200 research centers in 20 countries, making it the world's largest philanthropic source of funds for prostate cancer research. A *BusinessWeek* cover story surveyed Milken's "quest to cure cancer," reporting that scientists "are convinced they're close to unraveling [its] biological details. And Milken 'has done more to advance the cause' than anyone."

If that were not enough, Milken is the founder and chairman of Faster-Cures, a think tank, or, as its staff calls it, an "action tank," dedicated to accelerating cures and improving treatment results for life-threatening diseases. As with every Milken paradigm-breaking project, FasterCures has turned the entire research process on its head, identifying barriers to progress, engaging people and organizations in a more focused, cooperative effort, and proposing economic incentives and regulatory efficiencies to accelerate scientific discovery. As a result, in a November 2004 cover story, *Fortune* magazine called him "The Man Who Changed Medicine." The world would be a sicker, darker place without Mike Milken and his commitment to medical research. Lives are extended, families remain intact, and millions of people will enjoy more time together because of one man's personal, passionate efforts.

But this, of course, is not the whole story of Mike Milken. Critics and supporters alike will agree that his financial mastery forever changed the way American businesses functioned and helped set the scene for the immense economic growth of the 1980s. He revolutionized the junk bond market and helped finance some of America's greatest business minds of the past three decades—including Ted Turner, Ron Perelman, Carl Icahn, and Steve Wynn. As a result, Milken was named one of the "75 Most Influential People of the 20th Century" by *Esquire* magazine. There had been no one like him before, and nothing has been the same since.

Mike Milken broke paradigms.

He also broke the rules—and he spent twenty-two months in jail as a result. Critics called him the epitome of Wall Street greed in the 1980s. Yet because Mike Milken, at his core, is a genuine winner, he didn't let these failings define him. He could have gone down in history as the Real-Life Gordon Gekko; instead, he channeled his passion for people and become a latter-day Louis Pasteur.

Winners aren't perfect. They make mistakes. In fact, their mistakes are often bigger and more damaging than anyone else's, because they are taking greater risks. But what sets winners apart is that at the end of the day, they're continually trying to be better. To do better. To do more. To apply the principles of winning in a principled way. And in the end, they usually get it right.

In the final days of editing this book, Bill Gates, Melinda Gates, and Warren Buffett beat me to the punch. Winners usually do. As I was developing the narrative to explain and depict how winners are, above all, principled . . . they went and proved it beyond a shadow of a doubt.

Together, they are leading an appeal to the world's billionaires to give away at least half of their wealth to charity. Sounds ambitious, right? It is. But the payoff can be worth the sacrifice: *Fortune* magazine estimated that $600 billion would flow to charity if the four hundred people on the *Forbes* list of wealthy Americans all committed to "The Giving Pledge." For financial context, that sum could run the entire state of Florida for about ten years.

Typical of true winners, Buffett and the Gateses are leading by example. Gates has already contributed more than $28 billion to their foundation and has pledged to give much more. Buffett has pledged more than 99 percent of his wealth to charity. Yes, 99 percent! Buffett's public statement, written by the world's third-richest person, clearly articulates an individualized, personalized, humanized approach with a remarkably common touch:

First, my pledge: More than 99 percent of my wealth will go to philanthropy during my lifetime or at death. Measured by dollars, this commitment is large. In a comparative sense, though, many individuals give more to others every day. Millions of people who regularly contribute to churches, schools, and other organizations thereby relinquish the use of funds that would otherwise benefit their own families. The dollars these people drop into a collection plate or give to United Way mean forgone movies, dinners out, or other personal pleasures. In contrast, my family and I will give up nothing we need or want by fulfilling this 99 percent pledge . . .

Winners lead by example, and they understand the human dimension of everything they do. Buffett can't *personally* feel what today's economically stressed families are feeling, but he's so outwardly focused that he can, and does, still *relate*. It's not about dollars, just like it's not about the iPhone for Steve Jobs. It's about the human experience. It acknowledges life as it actually is, but appeals to something greater. Read on, because Buffett's expression of respect for others and humility over his own success are the words of a gentle giant:

> *I've worked in an economy that rewards someone who saves the lives of others on a battlefield with a medal, rewards a great teacher with thank-you notes from parents, but rewards those who can detect the mispricing of securities with sums reaching into the billions. In short, fate's distribution of long straws is wildly capricious.*
>
> *The reaction of my family and me to our extraordinary good fortune is not guilt, but rather gratitude. Were we to use more than 1 percent of my claim checks on ourselves, neither our happiness nor our well-being would be enhanced. In contrast, that remaining 99 percent can have a huge effect on the health and welfare of others. That reality sets an obvious course for me and my family: Keep all we can conceivably need, and distribute the rest to society, for its needs.*

Once more: *"Keep all we can conceivably need, and distribute the rest to society for its needs."* Here, Buffett is defining what truly makes a winner: *putting other people ahead of themselves and principles above all.* Whether you've made billions or live paycheck to paycheck, you can still *win*.

This book is not—and cannot be—about telling you the right principles by which to live. Everyone individually will be held accountable to the personal standards they set for themselves. And everyone is expected to adopt their own standards and then live by them. Winners understand that even they can't do everything they want. In the end, we are all only human. Even a workaholic like Donald Trump understands: "If you're interested in 'balancing' work and pleasure, stop trying to balance them. Instead make your work more pleasurable."

Senator Paul Tsongas (D-MA) was one of the most gracious people I have ever met. He was kind and caring. And in my mind, he achieved great things, including a run for the presidency that almost kept Bill Clinton from the White House. Tsongas was also a cancer survivor. He lived five years more than the foremost experts in cancer had predicted.

Despite the pressure and the struggles, he was able to do what many in Washington do not—he kept a balance between his work and his personal life. The Tsongas rule was simple—no matter what was happening in the U.S. Senate, he would leave to go home to have dinner with his wife and daughters.

Frankly, that is unheard of. Power players in Washington can barely contemplate putting down their BlackBerrys to use the restroom, let alone ignore a roll call vote on the Senate floor. But Tsongas was different. Tsongas wrote about the impact the decision had on his career in his book *Heading Home:* "You know, after 10 years in this town, all that I will be remembered for is the fact that I loved my wife." His wife replied, "And what's wrong with that?"[81]

Tsongas was right. In the drive for professional and financial success we tend to forget about things that should mean the most to us. Tsongas's decision certainly made a greater impact on the lives of his wife and children than another leadership title bestowed upon him by his Senate colleagues would have. He ended up losing a presidential campaign; he won the respect of his family. So tell me, is this man a winner or a loser?

THE OPTIMISM OF WINNERS

I've been fortunate to develop a relationship with Amway over the past year. Amway is one of the most successful direct-to-consumer businesses of the past half-century. Their products consistently rank near the top of every "best of" consumer list, generating more than $8 billion in global sales in 2010 alone. They must be doing something right. They're not just "global"—they're *everywhere.* In October 2010, as this book was being put to bed, I was invited to deliver speeches on back-to-back days before two huge but seemingly different audiences.

Day One was in Charlotte, North Carolina, in front of 6,000 IBOs from the Yager organization, and many of them were not native English speakers. Frankly, it felt like the United Nations on steroids: thousands of people speaking a dozen different languages but all gathered to celebrate a unity of purpose. My biggest lesson that day was to embrace the global diversity, keep the jokes simple, and to talk slowly so that the translators could keep up. But no one needed to have the word *freedom* translated. It clearly means the same thing in every language.

Not to be outdone, Day Two was in Louisville, Kentucky, before 15,000 IBOs from LTD, another Amway-affiliated organization, many of them freshly scrubbed college-age students intent on getting a firm financial footing rather than getting drunk. These kids would have made you proud—Junior Achievement all grown up.

You haven't lived, or died, until you have spent an hour trying to inform, entertain, educate, and survive an entire sports arena filled to the rafters with excited, motivated, dedicated people. No podium. No notes. No teleprompter. Just me, in bright red, white, and blue sneakers, running around a basketball arena in front of thousands of strangers. At least I had a message both audiences wanted to hear. I was asked to explain why, in a time of manic skepticism, people should still believe in a brighter tomorrow. These groups were as diverse demographically as you can get—one from around the world, the other from around the corner. Yet the only real difference between them was the color of their passports. The American Dream of economic freedom is alive and well everywhere. In fact, if Amway is any indication, it's thriving regardless of whether you're on Main Street or in Mumbai.

I was impressed and heartened by these two crowds not just because of their international diversity but because of their intellectual activity and commitment to make things better for themselves and their community. Rich DeVos's vision half a century ago of a global organization committed to community service as well as profit is flourishing. It used to be you had to come to the United States for a shot at the American Dream. That's changing. Media, technology, improving infrastructure, and increasingly stable political and legal systems, are all making it easier for people everywhere to have a shot at improving their station in life. Multinational companies don't provide job security anymore and, as a result, a rising generation of entrepreneurs everywhere is ready to bet on themselves and a rosy vision of the future.

While this language is clearly Amway-centered, I want you to imagine *you* every time you read a specific reference to Amway. Here's what I said:

THE TEN REASONS TO BELIEVE IN A BETTER FUTURE

1. America has faced incredible challenges over the course of its history, and overcome every one of them. A civil war, a move from an agrarian economy to an industrial one, two world wars, numerous foreign wars, a Great Depression, slavery, discrimination, terrorism . . . even the downfall of a presidency. The challenges we face today are daunting, but these too will be overcome . . . because that's just what we do.

2. America's best days are still ahead—and Amway is perfectly positioned for tomorrow. IBOs are the most optimistic people anywhere. They see the silver lining in every cloud. The economy is turning around, change is in the air, and while everyone else is paralyzed in fear, Amway is already moving forward.

3. Thanks to the events of the past two years, Americans have rediscovered the importance of freedom in their lives, and are demanding the right to decide their future. The more people desire freedom, the stronger the Amway model.

4. American innovation and can-do spirit are second to none—and thanks to technology, we can now reach 10,000 people in less time than it took to contact ten people just a decade ago. Technology=opportunity and opportunity=Amway.

5. Amway is already global at a time when other companies are struggling to take advantage of global opportunities. There's much we can share with the world, and the world still wants all things American. Let's not forget the U.S.-based company who helped design, build, and drill to rescue over thirty miners trapped for months in Chile.

6. Amway is the most family-friendly company on the face of the globe. No other business integrates and involves the family as much as Amway. Your children are brilliant. Teach them well, and they will teach you more than you can imagine. Amway allows, encourages, and even educates the next generation about economic freedom and the principles of prosperity. The more they learn, the better off they—and we—will be.

7. Amway is built just like America—on the belief of the power of the individual. We enjoy the freedom to pursue our dreams through free enterprise, and because of companies like Amway, we know that more and more people will achieve their own personal success stories in the years to come.

8. In an age of mediocrity, Amway is about exceptionalism: exceptional products, exceptional service, and exceptional people. We are the best at what we do—and the best always gets rewarded.

9. You will live longer than your parents. You will enjoy more years and a healthier life than they ever could have imagined. You will have more material wealth, but more important, you will have more freedom to do what you want and be what you want. You will be more connected to more people who share your vision—across the state, across the country, and around the globe. The only thing standing in your way . . . is you.

10. And the final reason is up to you. You decide. You tell us why the future is bright. You tell us why our best days are still ahead. This business is your business. Our future is your future. We're all in this together. So get going!

COMMUNICATING PRINCIPLES

Of all the Words That Work boxes in this book, none is as important as the one below. With faith and trust in business, government, the media, and many of the most important American institutions at an all-time low, these are the words that Americans want to hear—and the qualities they want to see—from you:

LANGUAGE FOR DEMONSTRATING PRINCIPLES

1. Accountability
2. Strict standards
3. Corporate culture
4. Moral compass
5. Social responsibility
6. Objective and unbiased
7. Uncompromising integrity
8. The simple truth
9. Chief ethics/ethical officer
10. Say what you mean and mean what you say

"Accountability" is the attribute most desired in the business community today—and unfortunately, it's also the one perceived to be most lacking. Accountability is about those in power answering to those who put them there. It's about making things right when they go wrong. And it's about never making the same mistake twice. People who *talk* "accountability" have an eager audience. People who *live* accountability thrive.

The lack of *"strict standards"* is what sunk BP, Toyota, Goldman Sachs, and other victims of the communication disasters of 2010. People want to know that your business won't bend to the wind as Arthur Andersen did to Enron. Standards alone are not enough; it's the diligence and rigor with which you uphold them that matters.

"Corporate culture" did not come into play as a powerful communication term until the accounting debacles of the early 2000s, but today it

has come to reflect a company's operating principles. Just as the way parents and children interact around a dinner table speaks volumes about their family dynamics, your company's corporate culture reveals the true nature of your company and the principles that guide it. Winners are acutely aware of their corporate culture and seek to define it as they define themselves. The most common corporate culture among winners: innovative, aggressive, and even disruptive.

"Moral compass" is to the individual what corporate culture is to the organization. It is desired (but not necessarily expected) of business and political leaders that they engage in socially acceptable behavior. CEOs who sleep with colleagues or use illegal drugs are unacceptable regardless of how profitable their companies have become. Without a moral compass, profits end up a higher priority than people.

"Social responsibility" is what Americans want more than good corporate citizenship. To them, social responsibility is defined first by respect for employees, followed by accountability to customers and service to the community.

"Objective and unbiased" defines the kind of information Americans want from their business and political leaders. They are looking to be informed, not spun. CEO letters in corporate annual reports that appear one-sided and lack candor will not just fail to resonate . . . they will actively undermine the credibility of even the most successful corporation.

"Uncompromising integrity" is hard to prove, but if people believe you have it, you are a winner in their eyes. Let me emphasize the descriptor *"uncompromising"*—it is just as important as *"integrity."* People and companies are judged not when times are good or the decisions are easy. What differentiates a winner from everyone else is the willingness to make tough decisions in tough times.

"The simple truth" is a phrase employed by Steve Wynn to describe what Americans deserve but aren't getting from their political leadership, but it applies to business as well. In fact, in a survey we did in 2010, *"the simple truth"* was the second highest desired value in politics after accountability. It represents fundamental, commonsense principles many believe have been lost in the complications and compromises of modern life—and it appeals to their desire to see those truths restored.

"A chief ethics/ethical officer" should exist in every corporation and organization in America. In essence, this person is the ethics cop, holding others accountable for their actions and behavior—an ombudsman but with C-level authority to instill accountability. From a public-relations standpoint, there is no title with more credibility. From the internal perspective, employees are most likely to listen to and accept decisions that are delivered by such an individual. The fact that a company is concerned enough about ethical integrity to create a position like this lends credibility and creates an environment of trust.

"Say what you mean and mean what you say" is exactly what Americans want their political and business leaders to do. It defines accountability in action. Warren Buffett is the best illustration of a business leader whom Americans believe most upholds this desirable attribute.

There is no single standard of winning. No secret recipe that—presto!—makes you a winner. However, there are many common traits of all winners. Together, they are factors you must incorporate in ways that suit your own style and objectives. You must *weigh* your passion against the importance of persuasion, priorities against principles, and people against profits.

You picked up this book. You've read to the end. That means you want to be a winner. But here, at the end, I must ask you (and *you* must ask *yourself*) . . . why? Is it for yourself, or is it for others?

Maybe you still haven't realized it, or maybe you have already figured it out, but this isn't really a self-help book. This is a *help-others* book. Every winner has elevated others, and in doing so, elevated himself.

It comes down to a simple, powerful word: *If.*

If you can apply the principles of winning in a principled way, then you'll have truly won. If you can put others before yourself, and in doing so lift yourself *and* others to a higher place, then you are indeed a winner.

My favorite poem, the very first poem my mother ever read to me, captures it all so well. Read it, apply it to everything you've learned in this book, and then set out on your own path to victory.

"IF"

by Rudyard Kipling

If you can keep your head when all about you
Are losing theirs and blaming it on you,
If you can trust yourself when all men doubt you
But make allowance for their doubting too,
If you can wait and not be tired by waiting,
Or being lied about, don't deal in lies,
Or being hated, don't give way to hating,
And yet don't look too good, nor talk too wise:

If you can dream—and not make dreams your master,
If you can think—and not make thoughts your aim;
If you can meet with Triumph and Disaster
And treat those two impostors just the same;
If you can bear to hear the truth you've spoken
Twisted by knaves to make a trap for fools,
Or watch the things you gave your life to, broken,
And stoop and build 'em up with worn-out tools:

If you can make one heap of all your winnings
And risk it all on one turn of pitch-and-toss,
And lose, and start again at your beginnings
And never breathe a word about your loss;
If you can force your heart and nerve and sinew
To serve your turn long after they are gone,
And so hold on when there is nothing in you
Except the Will which says to them: "Hold on!"

If you can talk with crowds and keep your virtue,
Or walk with kings—nor lose the common touch,
If neither foes nor loving friends can hurt you;
If all men count with you, but none too much,
If you can fill the unforgiving minute
With sixty seconds' worth of distance run,
Yours is the Earth and everything that's in it,
And—which is more—you'll be a Man, my son!

NOTES

2: The Nine P's of Winning

1. http://www.jimcollins.com/article_topics/articles/good-to-great.html
2. http://www.theage.com.au/articles/2003/11/20/1069027253087.html
3. http://nymag.com/daily/intel/2010/04/oprah_hardest_part_about_setti.html?mid=daily-intel–20100409

3: People-Centeredness

4. http://www.actupny.org/campaign96/rafsky-clinton.html
5. http://www.salon.com/politics/feature/2000/10/12/debate
6. http://dir.salon.com/news/feature/2003/05/07/kerry/print.html
7. http://www.destinationcrm.com/Articles/Columns-Departments/Insight/Required-Reading-Nordstroms-Class-of-Service-43256.aspx
8. classes.bus.oregonstate.edu/winter-07/ba495/ . . . /nordstrom%20pres.ppt
9. Ibid.
10. http://video.google.com/videoplay?docid=4436420281715600110#
11. *Women's Wear Daily*, March 15, 2002.
12. http://www.getmotivation.com/trobbins.htm
13. http://ezinearticles.com/?Tony-Robbins—The-Power-of-Questions&id=3534127
14. http://www.marketwatch.com/story/storm-clouds-gather-for-airlines-but-southwest-ceo-has-a-plan
15. http://www.forbes.com/2009/06/09/worlds-richest-women-walton-bettencourt-business-billionaires-wealth.html
16. http://archives.media.gm.com/servlet/GatewayServlet?target=http://image.emerald.gm.com/gmnews/viewpressreldetail.do?domain=2&docid=56132
17. http://politicalticker.blogs.cnn.com/2010/02/26/cnn-poll-majority-says-government-a-threat-to-citizens-rights/?fbid=VXZnfhrDp-z

4: Paradigm Breaking

18. The American Heritage Dictionary of the English Language, Fourth Edition
19. http://retailindustry.about.com/od/frontlinemanagement/a/mcdonaldsraykrocquotesbrandfranchise.htm
20. http://www.nytimes.com/2009/08/02/magazine/02cooking-t.html?_r=1&pagewanted=2
21. http://money.cnn.com/magazines/fortune/fortune_archive/2007/04/30/8405481/index.htm
22. http://www.usatoday.com/money/companies/management/advice/2009-06-14-andrea-jung-avon_N.htm

23. http://en.wikipedia.org/wiki/Ford_Model_T#cite_note-3
24. September 20, 2004 issue of Businessweek Magazine
25. http://www.washingtonpost.com/wp-dyn/content/article/2009/06/26/AR2009
062603457.html

5: Prioritization

26. http://www.charlierose.com/view/interview/8784
27. http://walmartstores.com/AboutUs/
28. http://www.businessweek.com/the_thread/brandnewday/archives/2007/09/walmart_
is_out.html

6: Perfection

29. http://news.bbc.co.uk/2/hi/health/3815479.stm
30. http://www.bts.gov/publications/national_transportation_statistics/html/table_04_
23.html
31. http://www.usatoday.com/money/autos/2010-01-08-prius-tops_N.htm
32. http://www.businessweek.com/news/2010-04-01/lexus-tops-mercedes-in-u-s-luxury-
auto-sales-in-march-quarter.html
33. http://www.breakingglobalnews.com/iphone-4g-problems-3/12211431
34. http://www.dailymail.co.uk/sciencetech/article-1289321/Apple-iPhone-4-Steve-Jobs-
advice-complaints-new-phone-loses-reception-held.html
35. http://blogs.wsj.com/digits/2010/07/16/live-blogging-apples-press-conference/tab/
liveblog/
36. http://www.businessweek.com/magazine/content/05_15/b3928109_mz017.htm
37. http://money.cnn.com/magazines/fortune/fortune500/2009/industries/182/index
.html

7: Partnership

38. http://en.wikipedia.org/wiki/Meditation_17
39. http://www.online-literature.com/donne/409/
40. http://content.usatoday.com/communities/greenhouse/post/2010/06/bp-tony-hayward-
apology/
41. http://www.washingtonpost.com/wp-dyn/content/article/2010/06/16/AR2010
061605528.html
42. http://www.democracynow.org/2010/6/18/hawyard_testimony
43. http://www.nytimes.com/2009/10/24/us/24prison.html
44. http://www.correctionscorp.com/about/
45. http://www.everymac.com/articles/q&a/macintel/faq/why-did-apple-switch-to-intel.html
46. http:ebay.about.com/od/ebaylifestyle/a/el_history.htm
47. http://www.ebayinc.com/sustainability
48. http://www.numberof.net/number-of-aaa-members/
49. http://www.goodhousekeeping.com/product-testing/history/good-housekeeping-seal-
history
50. Ibid.
51. http://www.washingtonpost.com/wp-dyn/content/article/2008/01/01/AR2008
010100642_pf.html

52. Ibid.
53. http://www.goodhousekeeping.com/product-testing/history/good-housekeeping-seal-faqs
54. http://www.consumerreports.org/cro/aboutus/mission/overview/index.htm
55. Ibid.

8: Passion

56. http://money.cnn.com/magazines/fortune/fortune_archive/2006/10/30/8391725/index.htm?postversion=2006102506
57. Ibid.
58. http://www.usatoday.com/travel/news/2007-05-15-airline-survey-usat_N.htm
59. http://www.cbsnews.com/stories/2007/08/30/sunday/main3221531.shtml
60. http://www.fastcompany.com/magazine/04/hiring.html
61. http://transcripts.cnn.com/TRANSCRIPTS/0109/14/se.55.html
62. http://en.wikipedia.org/wiki/Fight-or-flight_response

9: Persuasion

63. http://www.timesonline.co.uk/tol/news/world/us_and_americas/article6907681.ece?token=null&offset=36&page=4
64. http://business.timesonline.co.uk/tol/business/industry_sectors/banking_and_finance/article5355565.ece
65. Ibid.
66. http://www.nytimes.com/2009/07/15/business/15goldman.html?_r=1
67. Ibid.
68. http://www.washingtonpost.com/wp-dyn/content/article/2010/01/21/AR2010012101044.html
69. *The Charlie Rose Show*. April 30, 2010.
70. http://www.slate.com/id/2081042/
71. http://www.thedailyshow.com/watch/tue-april-19-2005/bee—hall-of-same
72. http://news.cnet.com/2100-1001-202143.html
73. http://en.wikipedia.org/wiki/Franklin_D._Roosevelt

10: Persistence

74. http://www.usatoday.com/educate/college/careers/Career%20Focus/cf3-22-05.htm
75. http://lifejourneycoach.com/2007/11/22/abraham-lincoln-on-success-and-failure/
76. http://www.brainyquote.com/quotes/authors/j/john_burroughs.html
77. http://en.wikipedia.org/wiki/Mike_Richter

11: Conclusion

78. Ibid.
79. Money-cnn.com, October 29, 2001.
80. http://www.usatoday.com/money/industries/retail/2004-09-23-costco_x.htm
81. http://news.google.com/newspapers?nid=1755&dat=19970123&id=wW4fAAAAIBAJ&sjid=GnoEAAAAIBAJ&pg=3006,2284677

INDEX